Hog & Hominy

ARTS & TRADITIONS OF THE TABLE

ARTS & TRADITIONS OF THE TABLE

PERSPECTIVES ON CULINARY HISTORY

Albert Sonnenfeld, *Series Editor*

HOG
&
HOMINY

SOUL FOOD
From
AFRICA TO AMERICA

FREDERICK
DOUGLASS
OPIE

COLUMBIA UNIVERSITY PRESS · NEW YORK

COLUMBIA UNIVERSITY PRESS

Publishers Since 1893

New York   Chichester, West Sussex

Copyright © 2008 Columbia University Press
All rights reserved

Library of Congress Cataloging-in-Publication Data

Opie, Frederick Douglass.
Hog and hominy : soul food from Africa to America / Frederick Douglass Opie.
p. cm—(Arts and traditions of the table)
Includes bibliographical references and index.
ISBN 978-0-231-14638-8 (cloth)—ISBN 978-0-231-14639-5 (pbk.)—
ISBN 978-0-231-51797-3 (e-book)
1. African American cookery—History. 2. African Americans—Food—History.
3. African Americans—Social life and customs. 4. Cookery, American—Southern style—
History. 5. Cookery—American—History. 6. Food habits—America—History.
7. Blacks—Food—America—History. 8. Blacks—America—Social life and customs.
9. Cookery, African—History. 10. Food habits—Africa—History.
I. Title. II. Series

TX715.O548 2008
641.59'296073—DC22   2008020309

DESIGN & TYPESETTING BY *uin dang*

THIS BOOK IS DEDICATED TO "Super," the nickname of my paternal grandfather, Fred Opie, Sr., whom I never met but heard so much about, as well as to Grandma Opie, whose minced meat and rhubarb pies kept me happy and full. The book is also dedicated to Luesta Duers, the gracious matriarch on my mother's side and my maternal grandmother. Finally, the book is dedicated to my wife, Tina, and my children, Kennedy Kwabena and Chase Asabe Opie. Thanks for helping me maintain a balanced life while I researched and wrote this book over the last seven years.

Contents

Illustrations

Introduction

The culinary tradition known as "soul food" has been widely celebrated, as jazz music has been celebrated, as part of African American culture. This book offers a broad look at the history of soul food, as it came to be called during the black power movement of the 1960s and 1970s, and at its social and religious meanings, particularly its relationship to the concept of "soul" itself. In recent years, many food scholars, food enthusiasts, cookbook authors, and others have debated what events, forces, and movements shaped the development of African American foodways, but few have turned their attention to tracing the concept of soul in African American foodways, where it appeared long before the name "soul food" was coined.

In the course of my research for this project, I have arrived at multiple definitions of "soul" and "soul food." As I understand it, soul is the product of a cultural mixture of various African tribes and kingdoms. Soul is the style of rural folk culture. Soul is black spirituality and experiential wisdom. And soul is putting a premium on suffering, endurance, and surviving with dignity. Soul food is African American, but it was influenced by other cultures. It is the intellectual invention and property of African Americans. Soul food is a fabulous-tasting dish made from simple, inexpensive ingredients. Soul food is enjoyed by black folk, whom it reminds of their southern roots. This book argues, then, that soul is an amalgamation of West African societies and cultures, as well as an adaptation to conditions of slavery and freedom in the Americas. African Americans developed a cultural identity through soul and the associated foodways of people of African descent over hundreds of years.

This project seeks to understand the history of soul and its relationship to people of African descent and their food within an Atlantic world context. This required investigating the traditions of Africans and the culinary traditions they absorbed from Europeans, especially Iberians. I also had to take into account the influence of Asian food. In doing so, I build on the pioneering work of Helen Mendes, Verta Mae Grosvenor, Sidney W. Mintz, Karen Hess, Howard Paige, Jessica Harris, and, most recently, Psyche Williams-Forson.[1] Additionally, I unearth and make use of often forgotten work by anthropologists and sociologists who have written about soul, among them, Ulf Hannerz, Lee Rainwater, and Robert Blauner.[2] Finally, I draw on recent scholarship on black power culture and politics by Doris Witt and William Van Deburg.[3]

The African American ideologues of soul food, with the exception of Verta Mae Grosvenor, failed to embrace and incorporate cuisines of other peoples of African descent migrating to the United States from the Caribbean after the turn of the century. Their concept of soul food evolved during the black power era of the 1960s and was largely exclusionary of other cuisines of the African diaspora present in U.S. urban communities. Partisans of the soul ideology juxtaposed southern black cuisine and southern black folkways against what they perceived as a dominant white culture, and they defined southern-based black cuisine as a marker of cultural blackness. But where does that place the equally African-influenced cuisines that began to proliferate in multiethnic communities of color in, for example, metropolitan New York as early as the 1930s? This book takes a more inclusive approach to the development of black urban food markers of identity that argues that jerked chicken, empanadas, patties, cucu, coconut bread, mafungo, mangu, chicharrones, ropa vieja, and fried plantains, to name just a few foods, are as much soul food as collards, Hoppin John, fried chicken, corn bread, and sweat potato pie. A trip to New York, Miami, Boston, Bridgeport, Hartford, or scores of other urban centers reveals that for every soul food restaurant today, there are many more Caribbean restaurants. And the cuisines of those restaurants are at least as African influenced as any southern soul food.

There is vast variety in African American cookery. I focus my attention on Virginia, the Carolinas, Alabama, Georgia, the Caribbean, and metropolitan New York, where many blacks and Latinos from these regions migrated between approximately the 1930s and the 1980s. My sources include travel accounts, government documents (including the WPA's

"America Eats" records, agricultural experiment station reports on food and diet in the South, and photographs), newspapers, magazines, autobiographies, and some ethnography. Employing the methods of social history and cultural anthropology, I also conducted some thirty interviews with African Americans and European Americans, most of them born before 1945 and ten of them members of my own extended family. These are oral histories of southerners talking about food—people like my ninety-five-year-old cousin, Gold, who was born in the South and raised by sharecroppers and domestic servants who cooked a variety of soul food dishes to sustain their families. They frequented jim crow eateries, feasted regularly at black church events, and recalled the growing popularity of the terms "soul" and "soul food" during the black power movement. Some never left the South, and others were southerners or the children of southerners who had migrated to metropolitan New York. I collected their histories to learn more about eating as it pertained to the Great Migration, the Depression, jim crow, the civil rights and black power movements, and the health fitness craze that followed. Interviews with kin and kith are too important to exclude simply because some historians may not like the idea of employing self-ethnography in a scholarly study. Instead, I made a conscious effort to temper the familiar interviews with archival sources and published primary sources.

The exploration of soul food that follows begins with the cultural exchange that took place between the Portuguese and African nations in the early years of the Atlantic slave trade. The first chapter describes the spirituality and rural folk culture of West African cookery, looking particularly at special occasions, such as religious ceremonies and weddings. In chapter 2, I move to the culinary history of enslaved Africans in eighteenth-century America, focusing on the influence of Europeans and Native Americans on African cooking in the New World and introducing the first simple but tasty soul food dishes made in colonial Maryland, Virginia, the Caribbean, and the Carolinas. Here, I describe how Africans in British colonial America who had access to raw food materials and free time drew on African cultures to create regional soul food cuisines. The chapter that follows traces the story of enslaved African Americans' cookery during the antebellum period, including descriptions of soulful, simple dishes made from rations, garden produce, and animals hunted on southern plantations. I consider black spirituality and soul food prepared on holidays and for religious revivals. The end of the chapter looks at the role of education in shaping the eating habits of African American farmers after emancipation.

Chapter 4 moves north with black migrants to consider how the Great Migration changed the eating habits of African Americans. Southerners living in the North continued the soul food tradition of cooking with simple, inexpensive ingredients in order to survive—and even to thrive, for cooking and selling soul food in both formal and informal spaces in the urban North became a lucrative business. The fifth chapter considers eating during the 1930s and 1940s and the survival strategies black folk employed during the Great Depression and World War II, while the sixth investigates how jim crow limited African Americans' options for eating outside their homes and contributed to the growth of African American–operated cafés, barbecue stands, and bar and grills. Important institutions in African American communities, these eateries played soul music, such as jazz and blues, and sold soul food: fried chicken, greens, corn bread, rolls, and sweet potato pie. These foods reminded people of their southern roots, and they formed the basis of the menu at the soul food restaurants that began opening in the 1960s.

Chapter 7 traces the evolution of the terms "soul" and "soul food" during the civil rights and black power movements, arguing that soul food became a cultural expression of the black liberation struggle of the 1960s and 1970s. It also discusses the critique by African American intellectuals such as Verta Mae Grosvenor of white southerners who tried to claim soul food recipes as their own inventions and property. Chapter 8 considers the seldom-discussed topic of African-influenced cuisines from the Caribbean on soul food in urban areas between the 1930s and the 1970s. The last chapter looks at the history of the health and nutrition movement in the African American community. The most influential agents of change were the Nation of Islam, advocates of natural food diets such as Alvenia Moody Fulton and comedian and activist Dick Gregory, and college- and university-educated African Americans. In the epilogue, I share some personal stories of how people have recently changed the cooking and preparation of traditional soul food dishes.

ACKNOWLEDGMENTS

Special thanks to several scholars who graciously read chapter drafts of this project and provided very valuable suggestions for improving the book; these include historians George Reid Andrews, Daniel H. Usner, Jr., William L. Van Deburg, Stanlie M. James, and Donna R. Gabaccia. I also wish to think all three of the readers provided by Columbia University Press. I appreciated their enthusiasm for the project and their suggestions for its improvement. I believe that the manuscript is now considerably stronger for the revision.

I also want to thank the many librarians who made my job as a historian possible: the librarians at the circulation desk at the Warren Public Library in Tarrytown, New York; Trevor Dawes, formerly of the Columbia University Library; Monica Riley in the interlibrary loan office at the Robert W. Woodruff Library of the Atlanta University Center; the Marist College librarians who handled my interlibrary loan requests; and the specialist collections archivists at Duke University and the University of North Carolina at Chapel Hill. Special thanks are also in order for the archivist at the Library of Congress in Washington, D.C., and at the National Archives in College Park, Maryland.

In conclusion, I want to acknowledge the support and encouragement of Dr. Rodney Ellis of metropolitan Washington, D.C. Dr. Ellis allowed me to participate in a men's fellowship health seminar held at a Temple Hills, Maryland, church in February 2000. My presentation entitled the "Origins of Soul Food" was the beginning of this book.

Hog & Hominy

CHAPTER 1

THE ATLANTIC SLAVE TRADE AND THE COLUMBIAN EXCHANGE

Starting in the 1490s, the Iberian (Spanish and Portuguese) scramble to exploit the land and labor of the Americas led to cross-cultural contacts among Amerindians (Native Americans across the American continent), Europeans, and Africans. This led to the creolization, or mixing, of cultures, as Europeans, Amerindians, and Africans interacted for the first time in the New World. The environment (topography, climate, etc.) and the availability of plants, animals, and fish both influenced the creolization process through the creation of regional differences. Other factors that affected creolization included contact with Europeans and Africans before and during the Middle Passage (travel from Africa to the Americas); a sense of self-identification as Africans with distinctive traditions; access to plants, animals, and fish; and group size and class status upon arrival. Because creolization was often an involuntary process, the effect of these influences on each individual varied.[1]

In the fifteenth through seventeenth centuries, there was a great deal of creolization and other ethnic mixing in the Atlantic world. African American cuisine—what African Americans in the 1960s would later call "soul food"—developed from a mixing of the cooking traditions of West Africans, Western Europeans, and Amerindians.[2] Historian Douglas Brent Chambers has shown in the case of the Igbo in Virginia that, contrary to popular belief, Africans in the New World did not face an entirely different environment: they had been introduced to American plants before their forced migration to North and South America and in general would have been "operating within a basically familiar agriculture" in colonial

America. Vegetables that African Virginians grew that were common to Igboland were kale, cabbages, mustard leaves, black-eyed peas (cowpeas), gourds, okra, spinach, squash, watercress, watermelon, yams, corn, pumpkins, and peanuts. These "were indigenous to the Americas but had been incorporated by people of Igboland probably by the early or mid-17th century." Yams, eggplants, bananas, plantains, rice, millet, cassava/manioc, and Melegueta peppers are other examples of African food crops in the era of the slave trade.[3]

Between 1450 and 1600, the Portuguese built trading posts on the west coast of Africa and slave labor sugar plantations on the African island of São Tomé in the Gulf of Guinea.[4] By the sixteenth century, the Spanish had established settlements in the Americas. On the African, European, and American continents, the majority of people shared a preference for preparing soups, stews, and breads; their diet consisted largely of grains. The African and Amerindian diets contained far more vegetables and legumes than the Europeans consumed. Many of the innovations in Atlantic foodways, particularly the introduction of exotic ingredients from the East, occurred as a result of years of cultural imperialism by foreign invaders.[5] Before 1000 B.C., North Africans and Celts settled the Iberian Peninsula. Phoenicians, Greeks, Carthaginians, and Romans controlled the region between 201 and 400 A.D. Ingredients found in Spanish dishes, such as olive oil, garlic, and pulverized almonds, were introduced by the Romans during this period. Seizing power in 711 A.D., the Moors ruled parts of Spain and Portugal for some eight hundred years; their cuisine had a great influence on Iberian kitchens.[6]

The Moors introduced into Iberian cookery a number of spices and herbs obtained through the Arabian spice trade. Before the European reconquest of the peninsula in 1492, the Moorish preference for cooking with liberal amounts of onions, garlic, and buttermilk dominated the Iberian world. Moorish cooks used cinnamon, cumin, turmeric, paprika, sesame seed, black pepper, cloves, and coriander seeds, among other spices. They were also knowledgeable about cooking with parsley, green coriander, marjoram, mint, and basil. Moorish seasoning techniques called for using spices and herbs to enhance, not dominate, the flavor of vegetables, fish, poultry, and red meat.[7] These spices and cooking philosophies of Moorish and Iberian origins became important in African cookery.

Several traditions that have influenced southern African American cooking can be traced back to the Arawak people of the Caribbean. The greatest concentration of Arawak islanders was within the larger Caribbean islands of Cuba and Hispaniola. The Arawak-Carib diet consisted of a lot of non-sauce barbecuing of meat on green wood grills called *brabacots*. The Spanish translated the word to *barbacoa*, from which came the English word "barbecue."

When the Spanish migrated to the Caribbean in the sixteenth century, they imported food and livestock from Europe.[8] For instance, they introduced peaches—of Persian origin—to the Americas, where the indigenous peoples cultivated them and popularized their consumption. The Spanish also imported large numbers of domesticated pigs and hens. Because the islands had no predators and there were many root crops to graze, the pigs thrived. Europeans quickly learned from locals how to smoke and barbecue pig meat. In 1555 one traveler described the residents of Santo Domingo as having great quantities of pork and poultry. The pork, he wrote, was "very sweet and savoury; and so wholesome that they give it to sick folks to eat, instead of . . . poultry."[9]

In addition to importing livestock, Columbus introduced sugarcane to the Americas on his second voyage in 1494. The Spanish cultivation of sugarcane in the Caribbean eventually led to the growth of the Atlantic slave trade and the importation of large numbers of West Africans. During the early stages of the Atlantic slave trade, eating traditions were exchanged as transatlantic links developed among European, African, Arab, and Asian traders.[10] Many of the eating traditions that shaped African American eating habits originated in West African cultures.

AFRICAN COOKERY

West African cooking (within the region presently made up of the republics of Senegal, Guinea, Sierra Leone, Gambia, Liberia, Ivory Coast, Ghana, Dahomey, Togo, Nigeria, Cameroon, and Gabon) between the sixteenth and eighteenth centuries remained "unmodified by European influences," writes one African American cookbook author.[11] I disagree and show instead that African cookery was significantly transformed by such influences, in large part stemming from the commerce that began as a result of, first, the Columbian exchange and, second, the African slave trade. Iberians introduced maize (as well as manioc) and new domesticated animal species, which increased the usage of fowl and pork in African kitchens. These introductions made notable and long-lasting changes in African cooking. African societies, according to one scholar, "absorbed and utilized new crops" such as corn and sweet potatoes "to support or to replace the basic diet." Arab traders, Indonesian islanders, and European slave traders all introduced foreign foods to Africans, who quickly made them a part of their diet.[12]

The Islamic religion's restrictions on pork consumption did have sway in some sections of West and Central Africa, but, for the most part, the influence of the religion did not hinder increased pork consumption. Among the Hausa of precolonial northern Nigeria, Islam was primarily an "urban phenomenon." Islamic Africans made up just 10 percent of those shipped to North America, making their influence rather minuscule.[13] In certain regions of Africa (urban areas without Islamic authorities and rural areas less affected by Islam), West and Central Africans viewed pork as a great delicacy, and African women prepared various parts of the hog for consumption. We know, for example, that pig meat was in high demand in Catholic-influenced Mozambique, where the Portuguese established a strong presence in the fifteenth century. The Dutch explorer Pieter de Marees tells us that, in Mozambique, pork was "as great a delicacy as Chickens" and was "given to sick people as food, instead of Chicken."[14] In addition to pork and fowl, the Portuguese introduced American vegetables to African farmers, particularly sweet potatoes and maize.

Previous to the arrival of the sweet potato, most West Africans used yams in the absence of bread. Soon many other substitutes were available. Indonesian traders introduced bananas, plantains, and the cocoyam from Southeast Asia; shortly thereafter, all three became part of the everyday meals of West Africans. This was especially pertinent in the equatorial forest regions. Because yams were such an essential part of this region's culinary traditions, some nicknamed it the "yam belt." As for plantains, we know that African cooks regularly ate roasted green plantains (and bananas). When the Atlantic slave trade introduced corn and sweet potatoes to Africa (along with other American crops such as pumpkins and cassava), the Portuguese used them to provision their slave-trading vessels.[15]

By the nineteenth century, the Igbo and Hausa people had incorporated corn and sweet potatoes into their fields. A similar transformation occurred among the Fulani. In northern Angola and the western Congo, it proved easier to grow and cultivate than indigenous crops (such as sorghum, millet, teff, and couscous [semolina]) during environmental catastrophes like locusts and flooding. It was not long before bread made with corn and sweet potatoes became the staple food of poor people in parts of Central Africa.

By the 1600s, de Marees observed women in the Congo making bread from both corn and millet: "In the evening they put this grain [millet] with a little Maize into water to soak. In the morning ... they take this *Millie* and put it on a Stone such as the Painters use to grind their Paint. Then they take in their hand another stone, about a foot long, and grind this Millie as fine as they can, till it becomes Dough and looks almost like baked Buckwheat Cakes. They mix this Dough with fresh water and Salt and make it into Balls the size of a couple of fists. They lay these on a warm floor where they bake a little; and this is the bread they eat."[16]

De Marees goes on to describe how women on the coast of Guinea accumulated capital selling corn bread to Portuguese enclaves in Angola and on the sugar-producing island of São Tomé. Calling them "the Negroes of the Castle Damina," he recalled how they made a popular maize bread called *Kangues* that sold well in local markets in coastal Guinea. The bread was made by wrapping the corn-based dough in a banana leaf and placing it under the cinders of a fire.[17] The bread was excellent, but it also sold well because the women had perfected a recipe that allowed it to be kept for several months, making it a perfect staple for the slave traders' long sea voyages.

West Africans were already cultivating two types of rice (one coarse and red, the other very small and white), when the Portuguese introduced Asian rice from the Far East. This most likely complemented rather than replaced the indigenous varieties. Groups between Cape Verde and the Gold Coast cultivated large amounts of rice. In fact, they cultivated so much of it that they became known as the people of the Rice Coast.[18]

In addition to corn, rice, and sweet potatoes, foreign traders introduced a new species of hen to West Africans.[19] The Guinea hen was perhaps the most important foreign animal introduced to Africa. The lean and dry meat of this game bird was considered superior to chicken and pheasant. Arab traders introduced it principally to cattle-raising societies like the Fulani of northern Nigeria. The Fulani mastered the art of raising large flocks of Guinea hens in the grasslands where they flourished. West Africans also incorporated the Guinea hen into many of their religious celebrations. The point here is that Africans were familiar with frying, baking, and making soups and stews with poultry before they arrived in colonial America.[20]

As mentioned, the Igbo and Mande were among the largest ethnic groups first to arrive in colonial Virginia, the West Indies, and the Carolinas. Information on the Igbo and Mande comes from the travel accounts of Europeans who explored the Congo, Guinea, Gambia, Ivory Coast, Ghana, and Nigeria. Although these authors were admittedly Eurocentric in their worldviews, they provide insightful descriptions of Igbo and Mande cooking.[21]

Along the Gold Coast, the Dutch explorer William Bosman identified West African societies as divided into five distinct groups: kings, chiefs, noblemen, commoners, and slaves.[22] Power came from controlling trading towns and cities, gold- or ivory-producing areas, the river tributaries, and trade routes across the Sahara that linked West Africans, Arabs, and Berbers. West African kings had two sources of revenue. First, traders paid royal tax collectors a percentage of their goods for the right to bring goods in or out of the empire. The second source was slavery: After 1600 West African kings made fortunes from the profits of slave traders who supplied European planters in the Americas with African slaves.[23] The intercontinental slave trade in Africa also provided the families of kings, chiefs, and noblemen with female cooks and kitchen staff. In precolonial northern Nigeria, almost half the population was enslaved. Slavery dominated the entire economy of the region, with the plantation sector absorbing the majority of slaves within most slave societies. The remaining slaves worked in the households of elites.[24]

Among commoners, female elders put a premium on teaching young girls within their families how to cook. A girl's mastery of cooking improved a common family's chances of obtaining a prosperous marriage alliance with a groom of some social standing. The female toddlers of commoners accompanied their elders into the forest to fish and to gather berries, herbs, tubers, mushrooms, and wild greens. Thus, at a very young age, African girls from nonelite family compounds learned how to live off the land. As the daughters of farmers and herdsmen, they foraged to supplement what the men produced and hunted. In West Africa, women gathered "bush greens," different varieties of spinach, collards, mustard greens, and the leaves of root vegetables like yams. They used them raw or in cooked vegetable dishes.[25]

The African cook used pieces of meat and fish as seasoning when he or she had access to them. Historian Robert W. July writes: "Protein deficiency, endemic in the yam belt, led to a general craving for meat, which in turn widened the limits of what was conventional fare."[26] Another researcher found that meat most likely represented "only a relatively minor part" of the commoner's diet in West Africa and the Congo. West Africans obtained meat from hunting if they lived in forest regions. Those in coastal regions consumed large quantities of fish, both fresh- and saltwater. Fish and oysters contributed essential protein to the commoner's diet.[27] Tradition in both forest and coastal societies obliged the head woman of a family compound to provide food and cook for her husband's relatives and friends. Family compounds consisted of one's immediate and extended family, including grandparents, aunts and uncles, cousins, and their off-spring. A village comprised several family compounds.[28]

IGBO TRADITIONS

The terms Igbo and Mande refer to two large families of languages spoken by a great number of West African ethnic groups and to the geographic areas they occupied. As mentioned, the Igbo originally settled in the northern part of the Niger River delta in what is today the Biafra region of Nigeria.[29] Igboland was the center of yam agriculture. "Igbo peoples were the yam growers par excellence in West Africa," according to historian Douglas Brent Chambers. Next to the yam in importance was the expressed oil of the African palm, which was used for frying and to make yam foofoo (a doughy paste made from pounded yams soaked in palm oil) and to flavor soups and stews. In addition, the bitter-tasting kola nut, which contained caffeine, was highly prized and served to guests. It would later be used as an essential ingredient in the original Coca-Cola soft drink recipe. Other important Igbo staples included rice, millet, and okra, used to thicken soups and stews. The Igbo also cultivated greens, watermelons, black-eyed peas (cowpeas), pumpkins, and gourds and raised domesticated animals for milk and meat consumption.[30]

The use of yam foofoo as bread and the palm tree for various food preparations is typical of Igbo cooking.[31] Explorer Joseph Hawkins observed that "if they possess rice, roots, and palm wine, a cow, a few goats or sheep, to afford them occasionally milk or meat, to feed themselves and entertain their friends, they enjoy consummate happiness." After the arrival of foreign traders, Igbos began raising and using corn as well as manioc and sugar. These adopted crops served as a complement to a yam-based diet rather than a supplement. In 1796 Hawkins recalled that Igbo fields had "a considerable quantity of large species of millet," manioc, sugarcane, and the "finest maize I had ever beheld." He also observed goats and sheep grazing in rich "pastures as far as the eye could reach."[32]

In 1796 the subsistence farming performed by the Igbo in the tropical climate ensured that community members regularly had plenty of healthy physical activity. Woman worked in the fields, pounded yams into foofoo and grains into flour, hauled water for cooking, and cooked for hours at a time in hot kitchens. Men, writes Hawkins, used knives "six to eight inches long" for everything from cutting timber, cleaning animals, and preparing plant foods to "digging, turning up the soil, sowing or reaping the crop."[33] Members of the Igbo communities located along the mouth of

FIGURE 1.1 *"Dining with Kaffir Chief."* Picture Collection, The Branches Libraries, New York Public Library, Astor, Lenox, and Tilden Foundations.

the Gambia and Niger rivers regularly engaged in hours of physical activity, maneuvering boats, casting and hauling in fishing nets, and processing their catches. With so much daily physical activity and the regular consumption of high-fiber and raw foods, obesity was apparently no problem among the Igbo.

The Igbo were familiar with cooking various types of fish and poultry in West Africa that they would later find when they arrived in the Chesapeake Bay. According to Hawkins, the rivers in Igboland were full of "lobsters, crabs, prauns, cray-fish, soles, mullets, &c. in great abundance while the thickets on their banks, afford the GUINEA-HEN, the MOOR FOWL, the ORTOLAN, and innumerable others."[34] Igbo hostesses also prepared an animal that in appearance looked like an opossum. "In shape and colour it resembled the OPOSSUM, except that it had no pouch or false belly; the hair also was much shorter—however, when dressed, it tasted deliciously," recalled Joseph Hawkins.[35] In short, Igbos cooks did not have that much adapting to do when they arrived in America. They had only to find an alternative to palm and kola nut oil for frying fish and poultry and making soups and stews in the Chesapeake Bay region.

Like the Igbo, the Congolese also cooked with palm oil, serving it with boiled rice and millet seasoned with a little meat, poultry, or fish. "The oil is so essential an article of food," observed Hawkins, "the Africans employ it in all their meals, with yams, rice, millet, fish, and even with beef and mutton."[36] Mullet dipped in a "palm-oil and hot pepper marinade" and then dried and smoked over a hot fire was a staple among coastal dwellers. On special occasions, like the arrival of foreigners, the Congolese entertained at banquets offering rice, roasted and dressed venison, fowl, and milk.

An Igbo hostess also cooked stewed meat and duck but served it with foofoo instead of rice. Cooks usually served stews in a calabash platter containing a large loaf of warm yam foofoo. The diners then squatted around the communal calabash taking turns breaking off a lump of foofoo with their fingers and rolling it into a ball. This was then soaked in the hot palm oil containing floating bits of meat and vegetables. Igbo people also used foofoo-covered fingers like forks or spoons to eat other stewlike dishes.[37]

MANDE TRADITIONS

Mande speakers (identified in the primary sources used here as Mandingo and Mandinka) lived in the geographic area of the present-day countries of Burkina Faso, Senegal, Gambia, Guinea, Sierra Leone, Liberia, the Ivory Coast, and Ghana, among others. As largely subsistence farmers and rice eaters, the Mande people, according to the expeditions in the 1790s of the twenty-four-year-old Scottish explorer Mungo Park, performed their daily share of physical activity, thus staving off obesity. "Few people work harder, when [the] occasion requires, than the Mandingoes," recalled Park.[38] The vast majority of their time was spent cultivating rice, couscous, a variety of vegetables, including corn, and the shea tree (whose fruit is crushed and boiled to produce shea nut butter). "The labours of the field," writes Park, "give them pretty full employment during the rains; and in the dry season, the people who live in the vicinity of the large rivers employ themselves chiefly in fishing.... Others of the natives employ themselves in hunting." We know from Park that before they arrived in the Carolinas and other parts of the Southeast the Mande hunted squirrels, "Guinea-fowls, partridges, and pigeons," foraged for insects, and raised milk-producing cattle. Park also recalls that a mainstay of the everyday Mande diet consisted of bowls of rice and couscous cooked with milk (or water) "flanked by copious bowls of cream and honey."[39] Again, the culinary transition that came with slavery in America was not drastic.[40]

By the nineteenth century, the Mande, like the Igbo, had fully introduced corn into their daily diets. A vivid description of how Mande women processed corn shows that it was a labor-intensive process requiring hard physical activity that kept them physically fit and lean: "In preparing their corn for food," the Mande used a "large wooden mortar called a *paloon*, in which they bruise the seed until it parts with the outer covering, or husk, which is then separated from the clean corn by exposing it to the wind; nearly in the same manner as wheat is cleared from the chaff in England."[41] The woman then took the freed corn, put it in a mortar, and beat it into meal. This process was used to make a variety of corn-based dishes in different countries. For example, Mande along the Gambia River made a type of cornmeal-based pudding using milk and water; it was called *nealing* and may originally have been made with millet. Park tells us that, during lean times, the Mande also ate for breakfast "a pleasant gruel called *fondi*" made from foraged berries and millet or couscous. Both nealing and fondi seem like precursors of the rice puddings and custards made so popular by enslaved cooks on Carolina rice plantations.[42]

In the book *Roots*, Alex Haley traced his family history back to the 1750s Mande village of Juffure. During lean times, villagers in Juffure survived on edible leaves, insects, rodents, and roots. The Mande developed distinctive dishes through cooking alternative sources of protein such as beetles and grasshoppers. "These would have only been tasty tidbits at another time of year, but now, on the eve of the big rains, with the hungry season already beginning, the toasted insects had to serve as a noon meal, for only a few handfuls of couscous and rice remained in most families' storehouses." After the rains and harvest came, the Mande diet changed drastically. The people then feasted on meat three times a day until they completed the harvest. The ability to locate food during lean times in West Africa proved very profitable to enslaved Africans in the Americas, where planters distributed niggardly rations that kept most slaves famished, forcing them to hunt and steal food in order to survive.[43]

One-pot meals were the most common among both the Igbo and the Mande. For example, the British slave trader Theodore Canot tasted an unforgettable mutton stew called *bonne-bouche* in the Mande town of Kya. Canot recalled: "The savory steam of a rich stew with a creamy sauce saluted my nostrils, and, without asking leave, I plunged my spoon into a dish that stood before my entertainers, and seemed prepared exclusively for themselves. In a moment I was invited to partake of the bonne-bouche; and so delicious did I find it, that, even at this distance of time, my mouth waters when I remember the forced meat balls of mutton, minced with roasted ground nuts, that I devoured that night in the Mandingo town of Kya."[44]

Mande women taught their daughters how to broil, roast, bake, and fry meats—a talent they would liberally exercise in slave quarters and big-house kitchens in the Americas. In Africa, Mande culinary arts called for jerking meat (salting and drying it in the sun) to conserve it. Among Mande living in the interior of the Gambia River region, salt was "the greatest of all luxuries," because their mostly vegetable diet "creates so painful a longing for salt, that no words can sufficiently describe it," says Park.[45] Perhaps this is the origin of the African-American love affair with salty foods that has resulted in a disproportionately high diagnosis of hypertension in contemporary communities of African descent in the United States.

Coastal dwellers among the Mande would smoke, fry, salt, dry, boil, or pickle fish or serve catches raw, much like their descendants forced to migrate to the West Indies and the Carolinas. The fish they caught in West Africa, writes Park, "are prepared for sale in different ways. The most common is by pounding them entire as they come from the stream in a wooden mortar, and exposing them to dry in the sun.... It may be supposed that the smell is not very agreeable; but in the Moorish countries to the north of the Senegal [River], where fish is scarcely known, this preparation is esteemed as a luxury, and sold to considerable advantage."[46] Mande women would purchase the dried fish at market and then add pieces of it to boiling water, vegetables, seasoning, and couscous to make a fish gumbo. The knowledge and practice of Mande gumbo making continued in the Americas with regional differences, especially in port cities such as Charleston, Savannah, Mobile, and New Orleans.

Like the Igbo, Mande people skillfully used vegetable oils like shea butter and palm oil to deep-fry and flavor poultry. Mande descendants continued the cooking technique in the Americas, only in the colonial South lard replaced the healthier palm oil and shea butter. Fried or curried chicken and greens were yet another culinary tradition passed on to African Americans and West Indians by their Mande forebears. West African women batter dipped and fried chicken, grilled it, and cooked it in a curry sauce. They commonly served chicken with collard greens and dumplings. African Americans also learned from their Mande ancestors the practice of using chicken innards (hearts, lungs, kidneys, and gizzards) in their soups and stews as flavor enhancers.[47] The African-American practice of eating chicken on special occasions is also a West Africanism that survived the slave trade. Among the Igbo, Hausa, and Mande, poultry was eaten on special occasions as part of religious ceremonies.[48]

SPECIAL OCCASIONS: FOOD AND AFRICAN RELIGION

Before Africans arrived in colonial America, they had a well-developed religious life that included "iconic foods served in ritualistic ways."[49] There are several keys to understanding the religious rituals that survived the

African slave trade and would shape the African-American concept of soul: spirituality, love, patience, hard work, and pride. These were essential components of what would later become soul food. First, West African religions honored and acknowledged God and the community's relationship to the spiritual world in everyday activities and on special occasions. Second, Africans held a belief that an honorable person showed reverence to God, community leaders, friends, and family through the use of music and food. As a result, West African ancestors incorporated music and food into their religious rituals and celebrations. Examples from different parts of West Africa and during different centuries illustrate this.

In general, we know that, on special occasions, hens were an important ingredient in many dishes. "The person who is to be made a Nobleman," writes Dutchman Pieter de Marees, "makes everything ready, such as food and drink in order to regale his guests well and give them a proper treat. He buys Chickens and many pots of Palm Wine, and sends to each Nobleman's home a Fowl together with a Pot of Palm Wine, so as to make them happy with him."[50] Africans sought to make their deceased ancestors happy with offerings of food as well.

The East Nigerian–born Olaudah Equiano (1745–1801) tells us that, in traditional Igbo religions and cultures, people had the practice of making "oblations of the blood of beasts or fowls" at the graves of dear friends and relations, whom they believed would "attend to them, and guard them from" evil.[51] An English naval officer and explorer, William Allen, observed that just before the planting of yams, villagers along the Niger River contributed an abundance of palm wine and game to a yearly yam-planting festival, while the inhabitants of the city of Accra, in the kingdom of Ghana, commonly hunted and prepared hare.[52]

Considered the most important religious event of the year in the Niger River region, the planting festival involved a multitude of villagers, who devoted a portion of their food and drink to their god as libations before the start of a communitywide planting season feast. A similar celebration occurred at the completion of the planting season. The "Marocho, which occurs about our Christmas period of the year," writes Allen, "is the greatest religious festival." The weeklong feast featured goat and poultry dishes as well as a steady succession of "dancing, singing, and firing of muskets."[53] According to de Marees, Africans in Guinea served chickens as a funeral repast. Women did all the preparations. "For having a good time together at the funeral: they cook a Sheep, as well as Fowls and other food which they usually eat."[54] There is no record of what Africans ate after

FIGURE 1.2 *"The Slave Deck of the Bark 'Wildfire,' Brought into Key West on April 30, 1860."* *Harper's Weekly*, June 2, 1860, Library of Congress, Prints and Photographs Division, LC-USZ62-41678.

they learned about the capture and exportation of a loved one, but we do know what slavers forced their captives to eat before and during the Middle Passage.

SLAVE PROVISIONS

As an eighteenth-century travel account explains, slave traders forced African captives to eat foods with both Old and New World ingredients onboard slave ships destined for the Americas. The enslaved Africans described in the following scene were native to the coast of Guinea: "The diet of the Negroes on board is a sort of pulp, composed of rice and horse-beans, with yams, boiled and thickened to a proper consistency, which is called a Dab-a-Dab, sometimes with meat in it, to this there is added a sauce, called flabber-sauce by the sailors, made of palm oil, mixed with flour and pepper; and there is an overseer with a cat of nine tails to force those to eat who are sullen and might refuse; an attempt to starve themselves being considered as the greatest possible crime, and receiving the severest punishment. This food is accounted more salutary, and nearer to their accustomed way of feeding than salt flesh."[55]

West African eating customs played an important role in the formation of African-American eating habits in what would become the southern United States. The consumption of yams prepared in various ways is distinctly African. The Igbo used foofoo to eat stews with their hands in a manner similar to the way we use utensils. African Americans in South Carolina would later use corn bread in a parallel way to sop (or soak up) a mixture of molasses and the grease produced by frying salt pork and to eat collard greens. Another parallel is how African women used shea butter and palm oil to season and cook most of their vegetables, legumes, chicken, and fish. African Americans in the South would later use fatback and salt pork in the same way to prepare vegetables and beans. The continuation of African culinary practices among African Americans can also be seen in the use of large amounts of salt and pepper to season food. These are Africanisms that stand apart from the influence of the Portuguese on African cuisine, which began in the sixteenth century.

Before the Africans' enslavement and forced migration to the Americas, the Portuguese introduced maize to the diet of Africans and increased the region's population of hogs and hens for consumption. By the 1600s, Africans had developed the habit of eating corn in various ways, including in puddings, breads, and porridges reminiscent of grits. In some instances, corn complemented or replaced African grains like millet. Groups like the Igbo, however, continued to eat primarily rice. Their knowledge of rice cultivation motivated rice planters in lowland South Carolina to seek them out by name when purchasing slaves. Africans brought their way of cooking long grain rice with them to South Carolina; in the kitchen, it was the African cook and her culture that made the greatest thumbprint on South Carolina recipes, not the European culture of the mistress.[56]

Among West Africans like the Mande people, meat consumption was seasonal. During harvesttime, meat was eaten three times a day. After the harvest, women used meat sparingly as seasoning in stews and sauces rather than as the main course. This practice continued among Africans shipped to the Americas. During dry seasons and famines in West Africa, insects like the locust replaced the large and small game that vanished during long droughts. As for chicken, it was generally served to guests and used as part of religious observances; this is another example of an Africanism that continued in the South.

In the Americas, Africans would continue some traditions, like eating roasted yams, while altering or creating substitutes for other traditions. Amerindians and Europeans influenced the food that the earliest Africans used to complement and substitute for their eating traditions before arriving in the Americas. Captivity and chattel slavery exposed the Igbo and Mande to various new eating habits and food preparation methods, but they largely had access to most of the ingredients familiar to them in Africa. And before they were forcibly sent to the Americas, African women had already begun cooking with imported crops, many of them from the Americas, such as corn, cassava, and pumpkins.

ADDING TO MY
BREAD AND GREENS

Enslaved Cookery in British Colonial America

For too long, Soul Food recipes were carried around in the heads of people grubbing for a living. They didn't have much time for writing cookbooks. But a lot is known about what people ate as they built this country. And from that, we can tell a lot about where Soul Food comes from.

—JIM HARWOOD & ED CALLAHAN—
Soul Food Cook Book

When and in what ways did Africans develop new cooking and eating habits after arriving in the Americas? In Africa, they had developed ways of cooking and eating related to their distinctive cultures and tribes. After being sold into captivity during the Atlantic slave trade, they were suddenly forced to interact with all sorts of people in a variety of cultural and physical environments. Exposure to new and different people, as well as to new and different plants and animals for producing food, caused them to "shift emphasis from their old staples to the *buckra*'s [Igbo word for white people] new ones."[1]

I limit my discussion here of this change to West Africans who were traded to the British colonies in the Carolinas and Chesapeake regions, with some discussion of the Caribbean. I chose this geographical focus the better to provide an in-depth analysis of the changes that occurred in African cookery over time. The total number of Africans imported into North America was approximately 481,000, or 5 percent of the 10 million brought into the New World. The apex of the trade was between 1701 and 1810. Most of the slaves that entered the Southeast did so through the Chesapeake Bay and the port at Charleston.[2] Scholarship done in the 1980s and 1990s on African identity in early America reveals that the first Africans came in loosely constituted ethnic groups that, in the process of adapting to slavery, created "distinctive regional common traditions." "First-comers" determined the predominate traditions in each distinctive region of the New World.[3]

Africans from the Bight of Biafra (Igbos) were numerically dominant in the slave trade to the Chesapeake Bay region, which included the colonies of Virginia and Maryland. Igbo made up about 40 percent of the Africans in the Chesapeake Bay region, one-fifth of the remainder being Western Bantu, one-fifth Mande, one-tenth Akan, and one-twentieth each Mande and Malagasy (Madagascars). Planters in the Carolinas and West Indies preferred slaves from Gambia and the Gold Coast (Mande people from contemporary Ghana), who dominated the culture of the Carolinas and West Indies, followed by slaves from the Congo, Angola, and Mozambique-Madagascar (contemporary Mozambique, parts of Tanzania, and the Island of Madagascar).[4]

I read travel accounts and memoirs concerning the above regions to look at the ingredients and techniques Africans used to create their cuisine before and after captivity and forced migration to the Americas. Throughout this study, I place particular emphasis on learning how Africans and African Americans cooked, presented, celebrated, and socialized with food.

During the early stages of the Atlantic slave trade, eating traditions were exchanged as transatlantic links developed among European, African, Arab, and Asian traders.[5] Many of the traditions that shaped African American eating habits originated in West African cultures. For example, the southern African-American tradition of eating dishes like grits and hot-water corn bread can be traced back to West Africans, who regularly ate porridges such as nealing, made first with millet and other indigenous grains and, after the 1600s, with corn that Portuguese slave traders introduced from the Americas. The African American tradition of eating corn bread with almost every meal can be traced back to West Africans, who began regularly consuming various types of corn bread after the 1600s. As mentioned, the African American preference for yams and sweet potatoes, pork, chicken, and fried foods also originated in certain West African culinary traditions. Rich seasoning, using herbs, heavy amounts of pepper and salt, meat, and cooking oil or lard, also has roots in West Africa, where both the Igbo and Mande liberally cooked with palm oil. In short, African preparation techniques and ingredients used in both everyday meals and on special occasions influenced African American eating traditions.

Of course, slavery and subordination to European masters who distributed rations to enslaved Africans also influenced African American eating traditions. In addition to providing rations, British masters in the southern colonies also granted enslaved Africans permission and the opportunity to cultivate gardens and to hunt and fish on Sundays. Before captivity, African women cooked largely with grains, legumes, some pork, poultry, salted fish, green leafy vegetables, herbs, onions, and hot peppers. Captivity and forced migration changed the diet of Africans in the Americas.[6] In the colonial South, the culture of the master class was British. As such, it makes sense here to discuss British foodways in the Atlantic world.

INFLUENCE OF BRITISH FOODWAYS

In the British Empire, produce such as potatoes, cabbage, beets, and turnips was traditionally considered food for poor folks and commoners. The English lower classes essentially prepared two types of vegetables: those they served hot, such as cabbage and turnips, and those they served cold, as in salad greens like lettuce, radishes, cabbage (again), spinach, and beets. English elites seldom ate any of these vegetables because they believed they caused flatulence and depression.[7] The English elites also believed raw fruit was unhealthy and caused fevers. As a result, they generally stewed or baked fruit until it was very soft, often using it in pies and tarts. The migration of this tradition is best illustrated by the number of different recipes for cobblers (also called bucklers in Virginia) found in southern cookery. For example, Louis Hughes, born into slavery in 1832 near Charlottesville, Virginia, recalled the peach cobbler recipe slaves used on a cotton plantation near Richmond where he worked. The peach cobbler was one of the prized dishes baked every Fourth of July (I will return to Fourth of July celebrations later). He published his autobiography in 1897, but his memory of the peach cobblers baked as part of the plantation's Fourth of July feast was crystal clear: "The crust or pastry of the cobbler was prepared in large earthen bowls, then rolled out like any pie crust, only it was almost twice as thick. A layer of this crust was laid in the oven, then a half peck of peaches poured in, followed by a layer of sugar; then a covering of pastry was laid over all and smoothed around with a knife. The oven was then put over a bed of coals, the cover put on and coals thrown on it, and the process of baking began. Four of these ovens were usually in use at these feasts, so that enough of the pastry might be baked to supply all. The ovens were filled and refilled until there was no doubt about the quantity."[8]

Africans adapted the culinary culture of the English as they prepared food for English planters in the Americas, particularly the English penchant for pies.[9] In addition to the predilection for pies, the British passed on to the Africans in early America the view that food quintessentially meant meat, particularly red meat. The "parochial food-traditions" of the English elites dictated that they consume an abundance of red meat and few raw fruits and vegetables.[10] English culinary tradition contrasted sharply with the Igbo and Mande traditions, which favored consuming the majority of a day's calories in vegetable and whole-grain form, with meat serving primarily as a flavor enhancer and not as the center of a meal.[11]

The Portuguese explorer Manoel Gonzales found that the "middling sort" dined "most upon butcher's meat," eating vegetables only as a supplement. The English were "indeed great flesh-eaters," downing large amounts of meat for dinner and supper. The English nobility most likely viewed the largely corn, potato, poultry, and pork diet of the Irish as the food of the colonized, because most Irish living under British imperialism survived on it.[12] The cooking and baking of the poor depended on lard and pork; indeed, pork was a favorite of the poor, because pigs could feed on just about anything and were therefore easy to raise.[13] Members of the British Empire continued to raise pork after they migrated to North America, and it remained an important staple.

THE CHESAPEAKE BAY REGION:
"LAND OF CULINARY NEGOTIATION"

In the Chesapeake Bay region, Native Americans (the Sapony, Mattaponi, and Pamunkey, among others) ate considerable amounts of plant foods, especially corn, their staple grain. They would salt, parch, steam, ground, roast, bake, soak, pound, and ferment corn and a host of other grains. Each of these methods changed the flavor, texture, digestibility, and nutritional value of the grain so treated. They also popped corn, used it to bake bread, and cooked whole ears of corn in the ashes of fires. As in Latin America, many tribes added ash to make hominy, which later emerged as a staple in the diet of black and white southerners.[14] In addition to hominy, Native Americans in the Chesapeake Bay region became well known for their bread, called *ponap*, from which pone bread (made with cornmeal and water) was most likely derived. They also ground nuts and seeds—for example, those of the sunflower—into flour from which they made nut bread from it.[15] Tribes in the Chesapeake Bay area were also known for their expertise in cooking with venison, their chief meat until the arrival of domesticated pigs with the Europeans. They made soups with venison, dried it, stewed it with hominy, and barbecued it. Amerindians in Virginia delighted in barbecued turkey and enjoyed other fowl, raccoon, rabbit, otter, turtle, and squirrel. They also roasted and dried oysters and used them in stews.[16] Sources show that after dining with American Indians upon their first contact, European settlers in the South then began incorporating their various corn and bean dishes, along with seasoning techniques, into their diets. Europeans and Africans also acquired from Native Americans methods for catching and cooking indigenous fish and wild game such as squirrel, possum, raccoon, rabbit, and bear. These are some of the most essential Native American influences on European and African American cuisine in the Chesapeake region.[17]

After several attempts, the British first established colonies in the Chesapeake region in the late sixteenth and the early seventeenth centuries. The overwhelming majority of British colonists in the region were commoners. Travel accounts provide evidence that settlers and their slaves learned how to hunt wild game such as turkey, raccoon, and rabbit and also how to cook local plant foods. Except for the turkey, most Africans had already hunted and cooked similar animals in West Africa. Africans had also cooked with oysters before arriving in the Chesapeake Bay region and the Carolinas.[18]

One historian argues that slave masters in the Chesapeake Bay region were not prosperous enough to grant their slaves the time and space required to cultivate their own subsistence crops as slaves in the Carolinas and West Indies did. In general, he says, Africans in the Chesapeake region largely depended on their masters for rations, such as corn and pig parts. Another study on the Chesapeake region contradicts this conclusion, insisting that Igbo slaves kept small gardens in which they grew plants common in Igboland or indigenous varieties that substituted for those too tropical to grow in the Southeast:

> Igbo in Virginia substituted "yams" for their old primary stable (*Dioscorea*), but maintained nearly all the secondary subsistence crops of their ancestral village agriculture, except for coco-yam, plantains and bananas (and tropical fruits such as papaws or papayas). The loss of plantains and bananas seems to have been made up with maize and meal, while butter and lard replaced palm-oil and cayenne replaced Melegueta pepper. Okra, associated with fertility as well as with proverbial knowledge in some parts of Igboland, and black-eyed peas (which in Virginia and indeed the entire South still bring good luck if eaten on New Year's Day), and squashes and watermelons and gourds and "greens" and others quickly reappeared and continued as staples of Afro-Virginian slave foodways.[19]

In addition to raising familiar African crops, slaves in the Chesapeake Bay region also hunted, fished at night (known in Virginia as "negur day-time"), and raised fowl to supplement their diets.

Primary sources on enslaved Africans in Virginia and Maryland also contradict the view that slaves did not receive the time or space to culti-vate gardens. Virginia school tutor Philip Vickers Fithian worked for Rob-ert Carter. The enslaved Africans on Carter's holdings made food out of weekly rations consisting of "a peck of Corn, & a pound of Meat a Head!" Most important here is the fact that, in addition to their rations, enslaved Africans on the Carter plantation grew produce in small plots allocated by their masters. Fithian recalled that on "several parts of the plantation" slaves cultivated "small Lots of ground allow'd by their Masters for Pota-toes, peas, &c."[20]

Another source documents similar scenes in Maryland in the late eighteenth century. Slave Charles Ball was born in Calvert County about 1781. He claimed that on "every plantation, with which I ever had any ac-quaintance," the masters and overseers allowed the slaves to garden, most often in "some remote and unprofitable part of the estate, generally in the woods." Ball explains that slaves supplemented their lean rations of "coarse food, salt fish, and corn-bread" during the spring in three ways: farming their "patches," fishing the Pawtuxet River, and fishing in the Chesapeake Bay. The river and bay provided slaves with an "abundance of fish in the spring, and as long as the fishing seasoned continued. After that period each slave received, in addition to his allowance of corn, one salt herring every day." Lean times for slaves in the Chesapeake Bay meant filling their pots in the slave quarters with fish from local waterways as well as the corn, potatoes, pumpkins, melons, onions, cabbages, cucum-bers, and "many other things" they grew in their gardens.[21]

SPECIAL OCCASIONS:
HOG-KILLING DAY AND THE FOURTH OF JULY

Chesapeake slaves, like those in other parts of the South, experienced both feast and famine. For example, Ball fondly remembers the fall of the year, when a feast followed the harvesting of the corn and the cotton, although this was followed by a very lean laying-up time when a slave's daily work regime and meat rations were drastically reduced. Between the harvest and Christmas, slaves on Ball's plantation survived on a diet of "Corn bread, sweet potatoes, some garden vegetables, with a little molasses and salt, as-sisted by the other accidental supplies that a thrifty slave is able to procure on a plantation." Ball argues, "A man who lives upon a vegetable diet, may be healthy and active; but I know he is not so strong and vigorous, as if he enjoyed a portion of animal food." December was hog-killing time, when slaves received a "tolerable supply of meat for a short time" as they gorged themselves on the parts of the hog that the master's family refused to eat: chitlins (entrails), trotters (feet), the snout and jowls, scrapple (the neck of the hog), "hog maw" (the mouth, throat, or stomach lining), and crackling or pork rinds (deep-fried skin, a by-product of rendering lard).[22]

In addition to the harvest celebration and hog-killing day in December, after 1776 slaves feasted on the Fourth of July as part of the national independence celebration. A barbecue, according to former Virginia slave Louis Hughes, "originally meant to dress and roast a hog whole, but has come to mean the cooking of a food animal in this manner for the feeding of a great company." It's not clear when it started, but southern planters early on began to commemorate Independence Day with a barbecue. As Hughes put it, "a feast of this kind was always given to us, by Boss, on the 4th of July." Hughes goes on to say, every slave "looked forward to this great day of recreation with pleasure. Even the older slaves would join in the discussion of the coming event." Perhaps Hughes was referring to the older slaves who were born in Africa, now looking forward to a feast that celebrated a freedom they had not experienced since they were forcibly taken to the Americas. "The older slaves were not less happy, but would only say: 'Ah! God has blessed us in permitting us to see another feast day.'" While white southerners celebrated independence from British tyranny, enslaved Africans co-opted the day to celebrate a brief respite from grueling work and hunger. Here is Hughes's description of how African Americans barbecued a hog and sheep on a Virginia plantation in either the late eighteenth or early nineteenth century:

> The method of cooking the meat was to dig a trench in the ground about six feet long and eighteen inches deep. This trench was filled with wood and bark which was set on fire, and, when it was burned to a great bed of coals, the hog was split through the back bone, and laid on poles which had been placed across the trench. The sheep were treated in the same way, and both were turned from side to side as they cooked. During the process of roasting the cooks basted the carcasses with a preparation furnished from the great house, consisting of butter, pepper, salt and vinegar, and this was continued until the meat was ready to serve. Not far from this trench were the iron ovens, where the sweetmeats were cooked. Three or four women were assigned to this work. Peach

cobbler and apple dumpling were the two dishes that made old slaves smile for joy and the young fairly dance.[23]

It is difficult to tell if Native American or African traditions influenced this early American barbecue performed by African Americans in Virginia. As mentioned, barbecuing was a favorite technique among Native Americans in Virginia. But we also know that before their arrival in the Americas, young women in Africa learned how to cook whatever wild game the men of their village or tribe brought home. African women cooked most meats over an open pit and ate them with a sauce similar to what we now call a barbecue sauce, made from lime or lemon juice and hot peppers.[24] The point here is that enslaved Africans in the Americas came from regions where feasts and famines were a way of life. They also came from regions where they barbecued on feast days. Thus barbecuing was another African technique that they had to adapt to the ingredients available to them as enslaved African cooks on white-owned plantations.

One book on family and community relations and experiences among whites and blacks in colonial Virginia argues that neither group understood the contours of the other's life in such areas as the kitchen. Similarities and differences "between black and white life have proven to be more elusive."[25] The 1717–1721 diary of the English planter William Byrd provides insights into the culinary lives of blacks and whites in Virginia. In the eighteenth century, Byrd, a lawyer, trader, and auditor, was the owner of several plantations totaling 26,231 acres and worked by an unnamed number of slaves.[26] Living on a large isolated plantation in colonial Virginia, Byrd was free to eat in violation of English parochial food traditions. No one from London could judge him for how he ate.[27]

Byrd, like most other elite planters in the colonial South, had a complete kitchen staff of enslaved Africans to prepare all his meals. Enslaved African cooks reserved their best cooking for the wealthy, where they had access to excellent cooking facilities and often the best ingredients money could buy. In general, enslaved Africans who cooked for the rich were female and received their training from the female elders within their immediate and extended families. Over time, the planter class took great delight in the traditional dishes made by African American cooks, such as hoecakes and fried chicken. These traditional dishes, argues historian Eugene Genovese, made their way to the tables of the rich and "became a much larger part of the upper-class preference than some among later generations of whites have wanted to admit."[28]

Byrd's diary entries from June 1720 to March 1721 indicate that his cooks made some dishes reminiscent of African traditions, such as "hoe-cake and onions." Enslaved Africans made hoecakes by baking bread in hot cinders on the blade of a hoe. This baking process is a facsimile of how African women in Angola and São Tomé had baked corn bread wrapped in banana leaves in the cinders of fires. In addition to hoecakes, African cooks in colonial Virginia served "stewed turkey," which was also reminiscent of stews made in West Africa. Enslaved African women in colonial Virginia were also observed cooking "fried chicken," "fricassee of hare," and "fried pork." All three of these meats were quite common in West African kitchens on the other side of the Atlantic. The only difference is that, in Africa, women fried with "the pungent castor-like" palm oil; in America, Africans adapted to frying largely with lard.[29] In addition to the African adaptations involving corn and various meats, African plantation cooks seem to have quickly gained the confidence of their masters' palates with a menu of essentially African dishes adapted to American raw materials.[30]

AFRICAN FOODWAY DOMINANCE IN THE CARIBBEAN

In the three decades following the end of Spanish hegemony in the Caribbean in 1650, British immigrants established large and highly profitable sugar plantations throughout the region. Most of the new sugar estates used enslaved Africans and a few white servants for labor. About one out of every four of the arrivals on the island of Barbados was an African who would work hand in hand with white *engagés* (indentured servants). Whereas indentured servants dominated during the first generation of British settlement, Africans became the majority labor force during the second generation, and their numerical dominance in the Caribbean continued to increase.[31]

Most of the earliest servants performed gang labor on plantations, first for joint-stock companies and then later for individuals. They worked twelve-hour days clearing new land, planting, hoeing, and harvesting cash crops. The artisans among them worked their trades and tended to receive better treatment than the unskilled did. The indentured servants were multiethnic European men and women in their late teens to early twenties who signed four- to seven-year contracts. Planters frequently bought and sold their labor, mistreated them, and forced them to live and work in Spartan conditions.[32]

FIGURE 2.1 *"A Representation of the Sugar-Cane and the Art of Making Sugar."* Library of Congress, Prints and Photographs Division, LC-USZ62-7841.

In general, the British viewed white indentured servants as possessing only slightly more importance than the free and enslaved Africans at the bottom of the colonial social order. It was the wealthy white planters, merchants, and professional men of property who wielded the most power and monopolized the best that colonial life had to offer. This, of course, included food. In the seventeenth century, most British planters in Barbados fed enslaved Africans potatoes, a thick gruel they called *loblolly, bonavist* (kidney beans), and "no bone meat at all; unless an Oxe died: and then they were feasted, as long as that lasted." The slaves hated their rations and loudly protested until their masters added a regular portion of plantains to their meals.[33]

In the Caribbean, British planters quickly became the minority to African slaves' majority. Many planters were so focused on returning to England wealthy that they made little effort to re-create English culture and, instead, in the words of one historian, "accepted the foreign diet as an aspect (and not necessarily an unpleasant one) of doing business in the Caribbean." He goes on to say, "Wild game, pork, lots of fish and shellfish, as well as many Native American and African foods dominated the exciting and diverse diet of this region." In general, slaves were allowed to retain and cultivate an African American cooking aesthetic.[34]

By one estimate, "80 percent of British imports of Gold Coast slaves went to Jamaica, the largest British sugar-producing region in the eighteenth century." In Jamaica, planters supplied slaves with weekly rations of salted fish and set small parcels of land aside for them to cultivate produce and raise animals, the bulk of the work being performed on Sunday. Slaves in Jamaica managed to raise fowl, pigs, vegetables, and rice.[35] What slaves did not use to supplement their rations, they sold on Sunday, the traditional market day and a free day for slaves. With their earnings they purchased salted beef or pork. They then combined the meat received as rations and purchased at market with produce from their gardens to prepare a spicy creolized stew they called *oglios*, or pepper pot. Charles Leslie, who traveled to Jamaica around 1740, noted, "The negro's common food is salt meat, or fish boiled with their vegetables, which they season highly with pepper."[36] A lack of utensils and kitchen equipment often necessitated cooking several items together; this may have been the factor that led to the development of the tradition of eating meat and vegetable dishes such as pepper pot and gumbo.[37] On Saturday night, hundreds of slaves would meet at balls that often lasted until Monday morning. A travel account from 1790 informs us that the cooks for these events prepared "a number of pots, some of which are good and savory; chiefly their swine, poultry, salt beef, pork, herrings, and vegetables with roasted, barbecued, and fricasseed rats," which they sold in small quantities out of gourds.[38]

What is interesting is how enslaved Africans in the West Indies appropriated the tradition of celebrating English holidays like Christmas for their own special occasions. They "greatly plundered" their masters' supplies of "poultry" for holiday meals. A nineteenth-century diary entry describes how one slave brought a turkey, another brought a pie and pudding or tartlet, and a third brought French preserves.[39] Planters also declared New Year's Day a holiday. The slaves on one plantation arranged an elaborate celebration, including a catered meal consisting of "cold roasted pea-fowls, turkeys, capons, tongues," and ham.[40]

Between the seventeenth and eighteenth centuries, European populations in the Americas decreased sizably as the rising economies in sugar production permitted wealthy planters to force poorer Europeans off their Caribbean land. Small, economically dislocated planters began to look for places to relocate. In 1660 Oliver Cromwell's rule gave way to the Restoration. To reinforce his power, the restored monarch, Charles II, distributed patronage in the form of proprietary colonies in the Americas.

Favored members of his court and those who had remained loyal to him during the Cromwell years received this honor. The British proprietors of the Carolinas used the offer of up to 150 acres of free land to attract seasoned settlers. As a result, sizable numbers of small planters from the Caribbean relocated to the new British settlement.[41] The majority of the early inhabitants of South Carolina were thus English émigrés who came from Barbados and the Bahamas with their slaves and an "appreciably Creole" mentality.

CULINARY FLEXIBILITY IN THE CAROLINAS

In the relocation, it was vital to slave traders that as many of their human cargo as possible disembark alive, so they took great care to feed enslaved Africans on their slave ships as far as possible with the food most appealing to their specific ethnic groups, despite the deplorable circumstances.[42] A passage from the book *Remarks on the Slave Trade, and the Slavery of the Negroes*, published in London in 1788, describes a dish that cargoes of Africans evidently ate during the long trip from Africa to the Carolinas. "Dab-a-Dab" is described as "a sort of pulp, composed of rice and horse-beans, with yams, boiled and thickend [*sic*] to a proper consistency" and served with "flabber-sauce" "made of palm oil, mixed with flower [*sic*] and pepper."[43]

Africans came to South Carolina early, both directly from Africa and by way of the West Indies. From the beginning they outnumbered Europeans; one estimate states that in 1715 South Carolina had 6,250 Europeans and 10,500 Africans. In 1749 there were 25,000 European inhabitants and 30,000 Africans. The 1775 figures show a ratio of ten to six: approximately 100,000 Africans to 60,000 Europeans. One chronicler wrote, "The missionaries [in South Carolina], accordingly, were confronted not only by some American-born Africans but also by masses fresh from Africa. The latter were again and again the leaders in revolts."[44] It is safe to say that the Carolinas had a slave population with a vivid memory of West African cultures and culinary habits.

Great numbers of Africans were imported to South Carolina to work the colonies' large rice plantations. South Carolina slaveholders supported rice cultivation because it proved to be a very profitable cash crop that also provided slaves with a "cheap, filling, nutritious food, for which the supplies could be grown by the slaves on a sustenance basis." South Carolina, according to one expert, "remained more African than elsewhere in the Colonies."[45] As a result, a creolized African cooking emerged there as slaves of different nations or tribes shared cooking techniques and developed dishes such as gumbo, jambalaya, and hopping John.

As in other parts of the South, gumbo played a vital role in South Carolina's creolized cooking. With roots in the sub-Saharan communal rice-based dishes, gumbo was a cook's way of making do with whatever rice, meat, and vegetables that was on hand.[46] A similar dish, hopping John consisted of rice, beans, peppers, and salt pork cooked to a stewlike consistency. (We know that, as early as 1742, South Carolinians cultivated Ethiopian or Guinea pepper from an African tree that planter and slave owner Eliza Lucas Pinckney claimed provided a "good Ingredient" in seasoning turtle, which became a southern delicacy.)[47] It is probable that hopping John evolved out of rice and bean mixtures such as the Dab-a-Dab served with flabber-sauce that sustained slaves during the Middle Passage.[48] The African American tradition of eating refined white rice instead of brown rice dates back to the antebellum period (brown rice is healthier because it contains essential vitamins, minerals, amino acids, and fiber that aid the body in the elimination process).

A detailed account of African American foodways in North Carolina comes from the journal of Scottish-born Jen Schaw. On the eve of the American Revolution (1774–1776), Schaw traveled from Scotland to the West Indies and North Carolina. In Carolina she visited John Rutherford's four-thousand-acre Hunthill plantation, located ten miles from Rocky Point, North Carolina, and thirty miles from Wilmington. The plantation had about 150 enslaved Africans, many of them artisans employed in various occupations, in the tar, turpentine, and sawmill industries, among others. The plantation comprised fields sowed with corn and other grains, fifty head of cattle, hogs, sheep, a sawmill, a smith's forge for iron work, a timber room, and water enough for two sawmills that produced twenty thouand feet of lumber a week. Schaw writes, "The Negroes are the only people that seem to pay any attention to the various uses that the wild vegetables may be put to." For example, they made bowls out of calabash, which "serves to hold their victuals."[49] West Africans in Gambia used calabash the same way. One historian tells us that the largest majority of enslaved Africans in South Carolina were "most closely associated with Gambia [followed by Angola]."[50]

Schaw noted that Rutherford distributed "a quart of Indian corn per day, and a little piece of land which they cultivated much better than their Master." In addition, slaves on the plantation raised "hogs and poultry, sow calabashes, etc. and are better provided for in every thing than the poorer white people with us." She goes on to say, "they steal whatever they can come at, and even intercept the cows and milk them. They are indeed the constant plague of their tyrants."[51]

The survival of African cookery depended on the region of the Americas where enslaved Africans disembarked. Those who lived and worked in the Caribbean or the Carolinas did so as a black majority with the opportunity and encouragement to grow African food plants and cook African-style dishes such as gumbo, pepper pot, hopping John, and jambalaya. Africans in Virginia lived in a more restricted cultural environment because they were in the minority, making up only 30 to 40 percent of the population.[52] Moreover, in the Chesapeake region, masters imposed greater restrictions on the raw food materials to which Africans had access. They had less time and space to cultivate subsistence gardens. In addition, they seemed to receive equally European, African, and Native American food influences. The inhabitants were constantly negotiating the culinary influences of whites, blacks, and Native Americans. In the words of one historian, "Whites in the Chesapeake may have eaten high on the hog while blacks ate low, but they both ate from the same hog." He goes on to say, "The hog from which blacks and whites ate was fed with Indian corn, a Native American crop. Such were the myriad of connections and influences that allow us to call the Chesapeake Bay region a land of culinary negotiation."[53]

HOG AND HOMINY

Southern Foodways in the Nineteenth Century

By the nineteenth century, the invention of the cotton gin and steam-powered cotton textile mills had revolutionized the North American South. In the now-independent United States, cotton emerged as the premier cash crop. By 1811 the cotton gin had expedited the processing of cotton, which led to more cotton being planted, which in turn required more slaves to tend and harvest it. As a result enslaved African labor gradually dominated the South, creating a belt of territory where blacks made up the majority of the population. The industrial revolution and the invention of the steam engine increased travel throughout the new republic. Much of what we know about African American eating traditions in the nineteenth-century black belt comes from people who crisscrossed the region on steamships and trains. The Virginia, Georgia, Alabama, and Carolina regions, though each unique, were united in their cuisines through the use of three main food sources: pork, greens, and cornmeal. Two further habits also connected the different regions: the cooking of poor-quality meats for a long time to break down the connective tissue and the use of salt pork to season fibrous greens, which required extensive cooking to make them tender and easy to digest.

In plantation regions, argues one historian, enslaved Africans "had quietly been making a life for themselves that included a healthy concern with cooking."[1] This endured despite the fact that masters generally distributed stingy allotments of rations. To supplement their meals, slaves in lowland South Carolina worked under the task system, which permitted them larger amounts of time to cultivate gardens and raise domestic animals. We already know that, in South Carolina, planters gave their slaves rice as a part of their food rations. For instance, in the 1850s Frederick Law Olmsted visited several rice plantations in lowland South Carolina. Planters there gave their slaves rice as part of their food rations during the rice harvest and on holidays. Olmsted observed that planters gave "the cracked and inferior rice that would be unmerchantable" to the slaves as rations.[2] In addition to rice, enslaved Africans received corn and sweet potatoes, "with the occasional addition of a little meat." Slaves in Charleston, South Carolina, recalled traveler Adam Hodgson, "prepare for themselves a little supper from the produce of their garden, and fish which they catch in the river."[3]

The Swedish novelist Fredrika Bremer had an opportunity to try some slave cooking on a Charleston rice plantation. While roaming near the rice fields one morning she spotted "a number of copper vessels, each covered with a lid, from twenty-five to thirty in number." The plantation cook had filled each vessel with "steaming food, which smelled very good. Some of them were filled with brown beans, others with maize pancakes," writes Bremer. "I waited till [the slaves] came up, and then asked permission to taste their food, and I must confess that I have seldom tasted better or more savory viands." As the slaves came from the fields, each one sat down and ate, "some with spoons, others with splinters of wood ... and each contained an abundant portion."[4] African Americans adapted pancakes from the Dutch. The Dutch traditionally made them from wheat flour, while southern African Americans used cornmeal to make hoecakes.

In the 1850s, Olmsted observed slave cooks in action on a large tobacco plantation further north, in Petersburg, Virginia. After an eleven-hour workday, slaves on the Gillin plantation returned to their quarters, where they cooked their own suppers. This tended to be "a bit of bacon fried, often with eggs, corn-bread baked in the spider [a frying pan with legs or feet on the hearth] after the bacon, to absorb the fat, and perhaps some sweet potatoes roasted in the ashes."[5]

In the nineteenth century, African-American cooks continued to grow and cook with yams and sweet potatoes. They used these staples like bread, just as their descendents had done in West Africa.[6] By the mid-nineteenth century, slaves in Virginia had influenced their masters to eat the tubers the same way. By the eve of the Civil War, African American cooks in South Carolina and Virginia had retained many African eating traditions and created new ones. Whites who lived and worked in close proximity to enslaved African Americans typically ate these same cheap, delicious, and filling dishes.[7] From the British African Americans acquired a taste for and the ability to make pies and puddings, which they made with both the African yam and the American sweet potato.[8] They also took pie making to another level with the baking of fruit cobblers from cast-off and foraged fruit and scraps of dough leftover from pie making done in the big-house kitchen.

SPECIAL OCCASIONS DURING SLAVERY

As slaves, African Americans only gorged on large amounts of meat and splurged on rich desserts on a few holidays and religious days during the year. For African Americans, then, good eating became associated with harvest feasts, Christmas, New Year's, the Fourth of July, religious revivals, and Sundays (their only day off during the week). On these special days, slaves received time to cook and garden, extra rations, and access to sweets. Most enslaved African Americans ate much smaller portions and very little meat during the week and did hard physical labor from dawn until dusk six days out of seven in extremely hot weather. Obesity thus was not the problem it is among African Americans today. The correlation between food traditions and religious events dating back to the antebellum period explains why spirituality is also associated with making soul food.

Like their West African ancestors, enslaved African Americans made special foods a part of their religious activities. The function of food at religious assemblies represents an important continuity between West African and African American religions. In the Americas, enslaved Africans continued to use sacred foods such as chicken as they adapted to the rudiments of New World Christianity in the South. African and southern American religious events, with their singing and abundance of food, played an important role in shaping African American religious tradition and the development of soul ideology.

Africans learned Christian theology not only from the preachers that masters hired but also from enslaved licensed and unlicensed preachers and exhorters. Peter Randolph, a slave in Prince George County, Virginia, recalled that, "Not being allowed to hold meetings on the plantation," unauthorized African American preachers would assemble "slaves in the swamps, out of reach of the patrols. They had an understanding among themselves as to the time and place of getting together."[9] Although the core of the enslaved Africans' religious activity took place in private in the slave quarters, praying grounds, and hush harbors (a place where slaves secretly met to practice their religion), public gatherings such as Sunday church services and revivals were also very important.[10]

It was not uncommon for masters to give their slaves permission and support to attend organized religious meetings such as Sunday church services and revivals. Annual revival meetings, which the Baptists called "protracted meetings" and the Methodists called "camp meetings," were morally sanctioned religious events that provided opportunities for all southerners to socialize, gather news, worship the Lord, evangelize, and feast. Church picnics and all-day preaching and dinner on the grounds became traditions basic to southern churchgoers, as most African Americans were by the mid-nineteenth century.[11] "By the eve of the Civil War," writes a preeminent historian of African American religious traditions, "Christianity had pervaded the slave community." He adds: "The vast majority of slaves were American-born, and the cultural and linguistic barriers which had impeded the evangelization of earlier generations of African-born slaves were generally no longer a problem. The widespread opposition of the planters to the catechizing of slaves had been largely dissipated by the efforts of the churches and missionaries of the South. Not all slaves were Christian, nor were all those who accepted Christianity members of a church, but the doctrines, symbols, and vision of life preached by Christianity were familiar to most."[12]

Religious workers regularly organized weeklong revivals that were often interracial, communitywide events. Fredrika Bremer described a camp meeting revival she observed during a visit to Macon, Georgia, in May 1850. "After supper I went to look around, and was astonished by a spectacle that I shall never forget. . . . An immense crowd was assembled, certainly from three to four thousand persons. They sang hymns—superb choir! Strongest of all was the singing of the black portion of the assembly, as they were three times as many as the whites."[13]

At sunrise, Bremer woke to the delightful sound of African Americans singing hymns and the delicious smell of frying ham and eggs, simmering red-eye gravy, steaming rice or grits, and baking buttermilk biscuits and corn bread. "People were cooking and having breakfast by the fires, and a crowd was already" gathering and filling the benches under the tabernacle for the seven o'clock morning worship service and the eleven o'clock sermon that would follow. "After the service came the dinner hour, when I visited several tents in the black camp, and saw tables covered with all kinds of meat, puddings, and tarts; there seemed to be a regular superfluity of food and drink."[14] Bremer's description of this Georgia camp meeting is reminiscent of travelers' descriptions of singing and feasting during West African religious gatherings, discussed earlier.

In some parts of the South before emancipation, the Church was the only institution in which whites permitted African American southerners to maintain their own peculiar way of satisfying their souls and bodies with spiritual and natural food. The autonomy of African American religious churches in the South naturally increased with the abolition of slavery. Moreover, the use of churches for community events drastically increased. Freedom for many African American southerners meant more time for church events like revivals and allowed for the addition of new events to a church's yearly activity calendar, such as Emancipation Day celebrations. But descriptions of Christmas feasts indicate that it was the most lavish of the yearly food-accompanying celebrations.

"Sundays and revival meetings," writes a historian of African American religion, "were not the only respites from work anticipated by the slaves. Christmas was the most festive holiday of all."[15] Masters generally granted slaves the week of Christmas off and gave those who wished it permission to visit nearby plantations where friends and relatives lived. They also furnished slaves with additional bacon and cornmeal rations, as well as flour and fruit for making biscuits, preserves, tarts, and pies.[16] Additional rations distributed for Christmas and time off from the fields allowed women to cook delicious dishes like ribs, hams, chops, chitlins, stews, soups, and sauces for their families and friends.[17]

Soul—Africanisms, spirituality, southern style, pride, love, care, and joyous hard work—cannot be understood without taking into consideration southern American religious rituals and oral traditions. During slavery, members of plantation communities brought the best of their first fruits and dishes to share with friends, family, and visitors. In the South, the most important religious celebrations coincided with the end of the harvest, when communities had an abundance of food and leisure time.

During slavery, foods cooked on Sundays and special occasions played an important role in southern African American religious traditions. Most slaves considered Sunday special because they could visit kinfolk on different plantations and make special meals that expressed their love for family and friends. Oral traditions allowed them to pass down instructions to the next generation on the intricate preparation of foods eaten on religious days: fried chicken, barbecued beef and pork, biscuits, pies, and cakes.

SHARED CULINARY TRADITIONS
BETWEEN AFRICANS AND EUROPEANS

Enslaved Africans did not develop their traditions within a vacuum. In some instances, whites, particularly white children, had intimate relations with blacks. Through close interaction, whites integrated many African religious and language elements. "Southern whites," argues historian John W. Blassingame, "not only adapted their language and religion to that of the slaves but also adapted agricultural practices, sexual attitudes, rhythm of life, architecture, food and social relations to African practices."[18] As masters adopted African foodways and slaves adopted the holidays and special occasions of their owners, black and white cultures in the South became more homogeneous.

By the nineteenth century, African Americans had clearly established a penchant for corn, rice, greens, pork and pork-seasoned foods, and fried foods. Over time, the planter class took great delight in the dishes of their slaves, such as chitlins; turnip greens, collards, and kale simmered with smoked pork parts; roasted yams; gumbos; hopping John, corn bread, crackling bread, and cobblers; and various preparations of wild game and fish.[19] Masters, claimed historian Eugene D. Genovese, "imbibed much of their slaves' culture and sensibility while imparting to their slaves much of their own. . . . Slavery, especially in its plantation setting and in its paternalistic aspect, made white and black southerners one people while making them two."[20] Accounts of food eaten by white planters support this assertion. For instance, on the tobacco plantation in St. Petersburg, Virginia, that Olmsted visited, enslaved Africans covered the big-house table with platters of hot corn bread, sweet potatoes roasted in ashes, and fried eggs. More enslaved waiters arrived from the cookhouse bearing plates of cold roast pork and roast turkey, fried chicken, and an opossum cooked in such a way that, according to Olmsted, it "somewhat resembled baked suckling-pig."[21] Traditionally opossum was one of several victuals that slaves obtained on their own to supplement their woefully inadequate slave rations. Former Maryland slave Frederick Douglass described how, when given free time, the "industrious ones of our number would employ themselves in . . . hunting opossums, hares, and coons."[22] Here, however, it is served by slaves to whites. Similarly, yams before the nineteenth century were part of what planters distributed as slave rations. But by the mid nineteenth century planters in the South no longer considered sweet potatoes and yams the food of slaves. At the Virginia tobacco plantation, Olmsted recalled, "There was no other bread, and but one vegetable served—sweet potato, roasted in ashes, and this, I thought, was the best sweet potato, also, I ever had eaten."[23]

The great complaint of the slaves was the monotony of their assigned diet of largely salt pork and cornmeal. In addition to raising chicken and pigs and hunting small game, they also responded by growing beans and greens. Through their own efforts they created heavily seasoned preparations of chitlins, collard greens, okra, and turnip greens and dishes such as hopping John. Genovese holds that enslaved Africans were not alone in enjoying these classic soul food dishes. Both poor whites and those in the planter class enjoyed them too. Blacks created the dishes, prepared them for their masters, and, in Genovese's words, "contributed more to the diet of the poorer whites than the poorer whites ever had the chance to contribute to theirs."[24] Speaking of poor whites in rural South Carolina, Olmsted observed, "Their chief sustenance is a porridge of cow-peas, and the greatest luxury with which they are acquainted is a stew of bacon and peas, with red pepper, which they call 'Hopping John.'" Poor whites, in Olmsted's estimation, seldom had any meat, he said, "except they steal hogs which belong to the planters, or their negroes, and their chief diet is rice and milk."[25] Food scholars generally recognize rice as a staple as an African introduction to the Americas. In Brazil, *Feijoada*, the staple of most slaves, was made from black beans, jerked beef, and rice slaves received as rations. They enhanced the rations used to make *feijoada* by adding spices and discarded animal parts like tongues, ears, feet, and tails from slaughtered farm animals. They also added *caruru* (cooking greens) and large amounts of pepper.[26]

Afro-Cuban cooks viewed a huge dish of cooked rice as an essential accompaniment to any meal they served. Without rice, Cubans of all complexions and classes regarded meat and other dishes at the table with indifference.[27] A similar attitude about the necessity of rice at every meal developed among black and whites in low-country South Carolina and Georgia.

Olmsted describes another example of Africans and Europeans sharing a culinary tradition among a steamship crew in Mobil, Alabama. "The crew of the boat . . . was composed partly of Irishmen, and partly of negroes; the latter were slaves, and were hired of their owners at $40 a month—the same wages paid to the Irishmen."[28] Olmsted observed, "so far as convenient" the ships captain kept the blacks "at work separate from the white hands; they were also messed separately." As members of the same working class onboard the ship, the black and white crewmen ate the same food. "The food, which was given to them in tubs, from the kitchen, was various and abundant, consisting of bean porridge, bacon, corn bread, ship's biscuit, potatoes, duff (pudding), and gravy."[29]

In Louisiana, working-class blacks and white shared similar culinary histories as consumers of foods purchased on the streets of New Orleans. In the Crescent City, African Americans wearing bright handkerchiefs as head wraps carried baskets and basins containing fried chicken and fish dinners that they sold to dock workers. Moreover, New Orleans residents sold out of their homes food typical of African American cuisine. "Those fresh from the gombo [sic] soup, and the ham, and the punch and julep, rushing back again.... I tremble to think of ... punches, and nogs, and soups, and plates of fish, and game, and beef and loaves of bread, that I have seen appear from side doors and vanish" for a dime each.[30] A similar commercial and culinary culture developed in nineteenth-century Brazil. In Rio, African Brazilian street vendors gained fame for the sale of a fish meal called *batatas doces*, described as sardines fried in dendê oil and broiled shrimp served with spinach, hearts of palm, and sweet potatoes.[31]

By the eve of the Civil War, whites in the South of all classes had accepted black cookery and made it part of their everyday cuisine. Nineteenth-century accounts tell us that whites who lived and worked in close proximity to slaves typically ate the same cheap, delicious, and filling dishes that slaves developed to temper the monotony of their food rations.[32] The same development occurred in Brazil, where black majorities shaped the cuisine of whites. By the mid-nineteenth century, *feijoada* was a staple of Brazilians of all classes. Travelers Louis and Elizabeth Agassiz noted that there was "no house so rich as to exclude" *feijoada* from the table. Depending on the region, the same could be said for corn bread, rice, and salt pork in the United States.[33] In short, whites and blacks influenced each others' foodways, if in different ways. Whites provided the material culture and adopted the culinary creativity of their African American cooks, coworkers, and neighbors. By the nineteenth century, the majority of the poor white population in the South enjoyed all parts of the hog, corn bread, greens, sweet potato pie, candied yams, and black eyed peas and rice. On the eve of the Civil War, poor white and black southerners were eating the same diet, based on greens, rice or corn, and skimpy amounts of meat.[34]

THE CIVIL WAR AND RECONSTRUCTION

During the Civil War (1861–1865) both Confederate and Union soldiers very often depended on African American cooks on the battlefield. Northern army officers put free-born blacks and runaways into segregated

FIGURE 3.1 *"Sweet Potatoe Planting—James Hopkinson's Plantation, Edisto Island, S.C., April 8, 1862."* Photographs and Prints Division, Schomburg Center for Research in Black Culture, New York Public Library, Astor, Lenox, and Tilden Foundations.

regiments, paid them less than white soldiers, and fed them inferior food. Union officers subjected African Americans to corporal punishment evocative of their enslaved experience and assigned them menial duties like cooking rather than combat. In a March 1863 letter from Washington, D.C., for example, H.W. Halleck, apparently a high-ranking member of the Northern strategic command, suggested ways to organize black troops in the field along the Mississippi River. He writes, following the example of one General Banks near New Orleans, that freedmen "can be used to hold points on the Mississippi during the sickly [malaria] season" and they "certainly can be used with advantage as laborers, teamsters, cooks, &c."[35]

Southern armies also used the labor of slaves and free blacks for menial tasks like cooking. President Jefferson Davis ordered planters to turn over one out of every ten slaves for voluntary war labor. These "Negro servants," as the Confederates called them, cleaned and cooked whatever soldiers caught, shot, and gathered as food.[36]

Pork and corn bread, sweet potatoes, and sweetmeats represented the most requested foods among Southern troops both black and white. In the Union army, African American troops requested additional corn bread and pork as rations. When commissary officials complied, southern-born white soldiers celebrated the change, while "their Northern-born comrades, accustomed to beef and wheat bread, complained bitterly."[37]

For most of the war, the South had no trouble producing food for its soldiers, though by its end, in 1865, Northern forces had advanced deep into the black belt, and pitched battles and foraging soldiers had ruined productive fields and reduced domesticated hogs and wild game almost to extinction.[38] Getting provisions to the field, however, represented the Confederate command's greatest shortcoming. There was a shortage of salt and other preservatives to keep the food and a shortage of money and transportation to ship it. Confederate forces were constantly short of cans, boxes, and barrels for shipping food to the battlefields. With the lack of regular food shipments, soldiers survived on handouts from civilians, rations taken from the remains of dead Union soldiers, and sustenance found foraging in the woods and raiding civilian homes and farms. Soldiers fighting along the Atlantic Coast also fished.

When they did obtain food, soldiers then had to confront a shortage of cooking utensils.[39] Some made them from the bottom halves of captured canteens and cooked meat on the points of sharp sticks. Others mixed meal and flour in turtle shells, calabashes, shirttails, and other makeshift containers. By the end of the war, many white soldiers who previously had no cooking experience became experts at creating what became southern delicacies after the war: huckleberry pie, roast pork, turkey, and opossum. For black southerners, preparing such dishes was nothing new.

FIGURE 3.2 African American army cook at work in City Point, Virginia. Library of Congress, Prints and Photographs Division, LC-B811-2597.

EDUCATION, CLASS, AND THE AFRICAN AMERICAN
DIET IN THE NEW SOUTH DURING RECONSTRUCTION

Various forms of tenant farming replaced plantation slavery. Sharecropping and tenant farming did very little to improve the nutritional conditions of the freedmen. Most southerners continued hearth-cooking practices and existed largely on simple diets reminiscent of the antebellum period. As one historian concluded, the "three M's, that is, meat (meaning salt pork), meal, and molasses, continued as the core diet."[40] Samuel H. Lockett, who traveled through Louisiana in 1871, argued that the people of the South needed to reform their eating habits:

> The greatest drawback to the people in the pine woods [referring to the South in general] is the manner in which they live, I mean the food they eat. Three times a day, for nearly 365 days of the year, their simple meal is coarse corn bread and *fried* bacon. At dinner there will be added perhaps "collards" or some other coarse vegetable. Even when they have fresh meat or venison, which they can obtain whenever they wish, it is always fried and comes to the table swimming in a sea of clear, melted lard. Chickens, eggs, milk and butter, all kinds of vegetables and fruit they could have, but have not. I really believe that the best missionary to send among them would be a disciple of A. Soyer, the great French cook. Let him preach "good health by good living," distribute throughout the Piney Woods and, in fact, throughout the rural districts of much of our southern country, dime cookery-books, and sell all the frying pans, and the mental, moral, and physical condition of the population would soon be immensely improved.[41]

Yet, Many African American sharecroppers and tenant farmers almost starved to death because they moved too often to be able to develop the type of gardens they had used to supplement their diets during the antebellum period. As a result, they ate very unbalanced meals full of saturated fats. In addition, beginning in the late 1870s, they began purchasing highly processed food staples. For example, groups of poor southerners increasingly turned to merchants for cornmeal and white flour. New high-efficiency roller mills increased the production speed of these staples, but they also stripped the processed grains of their healthy nutrients and fiber.

In the late 1880s, the U.S. Department of Agriculture—in collaboration with two historically black colleges and universities (HBCUs), Tuskegee Institute and Hampton Institute—performed dietary studies of African American farmers in the vicinities of Tuskegee in Macon County, Alabama,

FIGURE 3.3 Old African American couple eating at a table by a fireplace in rural Virginia. Library of Congress, Prints and Photographs Division, LC-USZ62-61017.

and Hampton in Franklin County, Virginia. These studies examined over a dozen families. Investigators visited each house for two weeks, "taking specimens for analysis, notes being made at the same time regarding the people, their dwellings, farm work [agricultural practices], habits, and the like."[42] These studies provide details about the eating traditions of southern farmers in the late nineteenth century.

For example, it appears that the majority of the farmers in the region of Tuskegee cultivated gardens where, during different seasons, they raised a variety of vegetables, including turnips, corn, collards, cabbage, and string beans. One recipe for "ol' cabin cabbage" said that everybody knew how to make this cabbage dish that left an odor so strong "that when tomorrow comes you kin tell you done had cabbage yesterday." The recipe described the odor as one of those "lingerin' smells that hides aroun' in the cornders an' oozes up outer of the cracks long after the cabbage done et up an' forgot about all 'ceptn them folks what can't eat cabbages an eats it anyhow." According to the recipe, the cook put on "the pot with a hunk er meat an' a cabbage kivered with water an' lets it bile an' bile till you can't tell the meat from the cabbage and cabbage from the meat."[43]

Farmers prepared collards and turnip greens more than any other vegetable because they had a much longer growing season and could be obtained at almost any time of the year. Good collard greens, according to
one cookbook, called for a ham hock, but the cook added that a "hunk
of fat back'll do."[44] To make southern-style collards, "Keep yo' meat an'
green stuff well kivered with bilin water an' let it all cook some two hours.
Don't bile fast but jes' let yo' pot simper along slowsome. A piece of red
pepper pod ain't gonter hurt the seasonin' none, an' use your gumption
when the bilin' air pretty nigh finished 'bout whether or not mo' salt air a
needcessity."[45]

African-American cooks did not restrict the use of fatback to cooking
cabbage and collards. One study of eating habits among African Americans in North Carolina, South Carolina, and Georgia showed that parents
gave crying babies a piece of fatback as a pacifier. Parents also introduced
fatty bacon, commonly called a "streak of fat and a streak of lean" and
other forms of pork into their children's diets at an early age.[46] Southerners used cured pork as a flavor booster, not as the center of the meal. As
Joyce White remembers from her childhood in Choctaw County, Alabama,
"Turnip, mustard, and collard greens glistened with a few slivers of ham
hocks, and so did crowder peas and butter beans. A meaty ham bone was
simmered with potatoes and green beans or with tomatoes, rice, corn, and
okra for delicious stews."[47] Like corn bread, sweet potatoes, and yams,
pork became part of the southern African American's diet during infancy.
This made it very difficult for many African Americans in their adult years
to imagine a life without it.

Very few African American farmers in Macon County, Alabama, owned
land in 1895 and 1896. Instead, most farmed on property owned by white
landlords. Their livelihood depended on how many bales of cotton they
could grow, and therefore they devoted little time to raising subsistence
crops. Generally, they dedicated their fields to cotton, with some corn,
sweet potatoes, and a few other food crops. Most of the residents in the
region around Tuskegee Institute, both black and white, ate a diet of "fat
salt pork, corn meal, and molasses." Farmers produced some molasses and
cornmeal and bought some from stores. Participants in both studies received a large amount of their nutrition from "unbolted [unsifted] corn
meal," which, in the late 1890s, cost about a cent a pound.[48] Unbolted
cornmeal, though processed, retained a large amount of bran, which plays
a vital role in maintaining a healthy colon.

Farmers also raised and killed their own hogs. In most cases, however,
the fat salt pork purchased in large quantities at southern markets came

FIGURE 3.4 Ten African American women in a cooking class at Hampton Institute, Hampton, Virginia. Library of Congress, Prints and Photographs Division, LC-USZ62-95109.

from meat-packing houses in Chicago and elsewhere. In Macon County, when a person referred to meat, he or she "always meant fat pork." The authors of the Tuskegee study wrote, "Some of them knew it [meat] by no other name, nor did they seem to know much of any other meat except that of opossum and rabbits, which they occasionally hunted, and of chickens, which they raised to a limited extent." One cook wrote that fried chicken was "hard ter larn a new cook ter do." The cook added that it is easier to fry greasy than not and the "cook what dishes up greasy fried chicken oughter go out an' wuck in the fiel' whar she b'longs."[49]

In Franklin County, Virginia, African American sharecroppers ate very little or no beef, mutton, or other leaner meats, because they believed that those meats would make them sick. In addition to fat pork and wild game was part of their definition of meat. Generally, cooks boiled game in water until the meat fell off the bone, then seasoned and baked or barbecued it. In Alabama, no barbecue was considered done unless the meat was "saturated with blistering sauces." For example, cooks in Eufaula, Alabama, basted the cooking meat, "whether it be pork, beef, lamb, kid, or chicken," with a "mixture of vinegar, mustard, catsup, Worchester sauce, olive oil, Tabasco sauce, lemon juice and whole red peppers in great quantity. The sauce is boiled for three minutes after mixture before being applied to the meat." The barbecuing and basting would last for hours, until the meat was an "aromatic brown."[50]

In addition to barbecued meat, those in close proximity to water consumed sizable of quantities of fresh, salted, smoked, and fried fish. In Franklin County, in the Chesapeake Bay region, families ate eel, herring, mullet, roach, blue croakers, trout, and perch. Except in Florida and Georgia, southerners considered turtle a favorite dish, typically cooking it in a pot as part of a soup or stew. Eel and frog were considered delicacies as well. Southerners seasoned and batter-fried them just like catfish. Fish and small game remained popular because one could cook and eat them in one or two meals, which reduced the chances that the meat would spoil and harm someone.[51]

FRIED FRESH TROUT

Slice salt pork thin and fry until crisp. Remove and set aside. Dredge trout in flour or roll in cracker meal. Sprinkle with black pepper. Fry in the hot salt pork fat until deep brown. Serve garnished with parsley and fried salt pork.

Pearl Bowser and Joan Eckstein, *A Pinch of Soul in Book Form* (New York: Avon, 1969), 225.

During lean times, some trapped and sold rabbits as a way of earning extra money. The poor consumed small game such as rabbits because they did not have the technological ability to preserve and/or refrigerate much of anything. In many parts of the South, people stored their perishables in small portable wooden cupboards or dairies with no refrigeration capacity. In addition, the poor grazing lands in the South raised comparatively few beef cattle and sheep. The meat that was procured was inferior to that raised in the Southwest and Midwest. One scientist involved in the study of black farmers in the South concluded: "The scarcity of fresh meat and the difficulty of preserving it doubtless goes far toward explaining the [preference for salt pork] in the dietary tastes and habits of the people in general in this region, if not elsewhere in the south."[52]

WILD HARE IN TOMATO SAUCE

1 cup meat from a young rabbit
flour for dredging

salt and black pepper to taste
bacon fat
4 scallions with tops, sliced
2 cloves garlic, crushed
sprig of fresh parsley
4 tbs. butter
2 tbs. Worcestershire sauce
2 cups tomato juice
½ cup milk
1 tsp. minced sweet basil

Roll rabbit pieces in flour seasoned with salt and pepper. Brown in bacon fat. Make a sauce with sliced scallions, crushed garlic, parsley, butter, salt, Worcestershire sauce, tomato juice, milk, and basil. Pour over the rabbit while it is still hot. Cook 2 hours in a covered pan, then remove lid and cook 15 to 20 minutes more, reducing the sauce. Thicken sauce with a little cornmeal mixed with water if it is thin.

Pearl Bowser and Joan Eckstein, *A Pinch of Soul in Book Form* (New York: Avon, 1969), 215.

Technological stagnation also explains the continuation of simple and primitive cooking methods in late-nineteenth-century southern cooking. Most southerners, black or white, could not afford a stove. Instead, they continued to cook in the ashes of a fireplace or with iron pots and pans over the hot embers of a fire. For example, in Macon County, Alabama, only two of the families in the study had enough money to own a stove, and, in Franklin County, Virginia, several women interviewed said they did not bake bread because they did not have an oven. Other women interviewed complained that store-bought, highly processed loaves of white bread lacked any kind of savory, mouthwatering appeal. Instead, they preferred various types of corn and wheat flour biscuits. Southerners made and ate biscuits sliced in half and stuffed with pork, fried eggs, cold baked sweet potatoes, and other items. Pone bread, johnnycakes, hoecakes, and ashcakes from the colonial period remained very popular because most southerners owned very few cooking utensils. Some recognized that consuming small amounts of ash and charcoal cured flatulence and upset stomachs. As a result, they sometimes ate pone bread baked in ashes without cleaning it off.[53]

In the 1890s, black farmers in and around Tuskegee, Alabama, were still preparing cornmeal in ways that dated back to the antebellum period.

"The daily fare," wrote John Wesslay Hoffman, agricultural chemistry and biology teacher at Tuskegee Institute from 1894 to 1896, "is prepared in very simple ways. Corn meal is mixed with water and baked on the flat surface of a hoe or griddle. The salt pork is sliced thin and fried until very brown and much of the grease is fried out." He went on to say, "Molasses from cane or sorghum is added to the fat, making what is known as 'sop,' which is eaten with the corn bread."[54] In general, among southerners, corn bread was the staff of life, and preparing the easy-to-make batter became a daily routine. Southerners usually ate corn bread Monday through Friday and biscuits on the weekend and on special occasions. In addition to ashcakes and hoecakes, southerners also made crackling bread, or fatty bread, out of cornmeal.

Farmers in Charleston County, South Carolina, made crackling bread in the wintertime during hog-killing days. The fat of the hog was cut into cubes and rendered in a wash pot set over a hot fire. The skin, writes Wendell Brooks, rises "to the top of the boiling grease, growing shriveled and brown." A cook would skim off these cracklings and then press them to remove excess grease. To make delicious golden brown crackling bread, an African-American recipe from North Georgia called for two cups of cornmeal with one cup of crackling. Add "salt, soda, buttermilk and enough water to make a soft dough (or use ⅔ cups of buttermilk). Bake pretty brown." Definitions and recipes for crackling bread varied across the South. For example, black farmers in Tuskegee, Alabama, made theirs with crisp pieces of fried bacon, cornmeal, water, soda, and salt and, according to Hoffman, "baked [it] in an oven or over the fireplace." Characteristically, cooks boiled or fried their food, and most dishes arrived at the table stewed or very crisp. According to Hoffman, many black farmers in the study suffered from various forms of indigestion because they consumed large amounts of fried foods.[55]

Fried pork and cornmeal in one shape or another appeared daily in the southern diet. A list of foods eaten by more affluent African American families in the study showed more variety, however, including dairy products, fruits, vegetables, and better cuts of meat. Those who ate greater amounts of fruits and vegetables tended to live near the influence of the Tuskegee and Hampton institutes. According to the food studies' government researchers, these families did not represent the average black belt residents. Apparently, increased educational opportunities and earning power improved the eating habits of southern farmers. In short, Tuskegee and Hampton improved the diets of the farmers within their sphere of influence. In addition, in contrast to those in Macon County, Alabama,

African Americans in Franklin County, Virginia, had greater access to fish and therefore healthier, leaner forms of protein.[56]

Historians still know very little about how diets changed after the Civil War and the role diet played in elite white- and black-led reform efforts at the turn of the century. There is a body of literature on food reform within the history of the vegetarian movement led by elite white reformers during this period. That movement, however, occurred principally in the Northwest and Northeast and made very few inroads among southerners, black or white.[57] Regarding white Southern elites, Historian Joe Gray Taylor insists that after the Civil War they did not shun black eyed peas, grits, or collard greens as white elites in the North did. He writes, "with the exception of New Orleans and possibly Charleston and Baltimore, the concept of fine food in the European sense hardly existed in the Old South." Instead, southern elites inherited from "British yeoman, from the Indian, and from the frontier . . . a preference for large amounts of different kinds of good food rather than a few dishes of presumably superb food." Taylor goes on to say, "the most striking fact about the diet of the New South, from the Civil War through World War II, is not that it changed, but how little it changed."[58]

The literature on the Tuskegee Woman's Club, started in 1895, and similar clubs at the Hampton Institute sheds very little light on upper-class black women's efforts to reform the African American diet in the South.[59] Most of these black self-help organizations were controlled by upper-class women. For example, the Tuskegee Women's Club only admitted female faculty members of Tuskegee or wives or female relatives of male Tuskegee faculty. Most of these women's clubs left a more substantial paper trail about their struggles to stop the tide of lynching that racked the country at the turn of the century than on their efforts to reduce the amount of fried foods African Americans were eating.[60]

African American Margaret Washington, the wife of Booker T. Washington and founder of the Tuskegee Woman's Club, was a typical progressive era reformer in many ways but not in all. She championed Tuskegee's mantra of "Bath, Broom, and Bible," that is, cleanliness and Christian morality.[61] She put great emphasis on developing biblical motherhood and wifehood in the rural women of Tuskegee, Alabama. What was different about her and other black reformers of the turn of the century, however, was a conservative black nationalism. The first lady of Tuskegee put particular emphasis on teaching black history and encouraging black landownership, which she believed would lead to black economic independence. Margaret Washington's focus on African American property ownership, which she called an obtainable goal, was a sharp contrast to other women's club leaders of the period who spent their energy fighting for women's suffrage. Yet there is evidence that crusaders at the Tuskegee and Hampton institutes encouraged African American farmers to produce most of what they cooked, consume less fried food and fatback, and diversify their diets. And, while they did not reduce fat and fried food consumption that much, black farmers close to Tuskegee and Hampton did grow more of what they ate, to the benefit of their diet. These farmers ate foods free of harmful pesticides. They also ate large amounts of fiber-rich cornmeal, while the lye that went into processing their hominy cleansed both the liver and stomach.

The Tuskegee Woman's Club did provide cooking classes through the college, but scholars provide no details about the instructional content of the classes.[62] Some insights, however, can be gleaned from Booker T. Washington himself. In a letter dated November 23, 1899, to one of his school administrators, Washington writes: "I call your attention to the enclosed bill of fare for the students. It seems to me that they are having too much fat meat; you will notice that they had bacon and gravy for two meals."[63] Like Professor Samuel H. Lockett before him, Washington wanted blacks to consume less salt pork and fat. Perhaps reducing the amount of fried foods was a goal of his wife's reform agenda and cooking classes?

Another insight into black reform movements and the southern diet comes from a look at the institute's menu. It shows that students at Tuskegee ate far more broiled foods than did African American farmers in Alabama, who seemed to have fried food with almost every meal. The Wizard of Tuskegee, as Booker T. Washington was called, was a micromanager in advancing his agenda. For example, he assigned African American Laura Evangeline Mabry the job of campus food critic, or dietitian. From Birmingham, Alabama Mabry graduated from Tuskegee in 1895 and stayed on as member of the school's staff until 1901. In a report to Washington on the institute's cafeteria dinner menu, she comments on the fare: "Boiled Peas. Boiled Sweet-potatoes. Stewed beef and Corn bread. The peas were boiled without fat. Enough hard corn was found in the peas to make them unpalatable and unattractive. The beef was not seasoned with pepper and salt, but the onions added much to the taste. Potatoes and bread were nice and hot."[64] Perhaps this menu reflects how Margaret and Booker T. Washington wanted all black folks to cook their food—though presumably with properly cooked corn.

Atlanta University graduate James Weldon Johnson also complained about the extent of fried food and fatback consumption among rural

blacks in Georgia. Johnson, an African American from the city of Jacksonville, Florida, did a stint as a rural teacher during which he boarded with
a family in Hampton, Georgia, thirty miles south of Atlanta. For the first
two or three weeks, his landlady served him "fried chicken twice a day,
for breakfast and supper." Thereafter the menu "steadily degenerated until
my diet was chiefly fat pork and greens and an unpalatable variety of corn
bread. For a while I lived almost exclusively on buttermilk, because I could
no longer stomach this coarse fare." He adds, "Then it was that I looked
longingly at every chicken I passed, and would have given a week's wages
for a beefsteak."[65] Again, we see an upper-class southerner complaining
that the lower classes fried too much of their food and did not include
enough variety in their diet.

In general, black southerners after the abolition of slavery continued
to exist on a diet of salt pork and corn bread. Emancipation did give them
greater access to poultry, however, resulting for some in the cooking and
consumption of fried chicken "for breakfast and supper." Fruit cobblers,
biscuits, turnips, sweet potatoes, and polk salad (also called poke sallet,
greens from the pokeberry or poke plant) were also familiar foods in black
southern homes. Some southern families ate polk salad boiled or floured
and deep-fried like okra. Others served peas, beans, cabbage, and greens.
Studies of late-nineteenth-century eating habits conclude that the poorest
families suffered not from an insufficient quantity of food but rather from
a lack of quality and variety. A special concern was the ability to obtain
fresh fruits and vegetables during the winter and early spring, when most
working-class families ate a monotonous nitty-gritty diet heavy on potatoes, cabbage, and turnips. High milk prices also put that source of vitamins and minerals out of range for most poor black families. One traveler
observed that those without milk to make butter would instead use "bacon
grease on the biscuits and corn bread, or you could dip it in the stewed
tomatoes." Thus, those with a cow or goat had better and more diverse
diets.[66]

Middle- and upper-class African Americans did share some eating traditions with poorer southern African Americans. For example, cooking
chicken, some form of corn, and one-pot meals was common to African
Americans of every status. In the 1880s, the family of middle-class African
American James Weldon Johnson preferred eating "soul-satisfying" dishes
such as gumbo, fried chicken, and hominy. Sausage and hominy or hog
and hominy was a popular breakfast. Gumbo and rice was an equally popular soul-satisfying dish. Johnson recalled the unforgettable experience of
eating some gumbo made by a Charleston, South Carolina, migrant named

Mrs. Gibbs. She made her Charlestonian gumbo in a large pot similar to those used in the old slave quarters. In it she put okra, water, salt and pepper, "bits of chicken, ham first fried then cut into small squares; whole shrimps; crab meat, some of it left in pieces of the shell; onions and tomatoes; thyme and other savory herbs." Then she slow cooked it for hours and served the gumbo over white rice.[67]

Johnson grew up living with his father, who was from Richmond, Virginia, and his mother and maternal grandmother, both natives of the Bahamas. "My grandmother was especially skillful in the preparation of West Indian dishes: piquant fish dishes, chicken pilau, shrimp pilau, crab stew, crab and okra gumbo, hoppin' John, and Johnny cake." Soups and stews remained important staples in many parts of the South because of their ability to feed several mouths with a small amount of meat or fish. While Johnson describes his grandmother's cooking as West Indian, descendants of slaves in the United States, Cuba, and Brazil prepared similar dishes with African ingredients like okra.[68]

In addition to rice, poor folk throughout history have also had an enduring relationship with fried fish. When fat or oil is heated to the high temperatures necessary for frying, its chemical composition changes, and the body's enzymes have trouble breaking it down. As a result, the body must work harder and longer to gain any benefit from a dish such as fried fish. As we now know, Africans along the Senegal, Gambia, Niger, and Congo rivers received a sizable percentage of their protein in the form of smoked, salted, and fried fish. This tradition continued in South Carolina and Virginia into the twentieth century. African Americans living near bodies of water ate lots of fish, both fresh and canned. After the turn of the century, canned salmon was so cheap that southerners purchased it to make salmon cakes or to eat plain. Similarly, they purchased canned oysters and sardines and ate them with crackers. Yet fried catfish and porgies remained the most popular fish preparation by far. "Southerners believed that God made fish to be fried," writes one historian of the South.[69]

After the Civil War, the consumption of fresh fruits and vegetables decreased as owners of large plantations were no longer required to grow them for slave rations. The orchard, across the South, insists one historian, "almost disappeared from the commercial plantation and was confined to the land of the provident yeoman farmer. As the twentieth century wore on, those who grew fruit found fighting insects and fungus a difficult and expensive proposition."[70] Commercially producing fruit orchards may have disappeared, but many African American families in the South continued to cultivate gardens that supplied their tables with fresh peaches,

berries, and grapes. For farmers who dedicated land to subsistence farming, like those around the Tuskegee and Hampton institutes, there were
thus healthy aspects to the southern African American diet. As I shall discuss, the tradition of subsistence gardening went with African American
southerners when they migrated north to states like New York.

SPECIAL OCCASIONS:
LATE-NINETEENTH-CENTURY REVIVALS

> After settling the question with his bacon and cabbage, the next dear-
> est thing to a colored man, in the South, is his religion. I call it a
> "thing," because they always speak of getting religion as if they were
> going to market for it.
>
> —WILLIAM WELLS BROWN—
> "Black Religion in the Post-Reconstruction South" (1880)

Religious traditions and eating on special occasions became even more established in African American communities after emancipation. There are
many different churches within most African American communities, but
the food celebrations remain consistent.[71] These events increased the association between soul and food in black communities: religion nourished
the soul while food nourished the body. African Americans at the turn of
the twentieth century were largely an agricultural group made up of hard-
working farmers and farmhands. Working off a heavy Sunday breakfast
or dinner on the grounds during a revival or on Christmas or New Year's
Day was much easier for them than for their descendants in the industrial
society of the late twentieth century.[72]

In 1895 and 1896 African American farmers in the vicinity of Tuskegee,
Alabama, generally worked "about seven and a half months during the
year," according to researchers from the U.S. Department of Agriculture.
"The rest of the time," says one researcher, "is devoted to visiting, social
life, revivals, [and] other religious exercises." During the "laying-by time,"
while the crops were maturing, African American farmers near Tuskegee held "bush meetings" and revivals and visited friends for sometimes
a whole week at a time.[73] Writing in 1903, W.E.B. Dubois insisted that,
at the turn of the century, the church represented "the social centre" of
African-American life: "This building is the central club-house of a community of a thousand or more Negroes. Various organizations meet here—
the church proper, the Sunday-school, two or three insurance societies,
women's societies, secret societies, and mass meetings of various kinds.

Entertainments, suppers, and lectures are held besides the five or six regular weekly religious services."[74]

Revivals and the centrality of the church in the lives of African Americans continued into the 1920s and 1930s. These were two important decades in American history, during which southern-born African Americans migrated to the North in large numbers. Most migrated in search of better-paying jobs and housing. Others fled to escape oppressive race relations and the jim crow policies that began after the end of Reconstruction.

THE NADIR BEFORE THE GREAT MIGRATION

Historians have called the period before the Great Migration (discussed in the next chapter) the nadir of race relations in the United States. In the late nineteenth century, conditions for black southerners became deplorable as northern politicians began dismantling Reconstruction in 1877, abandoning black southerners. Southern racists in the United States produced an abundance of anti-African-American literature, and bigots among predominately southern white Protestant church leadership declared the virtues of black subordination to whites in all facets of life. For black southerners, it became increasingly more difficulty to exercise their rights as U.S. citizens after northern politicians removed federal troops from the South.[75] For example, during his visit to the lower Mississippi region in the 1880s, Austrian writer and traveler Ernest Von Hesse-Wartegg asked, "What are these causes that have set Negroes on the move? Poverty and distress in the South since the war and bad treatment from planters and officials."[76]

In 1881 the *Weekly Louisianian* carried a story on why a group of African Americans had left North Carolina for Indiana. The black North Carolina natives explained that "although nominally free since the war, our condition in the South was in fact one of servitude, and was each year becoming worse." Economically, their wages were "only sufficient to sustain our lives with the coarsest food, cover our bodies with the poorest raiment, and shelter us in the [most] wretched habitations," they wrote. Politically and socially, "when the laws were not made to discriminate against us outright, they were so administered as to have the same effect." Local magistrates in North Carolina used every pretext to "send men of our race to the penitentiary, while white men were unmolested who committed the same offenses.... More and more each year we were deprived of our political rights, by fraud if not by violence. There was no security for our lives."[77]

Security for African Americans grew worse with the election of President Woodrow Wilson (1913–1921). Wilson demonstrated that he was either unaware or uninterested in conditions facing black southerners by staging the premier for the racist pro–Klu Klux Klan film *The Birth of a Nation* in the White House. Furthermore, he remained inactive during a number of race riots that happened during his administration, in East St. Louis, Charleston, Houston, Knoxville, Elaine (Arkansas), and Tulsa, in which hundreds of blacks were murdered. Over time African Americans learned that Wilson's silence in the midst of racist atrocities committed by whites was a deadly combination. It became clear that he was no champion of democracy and justice for all U.S. citizens. Taking their cues from the Wilson administration, officials at the local level around the nation remained apathetic to the complaints of the friends and families of African American victims of lynchings, arson, and beatings committed by both civilians and police officers between 1913 to 1922.[78]

Black folk were determined to defend their citizenship rights against white racist aggression. The assertiveness of African American veterans of the world war clashed with the determination of racist whites to reestablish the pre-WWI subordination of African Americans. In communities where riots erupted, supporters of the jim crow power structure encountered little restraint from local officials when they mobilized to crush outspoken and armed African Americans. Research on racial conflict across the country during the nadir indicates that southern whites were trying to regain self-confidence by practicing violent white supremacy rituals: beating, raping, shooting, lynching, and torching African Americans and destroying their important social and economic infrastructures.[79]

In the aftermath of several riots, one black southerner in 1921 concluded that African Americans, "especially the Southern wing of the race is tired of un-Godly principles being meted to us." He called jim crow an "un-American, unprincipled, and inhuman" system." He added, "No Colored man is safe here, no matter what his social, political, or financial status in the community. We are looked upon as outcasts, vagabonds, or anything other than an American citizen."[80]

THE GREAT MIGRATION

From the Black Belt to the Freedom Belt

When World War I started in Europe in 1914, food prices in the southern United States increased, and a business depression occurred that lasted until the summer of 1915. In addition, the boll weevil's destruction of black belt cotton crops and the flooding of some sections of the South and beyond led to a shortage of crops in 1916 and low demand for agricultural workers. There was also a "demand for labor in the North and higher wages offered there," according to a 1919 black migration study commissioned by the U.S. Department of Labor.[1]

For the first time in their lives, owners of large plantations in states such as Alabama had to tell their tenants they could not advance food to them and advised them to relocate. Food shortages, low wages, and unemployment resulted in the exodus of large numbers of African American wage-earning farmhands, sharecroppers, and tenant farmers, who supplied the lion's share of unskilled labor in the rural southern United States. In addition to economic factors, political forces also shaped their decision to leave the South.

In small towns and villages in states such as South Carolina, whites roughly handled and corporally punished African American residents. The 1919 Department of Labor migration study reported: "The beating of farm hands on the large plantations in the lower south is so common that many colored people look upon every great plantation as a peon camp: and in sawmills and other public works it is not at all unusual for bosses to knock Negroes around with pieces of lumber or anything else that happens to come handy." African Americans also regularly faced lynch mobs throughout the rural South. Seldom encountered before or during Reconstruction, incidents of lynching became quite common by 1910. The situation for blacks in urban centers was not much better. In southern cities, white public officials shamefully neglected public services and badly needed infrastructure improvements in African American neighborhoods. Harassing and humiliating to African American southerners, jim crow laws were a constant threat to civil rights, even within educational and recreational facilities.[2]

Many southern blacks traveled north by rail after receiving letters from friends and family testifying to better conditions and wages in the North. Others learned about the "real advantages of the North"—such as better educational opportunities, higher wages, and better options—through African American-owned-and-operated newspapers published in Chicago, Cleveland, Philadelphia, and New York. These papers kept black southerners aware of jim crow oppression, including lynchings and mob violence. By 1917 almost half a million southerners migrated to the North and Midwest to work in fast-growing basic industries. They created new lives for themselves in Kansas City, Chicago, Philadelphia, New York, and other major cities.[3]

Writer Langston Hughes, originally from Kansas, migrated to New York City to attend Columbia University, arriving there at the start of the Harlem Renaissance. In the 1920s African American artists such as Hughes, Zora Neal Hurston, Countee Cullen, Claude McKay, Alain Locke, Ethel Waters, Duke Ellington, and others received unprecedented and widespread support and enthusiasm for their work.[4] Artists of the Harlem Renaissance reflected a new radical consciousness associated with a "New Negro" movement that championed black culture and the ideology of self-determination.[5]

Many migrants traveled by rail from the black belt to the "freedom belt,"[6] as northern employers desperate for laborers provided free passage. African Americans accustomed to confronting jim crow policies while traveling acquired the habit of packing food for train rides. This allowed them to avoid humiliating treatment at segregated eating establishments that refused black customers or required them to go to a rear window of an eatery with a sign marked "Colored" over it (I discuss this in greater detail in a later chapter). Family and friends packed empty shoe boxes with cold sandwiches and other goodies. James Weldon Johnson remembered taking the train from Jacksonville to Atlanta. He wrote, "In those days no one would think of boarding a train without a lunch, not even for a trip of two or three hours; and no lunch was a real lunch that did not consist of fried chicken, slices of buttered bread, hard-boiled eggs, a little paper of salt and pepper, an orange or two, and a piece of cake."[7] In the 1930s Maya Angelou and her brother traveled on a train without adult supervision from California to Arkansas. "A porter had been charged with our welfare—he got off the train the next day in Arizona—and our tickets were pinned to my brother's inside coat pocket." Angelou recalled African American "passengers, who always traveled with loaded lunch boxes, felt sorry for 'poor little motherless darlings' and plied us with cold fried chicken and potato salad."[8]

Mothers, unaware of how long a trip would take, supplied relocating family members with enough provisions for the trip and more. South Carolinian Liza Bowman, as the story goes, must have spent days preparing for her son's move from one region to another. She prepared "tons of hoecake biscuits, pan after pan of cornbread, fried rice cakes, pickled vegetables, tomatoes, okra, beets, string beans, squash, and jar after jar of cooked beans." In addition, she sent along "cured and smoked bacon, slabs of salt pork, hams and jerk beef; she packed sacks of cornmeal, flour, grits, dried beans, and rice," dried fruit, and herbs.[9]

Lack of space for gardens in the North altered African American eating habits. In the South, people ate peas and beans of one kind or another two to three times a week. In the North, people ate them only occasionally and then often ate the canned variety because of the limited access to land and because the colder climatic conditions restricted their ability to grow inexpensive garden vegetables. In the North, cooks continued to make corn bread regularly, but for some unknown reason it became distinctly sweeter. Southerners dismissed the sweeter northern interpretation of corn bread as unfit for consumption. Over time, however, the corn bread of newcomers from the South became more northern in style, just like the migrants themselves.

Moving North provided African Americans with the opportunity to cook on more modern stoves than were found in the South. In addition, moving to the North required that the cooks who prepared southern food improvise and make do, which is the historical hallmark of African American cuisine. Except for the handful of wealthy migrants who prospered, most southern migrants continued inventing dishes that stretched and transformed what they could afford to purchase on meager working-class wages. Generally, this meant the continuation of the very unhealthy practice of eating the cheapest cuts of meat, particularly pork; seasoning legumes and vegetables with salt pork; and deep-frying chicken and other food.

Adam Clayton Powell, Jr., son of the pastor of Harlem's Abyssinian Baptist Church and former member of the U.S. House of Representatives, recalled his childhood days and the food he grew up eating in Harlem in his autobiography. Representative Powell was also a minister and became the pastor of his father's church. Both of Powell's parents were southerners. His father was born in 1865 in Franklin County, Virginia, at Martin's Mill, and his mother was born in 1872 on the campus of Christiansburg Academy, in Christiansburg, Virginia. The mother of the senior Powell was a "Negro-Indian woman named Sally," and his stepfather was a former slave named Dunn. In Franklin County, Virginia, the family rose to a breakfast of "fried fatback, cornpone cooked in the ashes of the fireplace, and coffee made of rye grains." In 1875 the family relocated to Coldsburg, West Virginia. After accepting a call to the ministry in 1884, the senior Powell attended seminary in Washington, D.C., and then served as the pastor of several Baptist churches in the Northeast between 1888 and 1908. In 1908 he accepted the job of senior pastor of Abyssinian Baptist Church in Harlem.[10]

The younger Powell remembers that, during his childhood years in Harlem, his mother stretched the meat or fish from the Sunday meal into dishes that lasted through the next Saturday: "A whole boiled cod, which I loathed, with its head and eye balefully looking at me, always offered its bones, tail, fins, and again that head as the basis of a New England fish chowder." When his father started fishing in the spring, his mother cooked fried "fish four times a week until the cold weather rolled in." Similarly, when rabbit was in season, "hucksters drove through the blocks with barrels of rabbits" for sale. His mother purchased enough rabbit to serve it in one form or another for a week. Culinary repetition also occurred when quarts of oysters and large smoked country hams arrived from relatives still living in the South. "Fresh greens were always cooked with this ham, from wild watercress in the spring to winter kale."[11]

Powell describes a time in Harlem "when it was a disgrace to bring in bread from a store and, for that matter, anything that was already baked." In his middle-class Harlem home, the family's black coal-burning stove "was a place of magic," where his mother made corn bread, biscuits, and muffins. For breakfast she fixed pancakes, salted mackerel, codfish cakes, and baked beans. The beans cooked "all night long on the back of the stove with plenty of black molasses on top and hunks of salt pork inside."[12]

Stories of eating from Powell's youth provide evidence that migration to the North did not alter African American cookery significantly. Migrants in the North continued to feel that breakfast should be a banquet, complete with ham, fried fish, eggs, sausage, bacon, grits, red-eye gravy, corn bread, and molasses. Lunch and dinner also remained the same, featuring large amounts of corn bread, greens, and various parts of the pig. For some migrants, cooking traditional dishes like pork chops with red-eye gravy, chitlins, trotters, snout and jowls, and hog maws reminded them of their past and their southern roots.[13] Some migrants, like the Powells, received pork by mail from relatives in the South who slaughtered hogs in the winter. Collards and cabbage seasoned with salt pork, fried chicken, and sweet potato pie carried with them similar memories of childhoods in the South.[14]

As members of Harlem's upper class, migrant families like the Powells could afford to eat like northern white elites or maintain their southern traditions. Studies on the city of Chicago by Tracy N. Poe, St. Clair Drake, and Horace R. Cayton show that black elites in that city could afford to eat very differently when they wanted to from working-class African American migrants who regularly consumed traditional southern food.[15] Two characters interviewed by Drake and Cayton, named Baby Chile and Mr. Ben, were a case in point. Mr. Ben recalls a dinner party at Baby Chile's apartment: "Baby Chile called us to the kitchen for supper—a platter of neckbones and cabbage, a saucer with five sausage cakes, a plate of six slices of bread, and a punchbowl of stewed prunes (very cold and delicious). Baby Chile placed some corn fritters on the table, remarking, "This bread ain't got no milk in it. I did put some aig [egg] in it, but I had to make it widout any milk."[16] In contrast, the social gatherings of the Chicago's black upper class featured food and beverage that was far more expensive than the traditional southern meal items that Baby Chile and Mr. Ben enjoyed. Speaking of northern elite African Americans in Chicago, Drake and Cayton write: "All through the year there is a continuous round of private informal parties and formal dinners. . . . On their tables one will find wild duck and pheasants in season, chicken and turkey in season and out, and plenty of their finest spirits and champagne."[17]

Perhaps members of the black upper class enjoyed fried chicken, yams, grits, and greens at home with their families and served more expensive foods at important social gatherings. The lower classes, however, made do with cheap ingredients almost all the time. An African American women living on the West Side told Drake and Cayton, "One thing, over here you can always get something to eat at the market like a basket of beans or tomatoes and potatoes for a dime, before they are graded." She added, "If you get more than you can use yourself, you can always sell or trade what you don't want."[18]

FIGURE 4.1 Negro tenant farmer eating breakfast in Creek County, Oklahoma. Library of Congress, Prints and Photographs Division, LC-USF34-035087-D.

FAMILY DIETS FROM SOUTH CAROLINA

South Carolina agricultural experiment station reports about family diets in the Piedmont and lower coastal plains areas of South Carolina provide excellent insights into the eating traditions migrants brought with them when they left the South.[19] Researchers studied black and white farm families in Marion, Florence, Darlington, Lee, Dorchester, Sumter, and Charleston counties. Some owned, rented, or sharecropped land; others worked as wage-earning farmhands. The records showed that the "dietary habits" of African American families "resembled those of white families in corresponding sections of the state."[20]

The focus here will be on the lower coastal region of South Carolina because records of food menus in black and white homes for summer, spring, fall, and winter are available. Not surprisingly, the spring and summer menus in the lower coastal region contain greater food diversity than the fall or winter menus. As for meat consumption, both black and white coastal farmers ate a lot of fried meats. A typical spring and summer menu primarily consisted of pork dishes such as "fried fat meat," "fried ham," "fried [pork] shoulder," and "fried side meat [salt pork and bacon]." African Americans cooked fried pork dishes in addition to boiled pork dishes such as boiled pork shoulder and boiled ham.[21] A similar study done in 1928 in the Mississippi Delta by Dorothy Dickins of Mississippi A & M, an HBCU, showed that blacks in that region also typically fried and boiled their food, with most vegetables "overcooked in fat" and meat "fried done and hard." Both meats and vegetables were "over-done as well as greasy," which at least in part explained "the high death rate, the frequent illnesses, and lack of energy" among African Americans in the Delta.[22] Coastal South Carolinians prepared vegetables, meats, and fish in a similar fashion to farmers in the Mississippi Delta.

Both white and black cooks regularly ate fried fish. During the summer months, however, white families ate shrimp dishes such as "fried shrimp" for breakfast and shrimp and stew for dinner. Similarly, gumbo only appeared on a white menu. For African Americans, shrimp appeared at only one time, and it was on a fall menu as the breakfast dish "shrimp and gravy." Side dishes also reveal ethnic similarities and differences in coastal South Carolina. Both black and white cooks regularly served corn bread, rice, and "okra and tomatoes" in the spring and summer months. Side dishes distinctive to white coastal cookery were "hambone with green beans," "stewed pears," potato salad, "squash with butter and cream," and "fried corn." In contrast, "hominy with fat meat gravy," "cabbage with fat meat," and "green beans boiled with fat pork" were all distinctly African American.[23]

In the fall and winter, common meats prepared among black and white cooks included fried pork, fried fat pork, fried pork shoulder, and more fried side meat. "Beefsteak" sausage, "liver hash," beef stew, salmon, and "salmon and gravy" appeared only on white menus. In contrast, "shrimp and gravy," oysters, fried rabbit, and pork stew cooked with pig ears, feet, and backbone appeared only on African American menus. These distinctive African American dishes were made in addition to southern staples such as fried pork and fried fat pork. White coastal cookery in the fall and winter included side dishes such as "dried peas cooked with fat pork," "field peas with fat pork," "turnips cooked with pork," cole slaw, baked sweet potato, "peach pickle," and "macaroni pie." The side dishes that were common to both black and white cooks were biscuits, corn bread, baked sweet potatoes, turnips, and what Africans Americans called "dried peas boiled with fat meat," which appeared as "dried peas cooked with fat pork" on white menus. The only distinctively African American side dishes on the menu were "collards boiled with meat" and "collards boiled with fat pork."[24]

A survey of the seasonal menus reveals that white coastal farmers economically fared much better than African Americans in 1939. This is evidenced by the appearance of luxury drinks and foods such as iced tea, jam, jelly, preserves, pies, cakes, and "jello with custard" on white menus. All these required store-bought sugar, baking powder, and spices. Coconut, bananas, "loaf bread," "bakers bread," cocoa, salmon (most likely canned salmon), and macaroni are other examples of luxury store-bought items that only appeared on white menus. The store-bought items that African Americans in coastal South Carolina apparently liked and ate were bologna, cheese, and crackers. When hog-killing meat was used up, both black and white families probably purchased their side meat, salt pork, and bacon from a store.[25]

The macaroni pie that appeared on white menus may possibly refer to macaroni and cheese.[26] There is another reference to the southern preparation of macaroni and cheese in the 1928 report about farm families in the Mississippi Delta by Dorothy Dickins. Dickins found that most African American women had never tasted macaroni and cheese and only a few cooked it for their families because they complained that it was too "starchy and gummy." Dickins goes on to say, "The majority feels that they have too little cash to spend on something which they perhaps cannot properly prepare or which, if they can, the family probably will not like."[27] What is interesting about this quote is that since the 1960s no African American feast I have attended prepared by southern-born women was considered complete without at least one large pan of labor-intensive homemade baked macaroni and cheese with bread crumbs on top. During research for this book, neither oral nor written sources provided an explanation of how and when the dish became apart of the culinary lexicon of African Americans.

Dickins's 1928 study found that, as African Americans improved their environment and education, the variety in their diets increased. As a result, the high school and college educated had more nutritious eating habits, with larger amounts of fruits and vegetables composing their overall caloric intake, than did their less-educated neighbors. For an uneducated African American in the Delta, an increase in income "generally means an increase in quantity but not necessarily an increase in variety of food. As environment and intelligence improve, variety of food used increases," writes Dickins.[28] For many black belt residents, migrating northward provided access to education and exposure to people from around the world. In their new environments, southerners worked and lived in close quarters with Jews, West Indians, Latin Americans, and Europeans. These "foreigners" taught southern African American migrants how to cook and enjoy foods—like macaroni—that back home they called white folks' food.

Over time they adopted foods such as macaroni and cheese and pancakes as their own.

AFRICAN-INFLUENCED CUISINES OF THE CARIBBEAN

Immigrants from the Caribbean who migrated to New York after World War I started a number of restaurants in East Harlem. (An extensive discussion of Caribbean migration to New York will come in a later chapter.)[29] Cubans in New York had a reputation for being epicureans. As one report noted, Cubans "love food, drink and delicacies of every kind, but it must be good." The Ideal, at Lenox Avenue and 115th, and Toreador, at 110th, introduced African Americans to traditional Cuban food like *agie el dulce*, a sweet chili con carne typically served with a side order of fried plantains.[30] One of the oldest Puerto Rican restaurants was Pascual Quintana's El Caribe, which opened in 1920 at 235 West 116th Street. It started off as a place where working-class folks would go to order a thirty-cent *mixta* dinner—meat or fish and rice and beans from a steam table—and a coffee. In 1927, a year before the start of the Depression, the restaurant relocated to Fifth Avenue, where new management changed the menu to attract wealthier customers. Famous Latin American professional boxers as well as locals came to enjoy traditional dishes such as *mafongo con chicharrones*, mashed green plantains mixed with mashed fried pig skin and covered with garlic, onion, and hot pepper sauce, and *pollo frito*, fried chicken served with fried plantains or fried potatoes and a salad. *Arroz con gallina*, chicken and rice seasoned with ham, salt pork, tomatoes, green peppers, annatto seeds, salt, garlic, and onions, was another popular dish.[31]

The Saturday special was *sancocho*, a stew made with sweet and plain potatoes; chicken, beef, and pork; green and ripe plantains; yucca; Spanish yams; and a typical Spanish sauce seasoned with annatto seeds, salt, garlic, and onions. Sunday's menu included *sancocho* plus *lechon azado*, oven-roasted pork basted with a mixture of annatto seeds, black pepper, salt, vinegar, and oil. "An individual ration of this dish, with an addition of fried plantains and salad (tomatoes and lettuce), usually costs 45 cts." Chefs at the restaurant followed the rural Puerto Rican custom of cooking with tubers and seasoning with pork and lard. Cooks at Fuentes, for instance, prepared rice with lard and saffron. They also made refried white, red, and black beans with salt pork, garlic, and annatto seeds. Other migrant cultures evidently influenced foodways in New York City's Puerto Rican diaspora: Fuentes's menu also included Virginia ham, Mexican tamales, and other foods outside traditional Puerto Rican cuisine.[32]

El Favorito was another well-known Puerto Rican eatery in Spanish Harlem. It was located at 2055 Eighth Avenue between 111th and 112th streets. Puerto Rican, African American, and British and French West Indian low-wage factory workers lived in the neighborhood; the great majority of the residents spoke Spanish. The spotless restaurant remained open twenty-four hours a day serving meals as cheap as thirty-five cents. El Favorito also sold traditional Latin American desserts such as flan, rice pudding, and sweet breads.[33]

Like many Harlem eateries, El Favorito did its best business on the weekend between 1 and 4 A.M., when "the merrymakers once more crowd the restaurant as soon as the theatre and the dance halls are closed." Following a night out on the town, customers ordered tons of "Puerto Rican style tamales" made from mashed green plantains stuffed with chopped chicken and veal, pepper, olives, and capers, wrapped in a special paper, and then boiled. A Sunday afternoon favorite was *paella a la Valenciana*. This saffron rice, meat, and seafood–based dish from Spain was very popular in both Cuba and Puerto Rico. It contained "trout, clams (in shells), shrimps, eel, and devil fish in an addition to chicken, olives and partially covered with pimentos." Non–Latin American offerings on the menu included traditional New England clam chowder, southern pig's feet, North American bacon and eggs, "and all kind of American sandwiches and desserts." [34]

In urban areas in and around New York, Europeans, Caribbeans, and southerners interacted in tenement houses, on the job, and on the streets, where they purchased new types of inexpensive good-tasting foods. Italian vendors sold pepper-onion-sausage sandwiches and Italian ices. Yiddish-speaking Jews sold *arbis*, knishes, and sweet potatoes. *Arbis* were large cooked chickpeas served with salt and pepper in paper bags for between three and five cents. Knishes were "crisp, brown-crusted cakes made of potatoes mashed with oil, onions, salt, and pepper and sell[ing] at two for 5 cents." Puerto Rican vendors sold meat patties filled with ground meat and garlic and finished with decorative crusts; the patties came in a variety of styles including "cuchifritos, moricillas, alcapurrias, and empanadillos de yucca." African American vendors sold soft-shell crabs, fried fish, and oysters.[35] Migration and immigration in short meant more than re-creating one's culinary traditions in northern urban centers such as New York and Chicago. It meant maintaining old inexpensive rural eating traditions and incorporating new ones from Europe and African-influenced ones from the Caribbean.

CASE STUDIES

What follows are case studies of various individuals who migrated North during their teens and twenties. Their stories illustrate the point that most often families and networks of extended families migrated North with time spent in more than one northern city before they settled. Most of the case studies are about people who became food professionals in the North, working as live-in domestics for white families. The majority of migrants worked as domestic. They were also quite entrepreneurial; it was not uncommon for domestic servants to have side jobs taking cake and pie orders and catering parties and weddings for the friends and associates of the white families who employed them full time. Other migrants went to work in the kitchens of hospitals and restaurants. Each migrant brought along his or her own food traditions, and their stories map episodes of southern migration to Harlem and Westchester County. The case studies are important because they provide essential biographical details about southerners whose written and oral histories I discuss in later chapters. Some of them are my older, southern-born relatives who adapted and mixed their culinary traditions as they moved North and passed them on to our family's northern-born younger generations.

Tillie Eripp

At age eighteen, a poor African American woman named Tillie Eripp migrated alone from Tampa, Florida, to Philadelphia. Writer Sarah Chavez interviewed her for the WPA Federal Writers' Project "America Eats," which was never published. New York City's WPA unit called their study "Feeding the City." In it, Chavez and other writers gathered insightful records about Depression-era food history. Chavez learned that teenager Eripp suffered desperately from loneliness after she arrived in Philadelphia. "Soon, through the help of a friend, she secured a job as a cook in a boarding house, where she remained for several years," wrote Chavez. She migrated from Philadelphia to New York in 1928, just before the Great Depression started. Her first job was operating a concession stand selling fried chicken at Harry Hansbury's speakeasy. Increasing demand for her chicken led her to move to a storefront space next to the speakeasy, where she ran Tillie's Chicken Shack.

Eripp struggled in getting the business off the ground, depending entirely on inexperienced help. "Once the success of the venture was assured she added to her menu, occasionally serving collard greens, pig tails, black-eyed peas, yams and hogshead," wrote Chavez. The restaurant served hot biscuits and coffee with every meal, "and each customer was permitted as many biscuits as he or she desired." Later she added spoon corn bread, a variety of vegetables, and salads to the menu. In 1932 she moved her place of business to 237 Lenox Avenue, just above 121st Street.[36]

Migrants from Windsor, North Carolina

Matilda Taylor worked as a schoolteacher in Windsor, North Carolina (Benjamin Outlaw's hometown as well). There, she raised four children—Luesta, Maggie, Bertha, and Dick—apparently alone. Bertha was the first to leave Windsor, migrating to Ossining, New York, in Westchester County, where she found a job working as a domestic doing cooking and cleaning for a wealthy white family. In 1930 Westchester County, the nation's "premier suburban region," had an African American population of 23,000.[37]

Luesta was the next to go, originally leaving Windsor to earn a teacher's certificate at North Carolina Normal School for teachers. She dropped out of school, eloped, and migrated with her husband to Philadelphia. Apparently Bertha sent word that she had jobs lined up for her sisters in Ossining. "My mother [Luesta Duers]," recalled Margaret Opie, "was the upstairs maid, and my aunt Bertha was downstairs, they all did domestic work. And one of the things you will find is that a lot of the women, especially black women, those were the jobs available to them." Luesta "did laundry, there was always a way in which they took the skill they had and marketed it."

The oldest child, Maggie, born in 1903, was by all accounts the best cook in the family (after her mother), renowned for making an abundance of great food out of scraps, handouts, and leftovers, all assembled in a black cast-iron skillet. Maggie married Charlie White of Windsor. The couple had a daughter named Katie and three boys named Booker, Charlie, and Horace before they split and Charlie began a second family with another woman in Windsor. Maggie, following the lead of her sisters Bertha and Luesta, migrated with her children to Ossining.

Eventually she found a good job working as a cook for a white family in Ossining named the Brants.[38] She rented a flat in the Italian immigrant section of the village. Katie, Maggie's only daughter and one of our family's best cooks, remembered her neighbors well. "You know I learned how to cook using Italian" seasonings like sage because the neighbors "used to give us food." Merchants "would give mama different things you know, meat leftover that they didn't sell."[39]

Migrants from Cloverdale, Virginia

Ella (Christopher) Barnett was born in the rural farming community of Cloverdale, Virginia, in 1915. When she was thirteen, she worked for a white women and her husband as a domestic in Cloverdale, and "they were as nasty as they could be to colored people . . . colored people had a hard time."[40]

Her largely absentee father, Claven Christopher, was one of the earliest members of her family to head north from Cloverdale in search of opportunity. "He worked in New Jersey but lived in Cloverdale, and he came home maybe once every two or three years," said Barnett. Claven Christopher worked as a cook in the railroad camps of the black workers who laid track in New Jersey and New York, including through the Tarrytowns. Apparently, railroad contractors laying track up north hired southern-born African Americans, paying for their passage north and providing wages in addition to room and board in work camps as far north as New York.[41]

Barnett's father was the best cook she knew of as a child growing up in Cloverdale. "He was one of the best cooks in the world. He was such a good cook that people named him Cook." Up north, people did not know him as Claven Christopher but instead by the name Cook. No one where he worked in New Jersey knew him as Christopher, says Barnett, "but all you had to say was Cook, and everybody knew him."[42]

Washington "Wash" Opia (a name later changed to Opie by a local official during a property transaction) came to Cloverdale, Virginia, as a railroad camp cook. He was a West Indian migrant that decided to purchase land and start a farm in Cloverdale after marrying Mollie Cox in 1898. She died, and he remarried, taking up with Fannie Christopher in 1913. She was an unwed mother with two boys to raise: Fred, born in 1908, and Neal, born in 1910. The couple had several additional children together. Lucy Demmie married Fred Opie. Barnett's sister, Martha, married Lucy's brother, Horace Demmie.[43]

Lucy Opie migrated from Cloverdale to North Tarrytown in the late 1920s or the early 1930s. In North Tarrytown, the majority of the southern-born migrants came from Virginia, the remainder from North Carolina, South Carolina, Florida, Georgia, and Maryland, in descending numbers. Most of them rented homes, creating a black enclave in the Valley Street section of town. They worked predominately at private homes for white residents as cooks, live-in domestic servants, chauffeurs, and laundresses. Others worked as laborers, truck drivers, and factory workers.[44]

FIGURE 4.2 *Left*, Fred Opie, Sr.; *right*, Jane Dimmie and Lucy Dimmie Opie.

All indications are that the first job Fred Opie, Sr., had in New York was as a heavy equipment operator with the construction crew that built the Rockefeller estate at Pocantico Hills. "I think that when John D. was developing Pocantico Hills . . . in the 1890s and early 1900s a lot of migrant workers from the South, black migrant workers from the South, came up to work primarily for the Rockefellers. Because there was a lot of manual labor that had be done," said Fred Opie, Jr. He added, "because until the war [World War II], General Motors did not hire black people."[45] As a result, most of the male migrants from the South in the Tarrytowns found employment at Pocantico Hills during the almost seventy-five years it took to build the miles of stone walls and dozen or more stone barns and houses and the mansion. Once the construction was completed, black southern women staffed the kitchens and cooked food for the Rockefellers and their guests.[46]

Lucy Opie did domestic work, particularly cooking. A superb cook, she prepared traditional southern dishes. What was unique about her cooking, according to her daughter, Dorothy, was that "the first ingredient she put in was a piece of love, stirred it up. Then she put in the ingredients, salt and pepper and whatever." In addition, as a southerner, she had the habit of cooking with a lot of lard and seasoning her vegetables with pork. She also continued the southern tradition of canning produce. "My mother canned everything, she did a lot of canning, she worked very hard."[47]

Lucy Opie was also an excellent baker, often preparing biscuits; hot cross buns; cakes; mincemeat, rhubarb, sweet potato, and cherry pies; and peach cobbler. Many of these baked goods were made from the fruits and vegetables grown in the family garden her husband kept. She and her husband also operated a storefront bakery in North Tarrytown until the Depression put them out of business. According to her son Fred Opie, Jr., "in Tarrytown there were not too many black businesses" like the one his parents operated. "Most of the black businesses were moving businesses, moving companies."[48]

In time, Lucy Opie sent for her brother Horace, who came to New York with his wife, Martha. After Martha arrived, she sent for her cousin, Ella Barnett, and her other sisters down in Virginia. Barnett explains, "My sister [Martha] got married and her husband's sisters were up here. And when she married their brother they brought her and her husband up here. Then when she got up here she brought her family up here, one by one." Barnett was thirteen when she migrated to New York.[49]

Nora Burns White

Nora Burns White migrated from Blaney, South Carolina, to New York City with two other girls in 1942. She was fourteen. White recalls, "My mother was a very smart person. But how she let me come to New York with two other girls" the same age continues to perplex her daughter. One of the girls lived in the Bronx, and she was down in South Carolina visiting her cousin. "Luis was going back with Mary and I said to my mama 'Could I go?' and for some reason or another she said 'yes.'" White's older sister, Luella, had already migrated to Harlem the summer before. But, "Luella did not know that I was coming to New York." [50]

Her mother packed a box full of "fried chicken, bread, and cake" to eat during the train ride, "enough to last us all the way to New York. I think it took us something like twenty-four hours to get there." She adds, "On the train then, there wasn't any place to eat on the train because it was segregated." Jim crow laws restricted black passengers to the coach car, and most of the other African Americans sitting there with the three young girls had similar boxes filled with food. "And we were in the coach, right there next to the [coal-burning] engine. And by the time we got to New York, everybody was so dirty and greasy."

They arrived at Penn Station without a clue as to how to exit the station, never mind how to get to Luella's apartment building. A boy just a little older than they asked them if they were lost and showed them how to get the A train up to 125th Street in Harlem where her sister rented a room. At this point in the interview, White yet again wondered, "What went through my mother's mind to let me go to New York?" Yet her mother likely realized that White would have better opportunities in New York than as the daughter of a single parent who tenant farmed in South Carolina.

Georgia, another roomer in the same building, originally from Roanoke, Virginia, worked as a cook for a private home on Amsterdam Avenue in Manhattan near Columbia University. She asked her employer if she was interested in hiring someone to help out in the kitchen. "She said yes and hired me, so of course I put my age up to twenty-one. . . . I think she paid me fifteen or twenty dollars a week," recalled White.

She learned most of her cooking skills working with Georgia on that first job.

Trained and inspired by her mentor, Georgia, at eighteen Nora White left her sister and the Harlem rooming house on 121st Street for upstate New York, where she worked as a cook for the family of a Dr. Kensdale, a scientist who worked on the Manhattan Project. When she questioned whether she was qualified for the job, she reports, "Georgia said to me, 'Oh no you can do it. Get yourself a cookbook, and add a little something, or take away a little something so that it taste right.'" She remembers learning on the job, like the time the Kensdale family requested eggplant Parmesan for dinner. White recalled thinking, "Oh my Lord! What am I going to do?!" So she went to the cookbook, found the recipe for eggplant Parmesan, and went ahead and fixed the meal; it turned out very well. She learned how to make a host of dishes using a similar tactic: the help of a cookbook and taste buds well versed in the southern African American culinary tradition of how to make something taste just right.[51]

Understanding what African Americans in the South used to make their food taste right is the key to explaining the uniqueness of down-home cuisine. In African American culture, seasoning was an art form passed down through oral tradition. It could only be learned through a lengthy apprenticeship like the one Nora White had with her mentor Georgia, an experienced cook, followed by years of practice. Ultimately, it becomes instinctive.[52]

African American children, mostly female, began their cooking apprenticeships at a young age, closely observing older cooks within their family and extended family. Over time, adults would assign chores of ever-increasing difficulty to acclimate the child to the art of cooking. "Because our recipes were seldom written down, we had to rely on momma's and grandma's experience and what we could learn by watching as they went about their chores in the kitchen," writes one author of a soul food cookbook. "The advantage of learning at grandmother's elbow is discovering things which are not found in any book." You learn how to season and cook food by being there when momma does it. Then one day somebody finally turns to you and tells you to make something and you do it. "For this reason the soul food cook usually knows instinctively how much salt to add, when the grease in the pan is hot enough, and how long before it's time to open the oven."[53]

South Carolinian Alexander Smalls learned how to cook while serving as his mother's "chief helper" in the kitchen on Saturday nights and Sunday mornings. "My mother and I would begin cooking about eight in the evening if there were pies or cakes or yeast rolls to be made. . . . By Sunday morning, breakfast and dinner were both happening at once—roast roasting, bacon frying, grits bubbling, potatoes boiling—so the kitchen was already a profusion of smells" by the time the macaroni and cheese and fried chicken were started. In addition to apprenticing in his mother's kitchen, Smalls also learned the art of seasoning and cooking from his grandfather, who was a great cook: from him, he learned how to season and cook catfish, "red-eye vinegar gravy with sage sausage," and "skillet rice with fresh parsley."[54]

Seasoning was learned by tasting other people's food and inquiring what ingredients and cooking techniques they used. It was during informal "kitchen conversations" that people exchanged family secrets for cooking fried chicken and other dishes. Some of the secrets were as simple as the use of a seemingly unlikely seasoning or marinade. For instance, one cook's mother marinated her chicken in peanut butter thinned with milk the night before frying it. In the morning, she would pat the chicken dry and fry it in seasoned cooking oil. Another secret was in the cooking fat. "Momma [saved] not only all bacon drippings, but sausage [drippings], too." If there wasn't enough to fry all the chicken, then she flavored her frying oil with it, which gave "an extra-special tastiness to the meat."[55]

Various amounts of spices and herbs, particularly salt and pepper, crushed red pepper, bay leaf, sage, and sugar, are partly responsible for the "down-home" flavor associated with southern African American cuisine. African American seasoning also depends on several fresh vegetables, including chopped scallions and/or onions and garlic. Apple cider vinegar and Worcestershire and Tabasco sauces are also staples in seasoning southern dishes. As mentioned earlier, the final component that makes African American food unique is the addition of pork flavor into dishes. Collards, kale, and turnip greens are seasoned with pieces of pork; fish, and chicken and are deep-fried in cooking oil made of or flavored with pork-based drippings (oil and sediment left in a pan after cooking bacon or sausage). Perhaps what's most southern about southern food is the inclusion of pork in some shape or fashion in just about every dish.[56]

Nettie C. Banks

Nora White eventually became a good friend and catering partner with southern migrant Nettie C. Banks. Banks was born in 1921 in the farming community of Samos, Virginia, in Middlesex County. Traveling to Baltimore to visit her sister and mother, who were working there that summer, she ended up staying. All three women earned money working as domestics. "In the South you kind of migrated to wherever you had relatives. My mother had a brother in Baltimore who had a big house."

While in Baltimore Banks attended public school. Later, the family returned to Virginia. "I was good at school and loved school. But the community did not have a high school; finally the ministers got together and built a high school. But they built it like in mid-county and you had to pay to get to the high school." During the Depression, there were a lot of Monday mornings when her mother could not afford the $1.50 per week bus fare. "I was embarrassed I guess … but that's when I decided I didn't want to do that anymore." So, at age seventeen she told her mother she would go to Philadelphia to find work. It was 1938. People used to go to Samos for vacation, and migrants like Banks would then catch a ride with them to Philadelphia.

In Philadelphia Banks met her husband, George, also a migrant from Virginia. They worked as domestics in Philadelphia until the end of World War II (her husband left to serve in the military), when a wealthy white family offered them "a job with more money and, we thought, better opportunity in [Ossining] New York." Most of the African Americans in Ossining in the 1930s and 1940s were southern-born, just like Nettie and George Banks. In my interview with her, she explained that she had relatives who had moved to New York to work as domestics for a white family. The family was looking for someone else to do the same kind of work. "And that's how we came, we had an interview," and they took the job as sleep-in domestics. "At the time that we came up, it was normal that we were sort of relegated, doomed to do house work."[57]

Firsthand accounts of migrants who settled north of New York City are evidence that Harlem was not always the final destination for southern migrants. Some stopped in Harlem and stayed with relatives until they located better opportunities. Many of them marketed their cooking skills to wealthy white families further north. Westchester County was attractive to southern migrants because jobs as cooks were much higher paying than were those in the South. By the time of the Depression, there were pockets of southern African American migrant communities in river towns along the Hudson River in places like Ossining, the Tarrytowns, and Peekskill. There were similar communities east of the Hudson in Mount Vernon, Elmsford, and White Plains. All these communities were accessible on the Harlem and Hudson train lines that carried passengers north of New York City several times a day.

In the host communities to which they migrated, southern migrants were introduced to new eating traditions, particularly influences from Italian immigrants. In Ossining, Katie Green learned from Italian neighbors how to season food with "Italian spices."[58] As a domestic, Nora White had to learn how to prepare new dishes like eggplant Parmesan that her white employers requested. The creolized eggplant that she cooked surely tasted different from the one an Italian American would have prepared. Nora's cooking up north was influenced by her mother's South Carolina cuisine, the kitchen traditions of her Virginia-born friend and mentor Georgia (who also taught her how to cook and modify recipes from books), and the recipes she found for foods like eggplant Parmesan, which were largely unfamiliar to southerners.[59]

Migrants from the South introduced southern traditions to African Americans born up north. Lucy Opie, for example, taught her northern-born grandchildren to carry box lunches when they traveled and to enjoy peach cobbler and mincemeat and rhubarb pies. Mincemeat and rhubarb pies were exotic alternatives to those made with apples that her grandchildren were accustomed to eating as New Yorkers raised in the apple-rich Hudson Valley region. After a couple of slices accompanied by a tall glass of cold milk, they grew to love them. In fact, they recall getting excited about going to Grandma Opie's house as children during the holiday season because her southern hospitality meant she would always offer something sweet like a slice of pie or cake served with a scoop of homemade vanilla ice cream.

SPECIAL OCCASIONS:
CHRISTMAS, WATCH NIGHT, AND HOMECOMING

Christmas for African Americans has traditionally been a very special holiday centered on sweets and offerings like chicken, ham, and a tableful of complementary side dishes. For those without much, Christmas might have meant little more than killing a chicken for dinner. Those in better financial condition celebrated with an assortment of meats and sweets such as "cakes, succulent pies, and luscious puddings."[60]

Ruth and Roy Miller, whose parents migrated north in the 1920s, shared with me their memories of holiday cuisine. Ruth was born in Harlem in 1932. Her mother migrated there from Savannah, Georgia; she worked as a professional cook. Ruth has vivid memories of her mother's holiday cooking. "We would have chicken and dumplings. We would have macaroni and cheese. We would have ... sometimes cabbage with some smoked meat; collard greens, actually many times all of the greens would be combined: collards, kale, turnips; candied sweet potatoes; and many times red rice, okra, and tomatoes.... We would have spareribs with cabbage and sweet potatoes." Roy Miller, born in Harlem in 1924, said, "That's interesting because that's a crossover. Because my [West Indian] aunts used to do red rice and all of that. I can't say that is a purely West Indian dish, it may be part of an assimilation. ... It emanated from the South, but my aunts used to do that beautifully also."[61]

Dessert was a celebrated part of the holiday menu. For dessert, "my mother made banana pudding, sweet potato pie, you know, apple pie, lemon meringue pie, and cakes," said Ruth Miller. West Indians made fruitcake, which was also traditional among southerners. Clara Bullard Pittman was born in 1948 in the very rural farming community of Pinehurst, Georgia. She recalls that on Christmas her mother made homemade fruitcake from what she grew in her yard. She also made "cakes and pies from scratch."[62] Making Christmas fruitcake was a long process, according to Benjamin Outlaw. When asked what Christmas was like growing up in Windsor, North Carolina, Outlaw responded, "Oh boy, it was like heaven." Mother "would start cooking her fruitcake, sometime about a month before Christmas. And she always made [either apple or grape] wine" and poured the "wine on the cake until Christmas ... building it up.... It was the best fruitcake I have ever eaten." Hattie Outlaw also made "all kinds of cakes: chocolate, vanilla, coconut, lemon." He went on to say, "Now Christmas was wonderful, she had everything you could mention, all kinds of meats." In addition, the family ate all kinds of vegetables at Christmas because the family raised their own vegetables, and "during the summertime she put that stuff up in a jar ... butter beans, snap beans, corn."[63]

On Christmas in Blaney, South Carolina, Nora Burns White recalled, "we always had a ham, you know, because we raised pigs." They also had "all kinds of cakes, that's when my mother would do some cooking because she would do some baking about a week before Christmas."[64] In Charlotte County, Virginia, Yemaja Jubilee's mother always made lemon icebox pies for Christmas. "She made it out of condensed Carnation milk, vanilla wafers: she'd squeeze fresh lemon juice in it, egg whites, sugar, and butter and she would cream that up and put it inside a vanilla wafer crust. . . . She did all this from scratch," says Jubilee, except for the vanilla wafers. It was called icebox pie "because you have to put it in the refrigerator for it to chill." The pie was only made on special occasions like Christmas. In addition to dessert, her mother also cooked capons for Christmas. A lady who lived down the street raised them. Jubilee's mother would stuff and bake them "the same way you did a turkey . . . the regular roosters were tough . . . but capons were tender and flavorful." Jubilee adds, "We always had ham on Christmas and Thanksgiving."[65]

In Virginia, Nettie Banks grew up with the tradition of eating pork and poultry on Christmas. If there was a ham left over from a hog-killing day earlier in the winter, her mother would boil that, and it would become a part of the Christmas feast. "Then they would have roast chicken. We didn't do a lot with turkey . . . people didn't have turkeys. My grandmother raised turkeys but we did not ordinarily have turkeys. We would have what they called fowl. And they would boil that then put it in the oven and baste it and bake it some. It was nice and brown." Before she migrated north in 1938, she recalled eating chitlins on Christmas if there were any leftover from hog killing. "You know they would make whatever was available."[66]

For Reginald T. Ward, Christmas in the city of Robinsonville, North Carolina, was similar to Christmas at Nettie Banks's home. Christmas meant ham, turkey or chicken, and barbecue, "chopped barbecue." Ward left North Carolina right after high school to attend the University of California at Los Angeles and later settled in the city of Mount Vernon, in Westchester County, New York. He explained that barbecue in New York meant barbecued ribs or chicken, "but in North Carolina barbecue, a whole pig is barbecued, cooked, and they chop it up with the different spices in it like vinegar and red pepper." At Christmas, Ward's mother would also make "oyster dressing" from leftover corn bread and bread, oysters, celery, onions, salt and pepper. "And some made sausage dressing."[67]

Joyce White recalled that for Christmas dinner in Choctaw County, Alabama, her mother "roasted fresh pork and made corn bread dressing, potato salad, and greens."[68] (Duke University's Stephen Erwin argued that collard greens were best when one ate them southern style. "It helps a great deal if one has pepper vinegar to sprink[le] over the collards before eating them and corn pone and fresh pork make collards a delight to eat.")[69] Joyce White's Christmas in Alabama would be filled with the "warming aroma of Chicken 'n' Dumplings, which was made with a big hen, since we seldom had turkey." Often her mother would "simmer the hen whole and then bake it in the oven with the corn bread, and that was our 'turkey,'" reflected White.[70]

Another African American southern religious tradition that should be mentioned is the Watch Night, or New Year's Eve service. Watch Night dates back to the end of the Civil War. In 1862 President Abraham Lincoln declared his famous Emancipation Proclamation, which set slaves in Confederate territories free as of January 1, 1863. As a result, African Americans across much of the South held religious services, many of them secretly, in which they praised and otherwise worshipped God as they watched the New Year and freedom arrive. Thus after 1863 African Americans regularly celebrated Watch Night and New Year's Eve in honor of Emancipation Day. Southerners carried their religious traditions with them when they migrated north.[71]

St. Clair Drake and Horace R. Cayton hold that the religious traditions of the rural South were "modified by contact with the complexities of a large northern city."[72] Yet southern migrants did not abandon their tradition of church membership. By 1945 the South Side of Chicago had about five hundred African American churches: "To the uninitiated, this plethora of churches is no less baffling than the bewildering variety and the colorful extravagance of the names. Nowhere else in Midwest Metropolis could one find, within a stone's throw of one another, a Hebrew Baptist Church, a Baptized Believer's Holiness Church, a Universal Union Independent, a Church of Love and Faith, a Holy Mt. Zion Methodist Episcopal Independent, and a United Pentecostal Holiness Church. Or a cluster such as St. John's Christian Spiritual, Park Mission African Methodist Episcopal, Philadelphia Baptist, Little Rock Baptist, and the Aryan Full Gospel Mission, Spiritualist."[73]

In addition to church membership, southern migrants brought with them a tradition of important yearly church programs and free food. Most likely to include free food were services on special occasions such as Easter, Thanksgiving, Christmas, and Watch Night. "In addition to these Christian red-letter days," report Drake and Cayton, "Baptisms, anniversaries, installations [of new ministers], youth nights, and choir nights" were well-attended yearly programs where down-home southern cooking was available in abundance for free.[74] In Chicago it was "not unusual to find a total of over 10,000 people attending" an important event at the four largest churches, and "an equal number distributed among the smaller churches."

African American churches in Chicago continually offered "concerts, pageants, plays, suppers, and other similar activities."[75]

As in the South, one of the most important events of the year was Watch Night service on New Year's Eve. This southern tradition had people filling church pews as early as 6:45 P.M. to secure a seat for a 7:00 P.M. Watch Night service at any of the five largest African American churches in Chicago. During the service the congregation sang hymns, listened to choirs, prayed, and worshipped until midnight. Then came an important part of the Watch Night service: the feast that followed the arrival of the New Year. Just after midnight, the members of the hospitality committee—the wives of the church—slipped into the kitchen to heat up food and then arrange it on the table of the fellowship hall, generally located in the basement or on the second floor of a church.

Frances Warren noted that, during her childhood, most families in the South ate black-eyed peas (cowpeas common to Igboland) and rice, especially at midnight on New Year's. For an unknown reason, some southerners believed "it was good luck." Warren was born in Atlanta in 1928 but spent most of her childhood in Miami, Florida. Her husband, Jim, grew up on a farm not far from Birmingham, Alabama, where blacks and whites followed the same New Year's eating traditions. Born in 1925, Jim believed that the black-eyed peas and rice on New Year's tradition had something to do with the influence of "black culture," but he was not exactly sure where the practice originated.[76] North Carolinian Reginald Ward said, "I don't care where you are, in New York" black folk on New Year's Day are going to eat "strictly pork." Tradition calls for cooking "black-eyed peas, hog head, a whole hog head now, pig tails, pigs feet." Ward went on to say, "You can go just about anywhere, and people who were born in the South, Georgia, Alabama, Mississippi, North Carolina, Tennessee," cook pork on New Year's Day.[77]

Having lived in California in the 1960s, Ward noticed that, "everybody born in the South was looking for pork" on New Year's. As a result, the price of smoked and pickled pork parts like pigs' feet and hog maws in California supermarkets became expensive around New Year's. Ward reported that pork, collard greens, and black-eyed peas seasoned with smoked or salt pork, along with "potato salad, candied yams, macaroni and cheese, and corn bread" were traditional dishes that southern black folk around the country ate on New Year's.[78]

A child of white southerners, Jim Warren was raised on the same type of southern cooking. He recalled that during the Depression that he would share meals with black farmhands at his family's farm in Alabama. In the process, he learned that his mother shared the same cooking traditions as black women. These traditions included those like New Year's dinners complete with black-eyed peas and rice, beans and greens cooked with ham hocks, and sweet potato pie.[79]

On New Year's, Yemaja Jubilee's mother oven-roasted a whole, hickory wood–smoked hog's head and prepared black-eyed peas. She explains, "We raised hogs, and when they harvested the pig they would put the head down in salt [for about six weeks] and then they'd smoke it." In Charlotte County, Virginia, "where I was raised, most of the people ate that or some kind of pork" on New Year's.[80]

Southern superstition established the tradition of serving hopping John in addition to other traditional dishes that depended on where the southern migrant community was from. Hopping John is a combination of black-eyed peas and rice, beans, red peppers, and salt pork cooked to a stewlike consistency. It is probable that the dish evolved out of the rice and bean mixtures such as dab-a-dab, the rice, beans, vegetables, meat, palm oil, and pepper dish that West African slaves survived on during the Middle Passage.[81] "On New Year's Day," in Virginia, recalled Lamenta Crouch, "we always had black-eyed peas and some kind of greens" along with "ham hocks or country ham." "Country ham" refers to the type of ham typically cooked on Christmas, "smoked ham, what they called the good old Virginia hams."[82] In Bertie County in northeastern North Carolina, Hattie Outlaw prepared her New Year's Day meal on the sixth of January, which she called "old Christmas." What is noteworthy here is that Hattie Outlaw's menu did not include pork. "Mama would make roast chicken, collard greens, desserts, and stuff like that," recalls her son, Benjamin Outlaw.[83]

HOMECOMING

After the start of the Great Migration in 1914, most southern-born African Americans who left for the North referred to revivals down South as "homecoming week." For instance, after moving up north, Joyce White, raised in Choctaw County, Alabama, recalled how "many of the people who had left our county years before would mark their return home by the revival at such and such church."[84] Churches typically held revivals in July and August after farmers had harvested their crops, when people had an abundance of food, money, and time for leisure. "I remember homecomings quite clearly" said Marcellas C.D. Barksdale, born in 1943 in Annandale, South Carolina. "My mother was a churchgoer and she would

FIGURE 4.3 Cooking fried supper for a benefit picnic on the grounds of St. Thomas's Church, near Bardstown, Kentucky, 1940. Library of Congress, Prints and Photographs Division, LC-USF33-030967-M4.

drag me [along], especially to the big events. We had the homecoming, pastor's anniversary, Easter program, and all of them were social as well as cultural and religious programs." He adds, "More often than not, when they had those big occasions, they would have these big eatings, as I called it. All the members would bring food, sometimes they would have commonly cooked food. The men would make a barbecue pit, put coals in and put a grill over it." There would be "potato salad and macaroni and cheese, and none of it was refrigerated, it's no [sic] wonder we didn't die from the mayonnaise." The food would be put outside on long tables with white tablecloths.[85]

Some churches held fish fries the day before revival Sunday. Southerners would rig large galvanized iron drums with charcoal burners. Deep cast-iron pans or skillets were placed on top to fry the fish a "rich golden brown," and it was served "piping hot." At one Mobile, Alabama, fish rodeo, "one thousand pounds of fish was fried and served to anywhere from six hundred to a thousand guest[s]."[86] Despite the popularity of a Saturday fish fry, revival Sunday and the start of a week of preaching and dinner on the grounds was the event of the year in most southern communities. Joyce White remembers Sunday was the big day and "all the families in the Negro community who were active in the church would prepare an array of dishes for the afternoon dinner."[87]

In African American religious tradition, men and women had different labor assignments. Men preached and were responsible for making a crudely built long table, while women were responsible for singing and cooking food to spread out on the table. There were often turf battles over who was the best cook in a congregation. These were a part of the culture and dynamics of a church family.

Joyce White remembers the competition well in her hometown in Choctaw County, Alabama. She observed that the womenfolk "would vie to outdo one another" with their "peach cobbler, blackberry pie, banana pudding, chocolate cake, pound cake, and sometimes even homemade ice cream." Although the culinary competition was intense, it did not disturb another important role African American church functions played in the South. Events like revivals were "soul-satisfying" affairs where African American southerners could pass time in "comfort and security" free from "the harsh reality of our Jim Crow world...."[88]

Southern African American churches established a tradition of continuous interchurch visiting that cut across denominational lines. Generally, when a pastor went to preach at a revival service that another church held, his congregation, choir, and soloist accompanied him. After moving up North, soloist Alexander Smalls, originally from Spartanburg, South Carolina, recalled performing at a southern revival.

> The best was to sing on a revival Sunday at a rural church.... There was never any pay for the soloist, but with a spread of food running from one side of the church to the other, money simply didn't matter. These sisters and brothers had harvested a table fit for Baptist Pilgrims full of the Holy Spirit and very hungry. Platters of beans and rice, turnip greens and poke salad, butter beans with chopped tomatoes and fresh onions, yellow squash casserole with brown bread crumbs, fresh beets in orange sauce, stewed greens beans and ham hocks, wild turkey in brown gravy, hams glazed in raisin sauce, all the fried young chicken a body could want, trays of deviled eggs, macaroni salad, baskets of biscuits, cornbread and hoecakes. Stacked-up pies, cakes (pineapple upside-down being my favorite), peach cobblers, and all kinds of Jell-O molds in every shade.[89]

Nettie Banks remembered scenes of her mother cooking for a church revival meal in Middlesex County, Virginia. "I can see my mother in the kitchen, with water just running down, she would be soaking wet." The women of the congregation spent long hot hours boiling and peeling potatoes, cleaning, cutting, seasoning, and cooking collard greens, chickens, and fish. In addition, there were the buttermilk biscuits, yeast rolls, and layer cakes, all made from scratch. Women would bring baskets of food with them to church, where they would spread it out on a long outdoor table on the church grounds, "and people came and ate." There were plenty of vegetables and "some people who were good at making corn pudding, ... brought corn pudding, macaroni and cheese, and chicken; chicken, of course, always chicken."[90] In addition to serving as a spiritual fueling station for the soul and a refuge from racism, revivals kindled a passion for African American foods like fried chicken, pound cake, cobblers, and sweet potato pie. "Sweet potato pie," wrote one WPA staffer, "is very tasty when made right. It should not be too stiff, so as not to choke you, having enough milk and plenty of butter, sugar, nutmeg, and vanilla or lemon flavoring."[91]

THE BEANS AND GREENS OF NECESSITY

African Americans and the Great Depression

UNEMPLOYMENT AND JOBS DURING THE DEPRESSION

Migrants from the South and the Caribbean came to New York, Chicago, and other northern cities during the Depression in search of opportunity. In their home regions, they worked most often as agricultural laborers, waiters, domestic servants, and porters. Up north, migrant men gained a foothold in the metalworking, automobile, meatpacking, and construction industries. Women most often worked as domestics and in commercial laundries, and the less skilled branches of the garment industry. Within a given industry, migrants were likely to be assigned the least-paying job on a piecework basis. By 1929, however, New York City, the center of the nation's wealth and finance, was in economic collapse. Migrants were hit particularly hard because many of the men worked in industries and occupations disproportionably affected by the Depression such as construction and the steel and automobile industries. Another problem was that migrant workers did not have seniority and were clustered in non- and semiskilled jobs; they were thus the first to be laid off when the Depression hit.[1] Conditions were only a little more favorable for African Americans in the public sector.

Drake and Cayton argue that the job discrimination in the postal service in Chicago ensured that whites dominated the best positions even though these were federal jobs secured through civil service exams. For example, in the postal service in Chicago in 1930, the largest percentage of African Americans worked as laborers (69.5 percent), clerks (28 percent),

FIGURE 5.1 Unemployed men in front of Al Capone's soup kitchen, Chicago, February 1931. United National Archives II.

and mail carriers (16 percent). In contrast, they made up only a small percentage of the more coveted positions of foremen and overseers (4.5 percent), inspectors (3.7 percent), and managers and officials (1.2 percent).[2] Economist William A. Sundstrom, studying unemployment percentages during the Depression, found that in the south blacks and whites had similar unemployment rates but blacks earned much less than whites performing the same kind of work. Moreover, in both the south and the north, females had lower unemployment rates than did males. Most notable is Sundstrom's finding that "within the North, unemployment rates were 80 percent higher for blacks than whites" and "in [northern] cities black men averaged 50 percent higher unemployment rates than whites."[3]

Many struggling migrants from the South and the Caribbean had to eat almost like vegetarians, surviving on produce grown in expanded family gardens. By 1930 most North Americans turned to public and private sources of relief. In New York alone, over fifty breadlines distributed food to the destitute. All over the country, private institutions such as the Salvation Army provided food relief. Organizations less known for altruism also provided relief during the Depression. For instance, Chicago mob boss Al

Capone operated a storefront relief kitchen that provided free soup, coffee, and doughnuts to long lines of unemployed men of various ethnicities.[4] New York–based evangelist Father Divine, perhaps an equally controversial figure, also fed the poor. The lion's share of food relief, however, came from local, state, and federal institutions.

Most migrants from the South who arrived in the North before the Depression had experienced noticeable improvements in their access to food luxuries, such as better cuts of meat and more sugar, poultry, and pasta. In contrast, friends and relatives who never left the South had been doing without such items for so long that many claimed to notice little change after the Depression hit. This was especially true in those regions of the South where people fished, maintained vegetable gardens, and kept dairy cows, hogs, and chickens. For southerners, the Depression generally meant the traditional southern African American diet. That diet, however, varied widely across the South and even within each region.

Malcolm J. Miller, the South Carolina administrator for the Federal Civil Works Administration (FCWA), summed up conditions in the South in the era of the Depression: "For sixty-five years the South has been the sweatshop of the nation. That's because we were afraid of the Negro. We wanted to keep him down—and did. But we dragged ourselves down, too." In turpentine-producing regions of Georgia, for instance, the FCWA's Lorena Hickok, a white Midwesterner, observed, "Half-starved Whites and Blacks struggle in competition for less to eat than my dog gets at home, for the privilege of living in huts that are infinitely less comfortable than his kennel."[5]

In general, the Depression dried up the economies of many communities. Many turned to the New Deal relief programs started after Franklin D. Roosevelt was elected president in 1932. Federal food relief came in many forms: emergency food stations, surplus food distribution programs, soup kitchens, breadlines, and relief gardens. Vegetables from a relief garden near Greensboro, North Carolina, went toward the mass production of canned soup distributed as relief. New Deal administrators established emergency food stations in communities facing imminent starvation. For instance, in 1938 the staff of an emergency food station in Cleveland, Ohio, passed out oranges, apples, and a pound of rice to starving residents.[6] According to African American singer and composer Nina Simone, the arrival of New Deal relief programs saved her tourism-dependent hometown of Tyron, North Carolina, from becoming a ghost town.[7]

THE SOUTH DURING THE DEPRESSION:
FARMING AND BARTERING

In 1933 the Federal National Relief Agency (NRA) chose Tyron for one of its surplus food distribution program area depots. According to Lorena Hickok, the federal government ran into problems with its surplus food distribution program. States with an abundance of an item would often continue to receive shipments of it while having difficulties getting what they lacked. This was the case with oranges in South Carolina and pork in Daytona Beach, Florida, where residents already ate too much of these foods.[8] Problems notwithstanding, however, many survived the Depression on government relief rolls and jobs with the NRA. Nina Simone's father and other men in Tyron received NRA truck-driving jobs. "Not only did the men at the depot get given a little extra food to take home, but the drivers built up a network of people who would trade food among themselves," Simone recalls. Families would trade what they raised in excess in their gardens as well as surplus food they received on the job. Drivers traded spare "collard greens, string beans, tomatoes and sometimes eggs" with drivers who had "more sugar or flour, say, than they needed."[9]

Some individuals depended on a combination of government relief and their own efforts. For example, many African American women worked as domestics, earning shamefully low wages. As one historian describes, "it was not at all unusual for them to 'tote,' that is, to bring leftovers from their employer's house home with them. When these women planned the meals, as they often did, the leftovers might be of good quality and considerable quantity."[10] In Savannah, Hickok observed, "if you hire a cook down here, that means you take on the job of feeding, not only the cook, but her whole family," because, before they go home, they "clean out your ice box every night." White patrons became so accustomed to this that they did their shopping and "marketing with that in mind. It's considered just as regular as tipping a waitress in Childs' [restaurant] in New York."[11]

During the Depression, Nora Burns White grew up on a farm, spending mealtimes sitting around the table with five siblings, the children of her oldest sister, and "somebody that just happened to be there at dinner time . . . and if any body came down at dinner time they sat down and ate."[12] As the child of a tenant farmer in South Carolina, White procured at least one big meal a week by wandering over to the landlord's door about a block away at mealtime on Sundays to take advantage of his southern hospitality.

White recalled, "I had a thing on Sundays . . . when the family would come to eat and I would be outside at our house I would be watching for

FIGURE 5.2 Federal food surplus distribution in Cleveland, Ohio. AP Image Collection.

the cars to come." Jokingly, she says, "I was always a greedy person." The water pump for both houses was naturally next to the landlord's house. So she would time her trip to the water pump based on when the landlord's family, the Rosses, were seated to eat their Sunday meal. "I would sit my pail down at the pump and go on up to the kitchen and open the door and say 'good evening.' Mrs. Carrie Ross would say, 'come on in Nora, sit over here.'" Nora would sit down to a typical Sunday meal in South Carolina: collard greens seasoned with salt pork, peas and rice, corn bread, ham, and fried chicken. "I'd get up when I was finished and say 'thank you ma'am,' get the pail of water, and go on home." This went on for years during the Depression before her mother figured out what was going on. "It seemed like their food was better . . . the best corn bread."[13]

In addition to feeding the children of their tenants, some southern planters provided meals for their black laborers. For example, Monday through Saturday Carrie Ross distributed freshly baked corn bread and coffee to the black farmhands that worked for the family in Blaney, South

Carolina. As a result, Ms. Carrie became an expert at baking large batches of mouth-watering corn bread.[14] Similarly, in Alabama, the parents of Jim Warren, born in 1925, regularly fed black hands on the family's cotton farm near Birmingham. "They would sometimes come in for dinner on Sundays. They would always ask mom to cook black-eyed peas."[15] During the Depression, it seems, southern hospitality prevailed over jim crow in the lives of some southern whites who cooked for and ate with the African Americans they knew intimately.

During the Depression, families also adapted their cooking to both lean times and the short periods of feasting that followed the arrival of state aid, bartered items, the harvest from a garden, or a hog killing. Nina Simone recalled that her family transformed a big garden into "a huge garden and finally a little farm. We had hogs, chickens, and a cow. Rows and rows of string beans, collard greens, tomatoes, corn and squash." During extremely hard times, her mother made vinegar pies out of apple cider vinegar and dough. She also prepared a lot of dumplings, an occasional chicken, and a "ton of beans." After a winter hog killing, the family gorged on salted, smoked, and roasted pork, served with dishes such as rice pudding, brown betty (baked pudding), and plenty of canned vegetables. "For the next few days the kitchen was filled with sausages, sweetbreads and hanging roasts and there was pork crackling with every meal."[16]

Those fortunate enough to have a subsistence farm carried on business as usual, and a handful of southerners even went through the Depression without the need for government relief. One was civil rights leader Ralph David Abernathy, who recalled his childhood as the son of an independent black farmer in Marengo County, Alabama, about ninety miles southwest of Montgomery. During the Depression, Abernathy's father took care of his family's food demands first, raising cattle, hogs, chickens, corn, and other produce; in addition, he raised 100 to 150 bales of cotton, which he sold at market. He killed thirty to forty hogs a year, maintaining a smokehouse filled with curing hams, and his farmhands preferred receiving pay in "hams rather than in cash because the hams were better than any you could buy." In addition to hams, the Abernathys went through the Depression regularly consuming beef, poultry, and milk, all of which were rare for most U.S. citizens. They also bartered eggs to the owner of the community country store in exchange for other food supplies like salt, flour, and sugar.[17]

Similar to Nina Simone's mother, Abernathy's mother furnished the family table with produce in season from the truck garden along with the meat and poultry the family raised. She spent hours canning corn, beets, tomatoes, black-eyed peas, beans, potatoes, sweet potatoes, squash, okra, collard greens, turnips, and mustard greens. She also canned peaches, plums, pears, figs, and apples from the family orchard. The laborious job ensured that "we had enough to eat in the winter, when most of the fruits and vegetables had to come out of a jar." Abernathy recalls, "On Monday, Tuesday, Wednesday, Thursday, and Friday, we would have ordinary meals—one meat, three or four vegetables, corn bread, butter, maybe some preserves, plenty of milk. And Saturday—well, that was a day when everyone was busy with special tasks . . . on Saturday we were lucky to get leftovers." Subsistence farming, money earned from cash crops, and frugality permitted the Abernathys to meet the basic necessities of a family with twelve children. Consequently, Ralph Abernathy recalls, "Everything I learned about the Great Depression was from a college textbook." [18]

Maya Angelou's grandmother operated a country store in Stamps, Arkansas. Like Mr. and Mrs. Abernathy, Angelou's grandmother used a combination of store profits, bartering, subsistence farming, and the preparation of nitty-gritty, good-tasting food to survive the Depression with dignity. In Stamps, Angelou writes, "the custom was to can everything that could possibly be preserved. . . . Throughout the year, until the next frost, we took our meals from the smokehouse, the little garden that lay cousin-close to the store, and from the shelves of canned foods." The family pantry shelves, in her words, "could set a hungry child's mouth to watering. Green beans, snapped always the right length, collards, cabbage, juicy red tomato preserves that came into their own on steaming buttered biscuits, and sausage, beets, berries and every fruit grown in Arkansas." During the Depression, her grandmother twice yearly supplemented the preserves and smoked meat with fresh liver purchased from a local white butcher with pennies, nickels, and dimes. "Since the whites had refrigerators, their butchers bought the meat from commercial slaughterhouses in Texarkana and sold it to the wealthy even in the peak of summer."[19] In contrast, in New York during the Depression most people barely made it, and blacks fared the worst. "There were very difficult times in Harlem during the 1930s," recalled longtime Harlem resident Rudolph Bradshaw.[20]

HARLEM DURING THE DEPRESSION

Even before the 1930s, the majority of Harlem's African American and Latin American residents lived on the margins. This was because white racists in New York City, who owned most of Harlem's banks and profitable businesses, worked to ensure the underdevelopment of the city's nonwhite (and non-Protestant) residents. For example, the owners of pharmacies, department stores, and restaurants refused to fill the more prestigious jobs in their businesses with African Americans and Latinos, and landlords and food merchants charged nonwhites higher prices for inferior living spaces and food. During the Depression, then, tough times only got tougher for African Americans in Harlem.[21]

To make ends meet, African Americans turned to strategies like rent parties. On a Saturday night during the Depression, one could always find buffet flats, rent parties, whist parties, and dances, where, for a small fee, one could purchase down-home food and dance to good music. Langston Hughes recalled: "The Saturday night rent parties that I attended were often more amusing than any night club, in small apartments where God knows who lived—because the guests seldom did—but where the piano would often be augmented by a guitar, or an odd cornet, or somebody with a pair of drums walking in off the street. And where awful bootleg whiskey and good fried fish or steaming chitterling were sold at very low prices."[22] The host of a party advertised an event by sticking brightly colored cards into the grilles of apartment house elevators. Some of the announcement cards were quite comical:

RIBBONS-MAWS AND TROTTERS A SPECIALITY

FALL IN LINE, AND WATCH YOUR STEP, FOR THERE'LL BE LOTS OF

BROWNS WITH PLENTY OF PEP AT

A SOCIAL WHIST PARTY

GIVEN BY

LUCILLE AND MINNE

149 WEST 117 STREET, N.Y. GR. FLOOR, W,

SATURDAY EVENING, NOV. 2ND 1929

REFRESHMENTS JUST IT   MUSIC WON'T QUIT[23]

Philadelphia rent parties were similar to those in Harlem. The family in need got the word out and then went to work preparing food for the event. Meanwhile, residents in the surrounding area scrounged enough money to buy a plate of food and prevent someone from being evicted. For very little money you could get homemade sweet potato pie, greens, and fried chicken, or fish, or some part of the hog. The type of meat you selected determined the cost of your plate. A bottle of Tabasco sauce and salt and pepper would be available to spice up a plate of food overflowing with warm "pot-likker" (the liquid produced when cooking salt-pork-seasoned greens).[24]

FATHER DIVINE'S PEACE CENTER
AND NAZARETH MISSIONS

Every Sunday Father Divine (aka the Reverend General Jealous Divine; aka George Baker) fed starving interracial groups by the hundreds for free in Harlem, while many other black preachers ignored their flocks' hunger pains. Most African American urban clergy avoided sermons that addressed racism, poverty, and the social conditions of blacks in America. Instead, their sermons focused on life after death and the need for spiritual conversion. Father Divine talked about conversion, but he also denounced racism and the inability of a country blessed with material abundance to feed its citizens.[25]

Divine was a migrant from the Deep South (possibly the Carolinas or Georgia) with a refined southern accent. He married white women and displayed "undiminished prosperity" during the Depression. Divine became famous for hosting banquets that fostered interracial dining.[26] White historian Carleton Maybee, who was a doctoral student in the history department at Columbia University during the Depression, recalled that "whereas other churches had seven sacraments, Father Divine had only one, eating together with other people." In short, he regarded his interracial banquets as Holy Communion. "Father Divine was extremely well known during the 1930s by the whole country for feeding people for free if they could not afford food." Opposed to any kind of racial segregation, Divine drew large crowds of blacks to his Harlem locations, "with a sprinkling of whites." In fact, Columbia University students and faculty quite often went to the banquets, says Maybee.[27]

At his opulent banquets Divine and his followers served first-rate roasted poultry, vegetable dishes, fresh fruit, and hot and cold beverages from morning to midnight. He was able to do this, argues one biographer, by using a scheme that some restaurants had used for years: serving courses of inexpensive filling foods before serving expensive meats. Divine instructed his staff to serve guests plenty of water, tea, coffee, and other beverages and provide plenty of time for talking and singing hymns. Next, they served starchy foods and some fruits and vegetables. By the time waiters brought out the expensive cuts of meat, most visitors were too full to eat more than a little. The meat would return to the kitchen almost untouched and would be frozen for upcoming feasts.[28]

Interviews conducted with people who ate at one of Divine's places provide a portrait at odds with the inexpensive food scheme theory. No one else describes any attempt to systematically fill guests with starches

FIGURE 5.3 Cook at Father Divine Mission, Harlem, 1935. Photographer, Aaron Siskind. Smithsonian American Art Museum, Gift of Tennyson and Fern Schad, courtesy of Light Gallery.

before serving more expensive foods such as meat. Harlemites Roy and Ruth Miller, their childhood friend Rudy Bradshaw, and Dorothy M. Evelyn said Divine operated pay-to-eat restaurants on the Upper West Side of the city during the Depression (and into the 1970s and 1980s). The main restaurant was underneath the viaduct on 155th Street in Harlem. There was another one on 81st Street, "and I understand that he had several oth-

ers in Harlem," says Bradshaw, born in 1926 in Harlem, the son of Caribbean immigrants. Evelyn was born in Harlem in 1924, the daughter of
Caribbean immigrants from St. Kits and the Dutch island of St. Martin.
She went to Divine's Peace Centers for meals on many occasions. According to her, they were located "all over Harlem." They charged ten to fifteen
cents for an all-you-could-eat meal "and you didn't have to tip them," remembered Evelyn.[29]

The price of admission, according to Bradshaw, was no more than ten
to fifteen cents. And you got an earful of Divine's followers declaring the
virtues of their pastor. "The price of going in," said Bradshaw, was saying, just like his followers, "peace, peace, peace, peace is truly wonderful."
So if you went to one of his restaurants, you had to be prepared to hear
people testifying about the goodness of Father Divine. Inside the restaurants, Divine's followers would be declaring "peace is truly wonderful,
Father Divine, you know, is God," recalled Bradshaw. "So if you wanted
to have a meal you had to be prepared to have a religiosity experience."
Bradshaw's friend Roy Miller, also the child of Caribbean immigrants,
added, "it was extremely clean, from what I understood, the cleanliness
was impeccable."[30]

Divine's Peace Centers were clean spaces where Harlemites could buy
very good, inexpensive, white-tablecloth, sit-down meals. Carleton Maybee remembers that the food was "in abundance, and very well cooked,
just simply delicious, no complaints about the food or whatever."[31] Father
Divine, insists Bradshaw, was not operating mere restaurants in Harlem
but "retreats from the rigors of the ... Depression." He goes on to say,
"When it's a recession in the white man's country, it's a depression in Harlem. Well, it was a depression for the white man back in the 1930s in this
country and in Harlem it was devastation." He maintains, "Those that had
a job, they were thanking their Almighty every day. Those that didn't, and
a lot of young brothers didn't ... guys like Langston Hughes, doing WPA
works, and people of his intellect and guys that didn't have his sort of intellect were doing much worse."[32]

Having a dime was precious because you had to find a place to sleep
and eat. People had to be sure and "make a meal count." As a result, folks
in Harlem would hunt for a Peace Center where they could get a meal for a
dime. "And some of the brothers, I understand, were smooth enough to go
through the mantra 'yeah right, truth, peace, truth is truly wonderful, yeah
right sister,' to get another extra plate and make his dime stretch into two
meals," Bradshaw commented.[33] Evelyn remembers that for "ten cents and
fifteen cents you get fried chicken, corn bread, macaroni and cheese.... It

was southern cuisine. Most of them must have been southerners because that's what they cooked."[34]

Going to a Peace Center for something to eat became a regular night out on the town for Evelyn and her friends. "Yes sir, for fifteen cents you could go get fried fish, all you could eat." Evelyn maintains that she did not feel any pressure to become a member of Divine's church. "I didn't intend on changing my religion for theirs. It was a public place and all you" had to do was repeat his famous saying "peace sister, peace brother." So you would say that, get your food, and keep on going. "Absolutely," remarked Evelyn, "he had a hell of a following."[35] At first look it may seem odd that Divine served traditional soul food dinners to the integrated northern groups that attended his Peace Center dinners. But as a southerner Divine was continuing a tradition and practice that migrants brought with them from the South and that extended all the way back to the antebellum period. For people of African descent, some foods like chicken, yams, and later others like macaroni and cheese became part of a lexicon of sacred foods identified with religious activities. For Divine, the love feast was religious praxis that required sacred southern foods.

Other churches provided food during the Depression, but not as southern as Divine's. For example, the Abyssinia Baptist Church where Adam Clayton Powell, Sr., served operated a soup kitchen. Similarly, St. Mark's Catholic Church on 138th Street fed its schoolchildren first and then distributed leftovers to lines of neighborhood children during the Depression and World War II. Evelyn lived on 139th Street, one block from St. Mark's. "Neighborhood kids would go there and get soup, and we called it prison bread at that time, brown bread; peanut butter on one side and jelly on the other. I will never forget that because I went on many of those lines. Not because I had to, but because my friends where going on line and I followed suit."[36]

THE DEPRESSION NORTH OF HARLEM

As an adult, Fred Opie, Jr., made numerous donations to the Salvation Army as homage to the work the organization had done in the Tarrytowns during the Depression, especially during the holidays. He would periodically say, "If it wasn't for the Salvation Army, my family would have never survived the Depression." His sister, Dorothy Opie, said that during the Depression and the war, "I can remember them knocking on the door, and they would bring us food for Thanksgiving and Christmas when we lived [in a cold water flat] down on Valley Street before we owned this house."[37]

FIGURE 5.4 U.S. government pork being distributed to jobless residents in New York City, October 28, 1933. The Emergency Work and Relief Administration hoped to have forty-nine stations in operation to distribute about 250,000 pounds of pork. AP Image Collection.

In Westchester County, business owners freely distributed leftover food to Maggie White. During the Depression and then the war years, "there was a scarcity of money, but they learned how to make do with a little," says Margaret Opie. Her aunt Mag, as she called her, lived over Nick's Market in Ossining, "and Nick would give away the soup bones ... in other words what you would call waste or scraps, she could make a soup out of that." She goes on to say, "That's one of things I remember about black people during the Depression, what other people threw off, black people could make do with, and make flavor[ful]." According to Margaret Opie, Aunt Mag "had flavor. She made you know that she loved what she was doing."[38]

Opie's Aunt Mag had two ways of cooking: one for the wealthy white family that employed her and one for her own family. When cooking for her own family, she "cooked for abundance and flavor, and [on a] limited budget." In contrast, when she cooked for the wealthy white folks, "every thing she needed was available to her." So much in fact that the Brandts, the white family she cooked for in Ossining, regularly gave her food to take home to her children. In addition, her Italian neighbors in her poor, working-class community gave her food to take home. During the Depression and then the war years, the welfare office in the village of Ossining also distributed flour and lard to needy families.[39]

As a single mother, Aunt Mag had to feed four boys and one girl, so she had to make the most out of what she could obtain. "Oh I remember she would cook chicken and dumplings and make pots of cabbage, and they were seasoned with ham hocks. And I always had to have a glass of water because she put red peppers in there and they were hot!" Aunt Mag filled her five children with "wonderful biscuits." "And she also made what we called spoon bread, which was flour bread in a big black skillet. And we would ... sop that with molasses. And she made home fries, and when she made home fries she probably do almost five pounds of potatoes ... in those black skillets." Opie goes on to say, "And back in them days, they cooked with lard. In contrast, when she cooked for the [Brandts], she used Crisco. So poor people did not use the same things as the wealthy people."[40] Another dish that blacks cooked for their families and friends and not for white employers was chicken. Psyche A. Williams-Forson, author of *Building Houses Out of Chicken Legs: Black Women, Food, and Power*, tells us that "cooking chicken, especially when it is fried, is a laborious process from start to finish. (For this reason, some women refused to cook chicken when they worked for white families.)"[41] Black women, however, joyously did the tedious work of frying chicken for church events.

SPECIAL OCCASIONS AND THE "GOSPEL BIRD"

By the twentieth century, Methodist and Baptist church people in the South served fried chicken, the "Gospel bird," as a traditional sacred food, for many years offered only on Sundays, holidays, and special events like camp meetings.[42] As I reported earlier, this was an adaptation of an Africanism: sources show that chicken played a similar role in West African religious celebrations and rituals. In the southern United States, fried chicken "was not cooked hard and dry, but it was sweet and juicy and could be easily digested and enjoyed," writes one WPA contributor from Virginia.[43]

Nettie Banks recalled that when she was growing up in rural Middlesex County, Virginia, black people fried their chicken with the lard they made during winter hog-killing days. When that ran out, they would use lard purchased from a store.[44] Yemaja Jubilee's family always had plenty of food because her father operated a country store in Charlotte County, Virginia. Traditionally, on Sundays, Jubilee's mother, born in 1926, cooked "fried chicken, macaroni and cheese, yellow chocolate layer cake, potato salad, and sometimes she did not have chocolate cake, she would have sweet potato pies, and home-made apple pies."[45] At age eighty-four, Benjamin Outlaw of Windsor, North Carolina, still had a vivid image of his mother's Sunday cooking. "Now I am going to tell you what we cooked. You cooked collards ... chicken, baked, fried, and pot pied, fish, rolls, sometimes a turkey, sometimes a geese, sometimes, a duck." He added, "vegetables now, sometimes she cooked cabbage, she cooked collards, corn, okras, and tomato pudding." For dessert, Hattie Outlaw made blueberry, blackberry, and strawberry dumplings: "we'd go out in the woods and pick them and can them up."[46]

Joan B. Lewis was born in 1935. Her mother was from Windsor, and her father was from Washington, both located in Bertie County, North Carolina. Her father did most of the cooking in the home. On Sundays, "we would have fried chicken, sweet potatoes, green beans, or my father made biscuits, and leg of lamb. Now my father was good about stuff. . . . Then with that we would have some kind of scalloped potatoes. Once in a while, my mother would make cakes for desert. My family really were not dessert people, we would just have peaches in the can."[47]

In his autobiographical writings, Stephen Erwin, a 1925 graduate of Duke University, former high school principal, and newspaperman, describes Sunday meals at his home in Harnet County, North Carolina, in which fried chicken played the leading part. "On Sundays the mainstay at the table was fried chicken along with sweet potatoes, collard greens cooked southern style with a hunk of pork meat, and biscuits and butter. Sometimes we had a large chicken stew, chicken dumplings cooked together in a large cast iron pot."[48]

On Sundays, chicken was also the center of the meal in Alabama. "Back then [the 1930s], chicken was the best of all meals to serve," recalled Ralph David Abernathy; "better than ham, better than pork chops, better even than roast beef or steak."[49] During his childhood in rural Alabama, his mother cooked fried chicken generally on Sundays; he and his siblings therefore "lived for Sunday." His mother also served it on the "grand occasion" when the preacher came to their home for dinner.[50] In Choctaw County, Alabama, and in most of the South, "every family was expected to feed the preacher at least once during the year" writes Joyce White. In addition to roast pork, rice with gravy, stewed tomatoes, corn, macaroni and cheese, corn bread, pies, and crowder peas with okra, White's mother always served fried chicken when the congregation's minister, Reverend Barlow, came to dinner.[51]

As the child of a Baptist preacher in Virginia, Lamenta D. (Watkins) Crouch ate Sunday dinner at different homes all over the state. She was born in 1947 in Greenbay, Virginia, in Prince Edward County, about nine- ty miles from Richmond, but her father accepted a call to pastor a church in Keinridge, Virginia.[52] In addition to this position, he also served as a pastor at several churches out of town. Lamenta Crouch spent many Sun- days eating at other people's homes. Most of the time she received a fried chicken dinner complete with sweet potatoes, greens, potato salad, succo- tash, and rolls. Crouch recalls what a treat it was to have "really, really tall hot rolls." Crouch never got sick of fried chicken. "Some had the knack of having fried chicken and the meat was tender. Some knew how to season it," she said. "Today I am very health conscious, but it is still very difficult for me to resist fried chicken." In addition to fried chicken and fixings, southerners in Virginia served Lamenta Crouch and her family pound cake, chess pie, and "very rarely apple pie."[53]

CHESS PIE

Before doing research for this book I had never heard of chess pie. I thought perhaps others might be interested in learning more about its ingredients and want to see a recipe.

4 oz. butter
½ cup brown sugar, packed
1 cup granulated sugar
3 large eggs
1 tbs. vinegar
2 tsp. vanilla
1 tbs. cornmeal

Melt butter and blend in sugars. Add eggs and other ingredients and stir until blended. Do not beat. Bake in unbaked pie shell for one hour at 350 degrees.

Like Ralph Abernathy, South Carolinian Alexander Smalls liked Sun- day best, the day his mother would make fried chicken. "I'd start thinking about Sunday on Wednesday. Southern fried chicken, fried okra, creamed corn, powdered buttermilk biscuits, a mountain of potato salad with sweet pickles ... caramelized brown onion gravy dripping off the largest roast loin of beef ever, the bowl of slow-cooked green pole beans with ham hocks" and fluffy Carolina long-grain rice. "There was no order or balance to Sunday dinner, health wise or otherwise, except plenty of everything and everything good," recalled Smalls.[54]

Nora Burns White was born in 1928 in Blaney, South Carolina, just twenty-two miles from Columbia. Her mother, a sharecropper and midwife, raised several girls alone during the Depression as a divorcée. Nora's eldest sister, Ella, did the cooking in the home. Nora recalled that a typical Sunday meal growing up was "fried chicken, usually some kind of vegetable, maybe collard greens, and macaroni and cheese and rice—two starches—I still do that today on most Sundays."[55]

The preparation of rice and collard greens on Sunday was not just a South Carolina tradition. Jamaicans also made similar foods on Sunday. Beryl Ellington was born in 1915 in the small rural village of Manchester, Jamaica. Ellington's mother had nine children, seven boys and two girls, whom she fed on produce and meat she raised. On Sundays she baked cassava "bammy" (or bread), fried plantains, and cooked goat's meat, rice and peas, yams, and collard greens. Rice and peas was made with "gongo beans," what Americans call pigeon peas, and Ellington's mother cooked the collard greens in a pot of water seasoned with onions, garlic, vegetable oil, and salt. On Sundays the family also had "yellow yam, or negro yam, and coco banana" cooked in a pot with a little piece of codfish, and a salad with lettuce and tomatoes.[56] A special Sunday meal was a tradition for southern-born blacks and West Indians. Fried chicken, collards, biscuits, and/or corn bread were the most popular items served by black cooks on Sundays following a long and soulful Protestant church service. It is easy to see how fried chicken's association with Sundays and church earned it the nickname "the Gospel bird."

CONCLUSION

Migrants tried to maintain their eating traditions as best they could despite the severe economic hardships of the Depression; this was particularly the case on Sundays and special occasions. Most often, however, unemployment and scarcity created incentives for migrants to accept food relief in the form of groceries and prepared ethnic dishes outside their culinary traditions. Food relief came from various public and private sources, including the government, white employers, churches and merchants, the Salvation Army, gangsters like Al Capone, and neighbors of various ethnicities. Indeed, I argue that the Depression created a climate in the United States that fostered a great deal of culinary exchange between black

Southerners and European, Latin American, and Caribbean immigrants in urban centers like New York and Chicago.

Times of scarcity ended with the Allied victory in Europe in 1945. After World War II, returning African American GIs and African American college students would open a new chapter in the cultural and political history of the United States. African American spaces such as churches, restaurants, and bars and grills provided sanctuary from the brutalities and offenses suffered under jim crow.

EATING JIM CROW

Restaurants, Barbecue Stands, and Bars and Grills During Segregation

Black folk bought and thoroughly enjoyed soul food long before restaurant owners and cookbook writers started using the term. Before the emergence of the civil rights and black power movements, African American cooks working at segregated restaurants, barbecue stands, bars and grills, and nightclubs helped establish consumer demand for what became known as soul food in the late 1960s. Jim crow policies ensured that black restaurants remained separate black spaces. For working-class blacks, these eateries enabled them to relax and recover from the stress of racial politics in North America.[1]

Many of the eateries owed their success to the jim crow laws and customs that restricted the public dining options of African Americans beginning in the late nineteenth century.[2] A number of the folks interviewed recalled the challenges of finding good food and service in restaurants before the 1954 landmark Supreme Court case *Brown v. Board of Education* that ended the principle of "separate but equal" and effectively began the slow death of jim crow segregation laws. Before 1954, African American parents raised their children to cope with jim crow restrictions. Eugene Watts, from Waynesboro, Virginia, remembers: "You didn't just walk into a white establishment," you stood in front until somebody came out and typically said, "Boy, are you lost?" It was then appropriate to stand, looking down at the ground, and politely reply, "No sir, I would like to get something to eat." African American elders made sure that before black youths went downtown, they clearly understood the particularities, dictates, and customs of buying food at a white-owned restaurant. Says Watts, African

FIGURE 6.1 African American sitting on bench at side of barbecue stand made of galvanized metal, 1939, Corpus Christi, Tex. Library of Congress, Prints and Photographs Division, LC-USF33-012032-M2.

American youths knew better than to "go through the door and try and get you something to eat" at a white-owned restaurant without first obtaining permission from an employee.[3]

BLACK COOKS, CUSTOMERS, AND SEGREGATION

An African American named Daroca Lane was a cook at a segregated lunch counter in the bus depot in the city of Alba, Alabama. Her nephew, Joseph Johnson, told me that as a child he worked there with his aunt Daroca. Black and white customers could order a piping-hot breakfast of sausage, eggs, and grits. At lunch and dinner Aunt Daroca served up mashed potatoes, peas, and chicken and dumplings, with sweet potato pie for dessert. It is ironic that most of the white owners of segregated eateries in the South filled their kitchens with African American cooks but often refused to sell food made by blacks to black customers.[4]

When black customers were permitted to eat in an establishment, jim crow segregation laws required that blacks sit apart from white customers. In her memoir, singer Diana Ross, who grew up in Detroit, remembers a trip she made with her siblings to visit relatives in Bessemer, Alabama, in the 1950s. "I dimly recall seeing signs on water fountains, in waiting rooms, and at movie theatres: WHITE, COLORED." She goes on to say, "There were so many indignities black people endured; everything was separate and unequal."[5] At the Alba bus depot, a sign posted at the lunch counter designated "colored" and "white" ordering and sitting sections. "You would order your food from the colored side, but you didn't come together," remembers Joseph Johnson. At other restaurants, white owners made black customers buy at a "colored" window at the rear of the building.[6]

Selling and purchasing food at the "colored" window of a segregated restaurant could be a degrading and even dangerous experience, says Eugene Watts; you never knew when some volatile white person behind the counter was going to "go off." For the slightest reason, white owners and managers might fly into a rage at the sight of an African American restaurant employee attending to an African American customer. They would sometimes claim the employee was taking too long, but mostly they would jump at any opportunity to unleash racist comments that articulated their contempt for both the employee and the customer. Managers often pushed their employees to dispense hasty service to African American customers, and African American employees sometimes rushed black customers so that they would get their orders in without incident.[7]

African Americans eating outside their communities remained on their best behavior, having been taught never to show any emotion no matter what kind of bad treatment they received from a white-owned restaurant. But, despite the outward appearance of deference, African Americans regularly resisted jim crow.[8] Interviews with southerners indicate that African American customers and restaurant employees did not simply capitulate to conditions in the South but employed what one scholar calls "infrapolitics."[9] In the case of segregated restaurants, infrapolitics included such everyday forms of resistance as theft, passing, and employing what one historian calls the "cult of Sambohood": using grins, shuffles, and "yassums" to get what one needed without violence. Infrapolitics describes the "daily confrontations, evasive actions, and stifled thoughts that often inform organized political movements."[10] For example, blacks working the "colored" window at white-owned restaurants regularly gave away food or discounted the food sold to blacks. Another form of resistance was to travel with someone light enough in complexion to pass as white and have that person get takeout orders from restaurants that would not serve black customers.[11] But the most common strategy for coping with the humilities suffered under jim crow was to buy food only from black-owned establishments, especially when traveling. Through word of mouth, blacks traveling across the country drafted mental road maps indicating where black communities and restaurants existed.[12]

For example, Joan B. Lewis recalls her first road trip in the summer of 1953 to Durham, North Carolina, to attend North Carolina Central University (NCCU), an HBCU not far from Duke University. She and her family drove from New York to North Carolina on U.S. Interstate 301. Lewis recalls that the road was very scenic, and you had to drive through a lot of little towns. But 1953 "was really a segregated time," and when you hit the jim crow state of Maryland, "you could not go to the bathroom!" If you did not know anyone in a jim crow region, "you could get gas at the gas station, but you couldn't go to get anything to eat," says Lewis.[13] If you drove into the District of Columbia, which was very racist, there were a number of African American sections of the city where you could eat. In the northwestern part of the city, the home of Howard University, an HBCU, two historic restaurants could be found not far from campus: the Florida Avenue Grill and Ben's Chili Bowl located on P Street. Both were popular African American–owned places where Howard students went for hassle-free down-home food. If you did not stop in the District, you kept driving until you reached the city of Richmond.[14]

In Richmond,[15] two popular eateries for African Americans were the Greasy Spoon and Johnnie B's. Located just a couple blocks from Virginia Union, an HBCU, Johnnie B's made the best bologna burgers, served with "fried onions, lettuce, and tomato, and if you want to, throw a little piece of cheese on there too, that's good right," recalls Yemaja Jubilee, who attended Virginia Union in the 1960s. "And the buns were big! They weren't like the buns now! I get excited talking about it," she says. They also sold milk shakes, "all different kinds of milk shakes." It was the kind of place where there were often lines going out the door to order food, "and it was black owned."[16]

Even those traveling far afield from such large cities as Richmond would have found African American neighborhoods and eateries like the Greasy Spoon and Johnnie B's. Jim crow ensured that African Americans almost "always lived across the railroad tracks" or in sections of a municipality called the lowlands, hollows, or bottoms, arguably short for the least desirable real estate in an area. One historian found that New Deal–era surveys tended to locate African American neighborhoods in areas where it flooded. As he put it, when it "rained, the water found its way to the places where black people lived."[17]

Most African American communities had at least one eatery where one could get down-home cooking. One of the best examples of these 1950s

FIGURE 6.2 Barbecue stand, Fort Benning, Columbus, Ga., December 1940. Farm Security Administration, Office of War Information, Library of Congress, Prints and Photographs Division, LC-USF34-056482-D.

eateries were the Cleveland, Ohio,[18] barbecue stands of Eugene "Hot Sauce" Williams, which were even featured in an article in *Ebony* magazine. In 1920 Williams, a childhood friend of Louis Armstrong and a one-time fish peddler in Louisiana, migrated from New Orleans to Chicago, where he became a cooper. Four years later he migrated to Cleveland in search of business opportunity. With no previous professional experience, he started a barbecue rib business after taking out a loan for fifty-eight dollars from "Cleveland's first barbecue czar," Henry "the Black King" Burkett. Williams returned to his native New Orleans around 1934, spending days "just drifting among cooks, gathering bits of information here and there on barbecue. One of the city's oldest chefs took an interest in him and let him in on his personal method of preparing tasty ribs." Returning to Cleveland with the culinary secret of making excellent ribs, Williams established two thriving rib stands that employed a total of twenty-five people.[19]

By 1950 he was grossing about $100,000 a year in sales as customers packed the two stands he operated "almost any hour during the six nights" per week they were open. He offered no delivery service, "but his spots often fill large orders from private parties and clubs," said the article in *Ebony*. Even Louis Armstrong was said to have phoned in an order for "300 large boxes of the flavory ribs." Most credited the success of his Cleveland barbecue stands to the secret way Williams flavored his ribs with "a dry spice powder and taste-tantalizing hot sauce." Only he knew the formula for the powder, which he personally sprinkled on all his pre-cooked meats. According to Williams, it was not just the ingredients he used: "It's the cooking that counts. Good cooking comes from proper tim-ing and the right amount of heat." His further instructions were to cook the ribs slowly over a low-burning charcoal flame, taking care to cook them thoroughly, but not long enough to dry them out.[20]

Joseph Johnson, a native of Alabama who operated a barbecue stand, argues that, in most restaurants operated by southerners, "you didn't have a lot of variety on the menu." Specialized dishes of fried fish, barbecued or stewed meat and rice, or smothered fried chicken (place fried chicken in a frying pan, add 2 cups hot water, let simmer for 30 minutes) and rice were some of the only dishes a lot of small, southern-operated restaurants offered.[21] The African American–owned Dew Drop Inn in Waynesboro, Virginia, for example, ran a Friday special on fried fish, grits, and collards, served all day long. In Greensboro, North Carolina, Barry's Grill was one of the most popular places in the city's African American community.[22] Betty Johnson of Attalla, Alabama, briefly attended North Carolina A & T, an HBCU in Greensboro, in the 1950s. Before the 1960 student sit-in movement at the Woolworth's and S.H. Kress store lunch counters, fear of white hostility dissuaded her and her classmates from ever trying to enter white restaurants in downtown Greensboro. Instead, they enjoyed the fried chicken and pork chops available at black-owned Barry's Grill.[23] In the city of Durham, African Americans lived in the Pettigrew community, where NCCU was located. Restaurants that African Americans patronized in the community were the Our Campus Grill, located on the NCCU cam-pus, and the Off Campus Grill, in the heart of the larger community. Both restaurants specialized in burgers and barbecue. Further south in the city of Athens, Georgia, there was another great restaurant for barbecue.[24]

African Americans Robert and Gladys Walker (who went by the names Bill and Geraldine) started a barbecue stand that specialized in hot pork sandwiches. Bill Walker first started accumulating capital in Athens work-ing for "white folks" at the age of ten. He took jobs "rolling an afflicted white man around in his wheel chair" for a dollar a week and then worked as a "houseboy for the white folks my mother worked for," at $2.50 a week. After that he took a job doubling as butler and chauffeur for friends of his mother's "white folks," where he earned $7 per week. When his employers fell on hard times, he left Athens for Atlanta, where he worked briefly at a barbecue stand, a fraternity house, and sundry other places for two years. "I was saving my money all that time to set up a barbecue stand of my own some day," he told WPA writer Sadie B. Hornsby.[25]

After Bill married Geraldine, the couple decided to open up a barbecue stand that would sell sandwiches, hash, Brunswick stew, and other dishes Bill had learned how to make when he worked at the barbecue stand in Atlanta.[26] No one is sure of the origins of Brunswick stew. Natives of Brunswick, Georgia, claim it came from there. Similarly, natives of Brunswick County, Virginia, say it was created in their region in the 1820s. Some suspect it is derived from Native American cookery, because the earliest recipes call for squirrel meat to make the stock of the stew, which is typical of Native cookery. Brunswick stew is "almost as necessary to a barbecue dinner as the barbecue itself," said one unidentified Alabama WPA writer: "Those parts of the meat unsuited to barbecuing form the stock of the almost-inevitable Brunswick stew. Added to the meat, in boiling pots, are canned tomatoes, and corn, potatoes, onions, bell pepper, black pepper, Worcestershire sauce, catsup, vinegar, lemon juice, butter and cayenne pepper."[27]

In Athens, the Walkers recalled digging their "first barbecue pit in our own backyard, and that good old meat was barbecued in the real Southern style." Southern-style barbecue required as much as fifteen to twenty hours of slow cooking over hickory or some other hardwood embers. Precooking preparation could take almost half that time. Both precooking and barbecuing required skill, but precooking, seasoning, and mixing the barbecue basting sauce drew on techniques passed down from West African ancestors, such as using lemon juice and hot peppers as essential ingredients. As in Africa, sauce recipes differed across regions of the South. "We done so much business that first summer," recalled Bill Walker, "that we decided to keep our stand going through the winter with home barbecued meat. We already had it screened but when winter come we boarded our pit up." In two years, the business literally grew out of a hole in the ground that was their barbecue pit into a corner restaurant. "When we sure opened up for business, I had 500 circulars distributed in a radius of 10 blocks around here, and then we went to work, day and night, to build up our trade."[28]

Flyers and word of mouth had the couple doing a brisk business in ten-cent barbecue sandwiches. In addition to barbecue, the Walkers sold corn bread, fish, cooked liver, bowls of hash and Brunswick stew, bottled beer, soft drinks, and candy. Geraldine Walker, originally from Bogart, Georgia, was raised on a farm not far from Athens. When she was old enough, she started doing farm work, which she never liked. Soon thereafter she went to work for a white lady for sixty cents a week, "helping with her work, such as toting water to the house, bringing in stovewood, and tending the food after she put it on the stove, to keep it from burning; She learnt me to make my first corn bread."[29]

Before she met Bill, she was married to her first husband and worked as a cook for five years. After the death of her first husband and her subsequent marriage to Bill, she kept on working as a cook for whites. "The reason I stopped working out was to help Bill in our barbecue stand," she recalled. They had to hire three delivery boys to serve customers who preferred their barbecue delivered. "Some of the nicest white people in this town send us their calls for lunches to be sent out to their offices and homes," declared Geraldine, "and to tell the truth the white folk buy more of our barbecue than the Negroes does." She added, "I've had at least a dozen calls for liver at the lunch counter, since I sold the last piece of it I had cooked up. These white folks around here sure do eat up liver fast as I can keep it cooked for 'em."[30]

Not far from Athens, there were a number of good black-owned restaurants in the city of Atlanta. This was especially true in southwest Atlanta.[31] One of the city's African American communities was an educational consortium called the Atlanta University Center (AUC), located in southwest Atlanta. AUC schools, located across from the Georgia Dome, included the Interdenominational Theological Center, Atlanta University (now Clark-Atlanta University), Morris Brown College, Morehouse College, and Spelman College. In the neighborhood surrounding the AUC complex were notable black eateries like Pascal's, as well as more humble holes-in-the-wall.[32]

Pascal's was down on Hunter Street (later changed to Martin Luther King Jr. Blvd.). During the civil rights movement, the restaurant served as a popular meeting place for black activists and politicians. Martin Luther King, Jr., Maynard Jackson, and Julian Bond, who all attended Morehouse, held strategy meetings over down-home cooking at Pascal's. According to Marcellas C.D. Barksdale, who attended Morehouse in the early 1960s, Pascal's was no dump. To the contrary, it was a white-tablecloth restaurant for middle- and upper-class African Americans in Atlanta, the "number-one so-called classy restaurant" for African American professionals. During segregation it remained the first choice for a Sunday meal for "Doctor and Mrs. so and so." In addition, well-to-do Morehouse students would also take their "public girlfriends" to Pascal's for Sunday dinner, says Barksdale. You could get full-course, great-tasting meals for two people for five dollars. In addition to formal dining, Pascal's also had a lunch counter and grill for casual dining.[33] Stanlie M. James, originally from Iowa, came to Atlanta in the late 1960s. She remembers eating grits and "sweet milk" for the first time in her life at Pascal's during her campus visit with her family to Spelman. For AUC students who could afford it, Sunday night fried chicken dinners at Pascal's were a tradition. But for those with less money there were neighborhood eateries, mom-and-pop corner places, that sold takeout.[34]

In most African American neighborhoods there was some type of "café, or cafeteria, or restaurant as you may call it," says Atlanta native and Morehouse graduate Alton Hornsby, Jr. "In my neighborhood [the Mechanicsville-Pittsburgh section] in Southwest Atlanta, I know there were at least three within a few blocks from my home. Indeed, my parents owned and operated a small place for several years which was called the Greasy Spoon." Hornsby remembers there was a bar that had about four stools and a "jar of pig's feet and other little sundry items." Most customers bought takeout "because we only sold sort of carry out items like fried fish sandwiches, chicken sandwiches, and barbecue sandwiches."[35]

In the 1950s and 1960s, AUC students "were trying to go some place and get good food off campus. Because the food was just institutional," says James. It was not like today where college cafeterias are operated like a food court with salad bars, pasta bars, and lots of options. When she was a student at Spelman, James goes on to say, "if they were having liver and onions, then that's what they were having."[36] Students at other HBCUs had similar complaints about the food in the college cafeterias. Before he moved to Atlanta and became one of Reverend King's deputies in the civil rights movement, Ralph David Abernathy led a student strike to protest food inequalities between faculty and students in the cafeteria of Alabama State College.[37]

Abernathy enrolled in Alabama State in the late 1940s on the GI Bill, after receiving an honorable discharge from the army. Reflecting on the cafeteria food at Alabama State, he remembers the students eating for lunch "heaps of steaming pork and beans—and nothing more, not even a piece of bread to sop it up." Dinner was not much different. He writes that the best dinner they ever had was Spam with unbuttered grits, while the faculty feasted on huge pieces of real country ham. "After several weeks of this fare, we were sick to death of it and were dreaming every night of fried chicken and biscuits." Abernathy was elected student body president in his sophomore year. Right away he organized a complete student boycott of the cafeteria, and it did not take long for the school's administration

FIGURE 6.3 "Hot Fish": Bryant's Place, Memphis, Tenn., June 1937. Farm Security Administration, Office of War Information, Library of Congress, Prints and Photographs Division, LC-USF34-017593-E.

to act: the next time the cafeteria opened at Alabama State, students "saw huge platters of fried chicken waiting at the counter."[38]

At Virginia State and Virginia Union, faculty and students ate the same class of food, but that didn't mean there were no complaints. At Virginia State, students ate what they called "wonder meat" because "we wondered what it was," says Lamenta Diane Watkins Crouch, a 1970 Virginia state graduate.[39] Her older sister, Francis Ann Watkins Neely, graduated from Virginia Union in 1967. "I really did not like the lamb chops" that they served in the cafeteria. "My husband went to Howard University and he told me that the meat that they served in the student cafeteria there he believed [was poor-quality cuts that] came from the federal government." In general "we southerners just did not like the lunch and dinner menus in the college cafeteria," says Neely.[40] The food at Virginia State, according to her younger sister, "was not seasoned the same as home," and there were a lot of "starchy foods including potatoes served with just about every meal and lots of pasta."[41] "My mother was a really good cook and that's what I grew up on," says Neely. "We southern students were always receiving care packages from home filled with good food. So we always knew some-body on campus who had just received a care packages so we would go and eat that instead of the cafeteria food." The northern students, she said, who had fewer options, seemed to say very little about the cafeteria food but ate at the Union a lot more often than the southerners did.[42]

College students, white or black, gripe now and then about the quality of cafeteria fare. Yet the tendency may have been greater among southern students raised on elaborately seasoned traditional downhome food, food that was different than the cuisine that black students with parents native or acculturated to the north grew up on. The chief complaint of HBCU students was the bland taste of the food and repetitive menu. As Watkins Crouch recalled, "If there was chicken and vegetables served one day, we knew there was going to be chicken vegetable soup the next day."[43] Most scholars accept that HBCUs received far less government funding than did white institutions. As a result, HBCU administrators had to use leftovers in soups and stews to reduce their expenditures. The bland nature of mass-produced institutional food, inadequate funding, and poor-quality meats made it difficult for cafeteria meals at HBCUs in the south to compete with traditional southern cooking.

In the South, disdain for institutional food, even black institutional food, and the hostility blacks encountered in white spaces helped main-tain culinary traditions in the African American community. Similar fac-tors ensured the proliferation of black culinary traditions in the North. There, African Americans "accepted a certain way of life, but we did not think of it as segregation," Diana Ross writes of Detroit in the 1940s and 1950s. She grew up in an all-black urban neighborhood and accepted seg-regation until the defiance of people like Rosa Parks and the forging of the civil rights movement.[44] In suburban Westchester County, African Ameri-cans grew up in quasi-segregated housing arrangements, typically living next to largely poor Italian, and some Latin American immigrants. In both urban Harlem and suburban communities in Westchester, racist whites made it very clear whom they wanted to serve in their dinner clubs and restaurants.

HARLEM IN THE 1950s

Before 1945 restaurant chains in New York City refused to serve African Americans and restricted their employment options, refusing to let them serve behind luncheonette counters. Furthermore, until the passage of antidiscrimination laws after World War II, African Americans in New York restaurants endured "inferior service, especially in terms of seat location [if they were seated at all], personal treatment, and length of wait," writes one historian.[45] This was not the case in Harlem, which was a hotbed for communist and other radicals who protested against second-class treatment anywhere in that Upper West Side African American community. Harlem, with its amazing jazz clubs and restaurants, remained a great place to socialize in the 1940s and 1950s. There was Tillie's Chicken Shack, Well's (for chicken and waffles), the Red Rooster, Jock's Place, and the Bon Goo Barbecue.

The Bon Goo Barbecue opened in 1938 and became a very popular Harlem eatery. It was located at 717 St. Nicholas Avenue, north of 145th Street in the heart of Harlem's bustling nightclub district. An African American man named Lamar operated the restaurant, whose clientele included "most of Harlem's celebrities and a mixed group from the middle working classes, including both white and black." At the Bon Goo Barbecue one could order golden brown spare ribs for thirty cents and chicken or roast lamb for thirty-five cents, all served with spaghetti, coleslaw, and bread and butter. The menu also included "pig's feet and ham for those who desired them." Take-out orders, called the "Housewives' Special," could be purchased in larger portions: for example, whole chickens could be purchased for $1.70. The twenty-four-hour restaurant did its best business at night, after clubs like the Savoy and Renaissance Ballrooms had closed.[46]

Saxophonist Carmen Leggio recalls hanging out at the Metropolis and the Cooper Rail in addition to the Savoy and Renaissance ballrooms in New York. The Metropolis was located just a couple of blocks from Birdland, a jazz club in Harlem named after jazz giant Charlie "Bird" Parker.[47] The Metropolis was one of the late-night stops, a "winding-down place for the African American swing musicians," says Leggio, who was born in 1927. It was located on Seventh Avenue, and across the street was a southern food restaurant called the Cooper Rail. In the 1950s the police left the club and the restaurant alone despite the drug pushing and using that went on there. Artists like Ben Webster, Henry Red Allen, Charlie Schafer, and Ornette Coleman hung out at the restaurant all night long, talking jive and eating pigs' feet, black-eyed peas and rice, collard greens, and fried chicken.[48]

Not far from the Cooper Rail, on 120th Street and Seventh, or Lenox, Avenue, was a place called Creole Pete's. It served as a popular restaurant for those living in boardinghouses without kitchen facilities. Rudy Bradshaw recalls, "It was very difficult for a lot of brothers and sisters in Harlem ... to get a room with a kitchenette; if you did not have a room with a kitchenette and just had a hall room, that meant that the bulk of the brothers who were bachelors in those days had to find a certain place where they could eat their dinner, and Creole Pete's was one of those places." It was not a "top-of-the-line Harlem restaurant," but you could get a good yet inexpensive home-cooked meal with friendly service. Pete, the restaurant's owner, migrated to New York from New Orleans.[49]

Tillie's Chicken Shack also provided inexpensive meals with dignity for a diverse clientele. Red-and-white-checked cloths covered plain tables, and old hit songs and pictures of the artists that sang them covered the walls. The Chicken Shack had a piano "used constantly by the musically inclined," and a kitchen equipped with old-fashioned iron pots. Tillie's multiethnic patrons, many of them socialites, entertainers, politicians, and other celebrities, consumed "400 chickens and 200 pounds of fat" per week from Arthur Addison's kosher market.[50] Tillie purchased her other groceries from the A&P next door to her business.vLocated at 237 Lenox Avenue, just above 121st Street, the Chicken Shack became famous for its fried chicken dinners served with yams, hot biscuits, and coffee, all for a dollar. "It is difficult to estimate the number of biscuits consumed by a single patron," writes WPA author Sarah Chavez, "but the piled-up plate returns to the kitchen empty." In addition to fried chicken, the menu also included black eyed peas "cooked southern style, boiled with hogs head or pig tails."[51]

In hash houses in Manhattan's Bowery neighborhood and from street vendors throughout the city, African American customers could also expect good-tasting inexpensive food unaccompanied by the hassle of jim crow racism. In addition to goulashes, stews, and ragouts, customers also feasted on dishes familiar to African American southerners, such as pigs' knuckles and snouts, beef tongue, and liver. WPA writers Irving Ripps and Macdougall observed firsthand that no color line existed in hash houses. In one restaurant, Ripps reported, eight thousand people a day ate "tremendous quantities of simple" food, twenty-four hours a day. For as little as between two and four cents you could have fishcakes, spaghetti, clam chowder, hamburgers, macaroni and cheese, and french fries. These foods, especially the greasy and unhealthy french-fried potatoes, were modern introductions to African American cuisine from European immigrants. Over time, the easy-to-make deep-fried potatoes would, in many instances, replace the traditional southern and labor-intensive home fries, which typically called for chopping and dicing red or white potatoes, adding onions, peppers, garlic, and seasoning, and then slow-cooking them in a frying pan for nearly an hour. At Bowery hash houses, dessert, usually "incredible quantities of rice pudding or large cuts of pie," was likewise priced below five cents. The inexpensive menu attracted a diverse crowd of poor folk, but restaurant owners enforced no color line.[52]

In the 1940s and 1950s African Americans and Puerto Ricans where just starting to migrate from other parts of New York City, slowly gaining footholds in once predominately Irish, Italian, German, and Jewish neighborhoods in the South Bronx. "By 1950, there were almost 160,000 African Americans and Puerto Ricans in the borough, 91 percent of then in the South Bronx, concentrated around Prospect and Westchester avenues where their compatriots had settled years earlier. Later arrivals joined them as migration from the rural South and Puerto Rico continued," writes historian Evelyn Gonzalez.[53]

Kwame Braithwaite, an activist, photographer, and expert on the history of jazz in New York City was born in Brooklyn. His family, migrants from Barbados, lived in Brooklyn for about a year before moving to Harlem and then, when he was five years old, in 1943, to Kelly Street between Longwood Avenue and 156th Street in the Bronx. "It was a very mixed block," says Braithwaite, with people from Caribbean and the South. He remembers his Barbadian mother "used to make the best coconut bread ever and [she] ... used to make it in two forms ... either like in a bun or in the pan. She used to sell them. Everybody used to come around here. ... People used to come by and place [an] order." His mother was also renowned for cooking cucu, an okra dish from the Caribbean made with cornmeal and okra and served with boiled salt fish. She also made pigs feet with a sauce that was too unfamiliar to the New York–acculturated Barbadian American Braithwaite; he admits, "I didn't eat [them]."[54] African American Frank Belton's family moved to the Bronx in 1948 from South Jamaica, Queens, when he was nine years old. In Queens, the family had lived in a mostly African American community. Much to his surprise, they moved to a largely Puerto Rican neighborhood on Chisholm Street, in the South Bronx. "I went to the grocery store one day and the guys were up there talking. I didn't understand a word they were saying [laughter]." When he started school, he also noticed that a fair number of his classmates were Puerto Rican and thus came to the conclusion that "it was basically a Puerto Rican population in the South Bronx." On Chisholm Street, there "was a kind of mixed population" of largely African Americans and Puerto Ricans, with Italians, "a couple of Irish" and one Jewish family that remained in the neighborhood until about 1952. "They were the last Jewish family to move off Chisholm Street. But the Italians, they stayed, even up until the time I was in college, there were still three Italian families still living on the block." He says, "the Italians did not move, they held their ground."[55]

Nathan "Bubba" Dukes, a Bronx basketball legend, recalls trips to Johnson's Barbecue as a child for some down-home southern take-out. Duke's family had moved from Columbia, South Carolina, to the South Bronx's Prospect/Tinton Avenue area in the 1950s. His father was a superintendent of a tenement house not far from Johnson's; the owner of the restaurant was also a South Carolinian migrant. Bubba Dukes loved living in the tenement housing because "every Friday, especially during the summer times, what would happen was, we would go around the corner on Tinton Avenue, [and] 161st Street ... and there was Mr. Johnson's rib, chicken, and potato salad place. And the lines would be backed up"[56] I argue that eateries like Johnson's Barbecue and similar venues selling Caribbean cuisine provided spaces that helped forge cordial relations and cultural exchanges among different ethnic groups and nationalities in the multi-ethnic neighborhoods of Harlem and the Bronx. As Paul Gilroy as shown, language proficiency, class, traditions, and housing patterns determined the amount of relationship building and cultural exchange that occurred in leisure and work spaces.[57] More segregated sources of down-home food developed further north, as southerners and Caribbean immigrants settled in Westchester County.

WESTCHESTER COUNTY

Interviews with Westchester County residents make it clear that jim crow customs prevailed in most parts of metropolitan New York.[58] Some white-owned restaurants in Westchester flatly refused service to African American customers, while others provided such hostile service that "word got around" not to go into specific bars and grills, says Alice N. Conqueran. Conqueran's parents migrated to North Tarrytown from the French Caribbean Island of St. Lucia before the Depression. Alice was born in North Tarrytown in 1926 and spent her early childhood years living in the same cold-water flat as my father and his family.[59]

She remembers that when you walked into some restaurants in the county, "you got the message" that you were not welcome. Scharff's Restaurant in White Plains was like that in the 1940s and 1950s, for instance; it just didn't serve African Americans. In the South, jim crow racial hostility in restaurants was "open, but in the North it was subtle, but it was here," says Conqueran. "You knew where you stood in the South, but in the North, you weren't sure." The very popular Wonderful Bar in Tarrytown was another example. This white-owned bar and grill served American cuisine. "I can remember when blacks were not served in the Wonderful Bar," says Conqueran, "this is going back to the 1940s and 1950s."[60]

As Conqueran says, "You have to remember, in those days we weren't as welcome in restaurants."[61] As a result, many African Americans patronized businesses such as black-owned and -operated bars and grills. Born in 1935, Margaret Opie argues, "because of segregation, black people would go, [I] am talking about young people like us, you would go to these bars not so much for drinking, but to get good food." Most of the African American bars and grills in the county also had live music on the weekends.[62]

In metropolitan White Plains, an area with a sizable African American community, there was Tark's on Central Avenue in White Plains proper, Farmer's on Tarrytown Road in Greenburg, and Fields' Rotisserie, also on Tarrytown Road. All were African American–owned and -operated bars and grills. Fields' was owned and operated by John Fields and his wife; it remained a family-owned business until it closed for good in the 1980s.[63]

"The bill of fare," says New Rochelle native Christopher Boswell, "consisted of ribs . . . cooked on a rotisserie and given the barbecue treatment before you served them, and they also served fried chicken." Boswell worked as a cook at Fields' in the 1960s. In 1910 His father had migrated from Trinidad to New Rochelle, where he worked as a bank courier in the old Huguenot Trust Company. His mother was from Chicago but migrated in the 1920s to New Rochelle, where she worked as a housekeeper at the old Bloomingdale's. Boswell remembers that people used to come to the window at Fields' when it had a "fry-o-ladder" and watch him cook. He would simultaneously fry thirty or more pieces of chicken while bystanders stood in stark amazement, wondering how he knew which pieces were ready to remove from the oil. It was simple, says Boswell: cooked chicken floats on hot oil "when it's done, the same is true with fish."[64]

Fields' did a brisk business, especially on Fridays and Saturdays, when it offered live jazz. The place also had booming business on Sunday afternoons, when African American couples in the 1950s and 1960s traditionally went out for lunch or dinner and a movie. Greenburg resident and photographer Gordon Parks was a regular at Fields' on Sundays. In addition to chicken and ribs, Fields' served fried shrimp, collard greens, sweet potato pie, and delicious rolls. Customers would rave about the rolls, though Boswell says, "I guess I can say this now, they were store-bought rolls." And the sweet potato pies, "frozen, store bought," he confesses. "Nobody knew

[and] nobody" ever suspected that some of the down-home food was not made in-house. It was the Fields' family secret. The other bars and grills in the area, Farmer's and Tark's, had smaller food menus, and people went to them principally for the liquor. According to Boswell, "Fields' was the place in the area" for southern food and live jazz.[65]

Similar venues for food and live jazz existed in the African American sections of the Westchester towns along the Hudson River. There was Club Six, owned by southern migrant Martin Cotton and five other African American business partners (hence the name). This African American honky-tonk, located under a bridge just up the road from the Tarrytown train depot, provided live hot jazz played by local virtuosos. Bass player Benny Molten, drummer June Bug Lindsay, and saxophonist Carmen John Leggio, all from North Tarrytown, along with piano player and Yonkers native Ketter Betts, began their careers playing local venues like Club Six before going on to join big-time bands with jazz legends Maynard Ferguson, Gene Krupa, Benny Goodman, Duke Ellington, Lester Young, Buddy Rich, and others. In addition to great music, Club Six had "a lot of soul food and really good eating" says Alice Conqueran. Like the Greasy Spoon in Atlanta and the one in Richmond, Club Six was a place where you could get fried chicken and just about anything else on a sandwich.[66]

Alice Conqueran remembers that De Carlo's was up the street from Club Six in the middle of Cortland Street's African American neighborhood. De Carlo's, she says, "used to be a poolroom and then became a bar." North Tarrytown native Mary Tweedy used to be the cook at De Carlo's, where you could order fresh fried porgies and other items.[67] According to Margaret Opie, before the end of de facto segregation in Westchester, "black bars had to have food" because white restaurants did not serve African American customers or, if they did, they served them with such haste and hostility that you did not want to go back. Thus African American bar owners usually looked for someone whose reputation as a cook could draw customers, someone who could really "throw down," says Opie. "Usually it was a separate person that had that concession in the bar." In short, these concessions of really good southern food were important "appendices to these places."[68]

If you took the train from Tarrytown ten miles north along the Hudson, you would arrive in the village of Ossining, the home of Sing Sing Prison. At one time, the village of Ossining was officially called Sing Sing, named after the Sing Sing Indians who inhabited the small hamlet just thirty-five miles north of New York City. African Americans would frequent a neighborhood bar and grill in Ossining called Bar Harbor, located on Hunter

Street just a couple of blocks from the railroad station. The prison was a stone's throw south of Bar Harbor on Hunter Street. Two southern-born brothers, Raymond and Walter Cook, originally from Virginia, owned the establishment.[69] If you continued north on the train along the banks of the Hudson for another twenty minutes, you would eventually make your way to the city of Peekskill. Here, African Americans, especially from Ossining and the Tarrytowns, went to Green's Bar and Grill to dance and dine with African American residents of Peekskill. Howard Green owned and operated the bar and grill. According to Joan Lewis, Green's, located in downtown Peekskill, was nicer than Ossining's Bar Harbor and Tarrytown's Club Six and De Carlo's. All these clubs had essentially the same type of southern food: fried chicken, potato salad, corn bread, greens, sweet potato pie, and layer cakes.[70]

Mom-and-pop operations, bus stop lunch counters, and bars and grills represent the modern origins of the restaurants that started appearing with the phrase "soul food" in their signage and other marketing materials in the late 1960s, 1970s, and 1980s. African American cooks in what I call pre–civil rights, black power, and soul institutions established the definition of a good menu in restaurants that specialized in southern food. In the South, African American women reserved the labor-intensive process of making rolls and sweet potato pies for special occasions: Sundays, holidays, church events, weddings, and funerals. In commercial establishments throughout the 1930s, 1940s, and 1950s, "southern fare" became synonymous with fried chicken or fish on a sandwich, chopped barbecue, rolls or biscuits, collard greens, sweet potato pies, and cakes. Thus special-occasion foods became the food that these honky-tonks and restaurants sold to African American consumers. It was food that was easy to market because it was relatively inexpensive, it tasted good, and it was attached to memories of special times spent with family and friends in tight-knit African American communities. It was also food that could be obtained without jim crow restrictions.

African American responses to de facto jim crow in New York were similar to those of blacks in the South. African Americans in New York kept mental ratings of the restaurants where they lived. White-owned restaurants were rated on their food, service, and civility toward black customers. The African American rating list also included all the black-owned restaurants where one could obtain down-home southern food and, with favor, southern hospitality. Thus African Americans visiting other communities, from New York to Atlanta, learned from each other the best places to eat before 1954, when lunch counters and restaurants in North America were desegregated.

FIGURE 6.4 "White" and "Colored,": Durham, N.C., May 1940. Farm Security Administration, Office of War Information, Library of Congress, Prints and Photographs Division, LC-USF33-020513-M2.

Joan Lewis, the Ossining native who went south to attend NCCU in Durham, provides interesting insights into the significance of the 1954 Supreme Court decision officially ending segregation in the United States. When she went to Durham in the summer of 1953 to start her freshmen year, city restaurants and the bus depot lunch counter were all segregated. "Now everything changed. I was down there in 1953; in 1954 when we came back after the summer, for the next year, all the signs were gone because they had to integrate in 1954." The change in racial tolerance was drastic, says Lewis. In Durham, white restaurant owners changed their behavior toward African American customers, and "you could do what you wanted to do," says Lewis. She recalls that during her first year, "we were sitting way up in the balcony, they put the black people up in the balcony at the theatre downtown." The "next year," however, "we came and we could sit anywhere we wanted to sit." Similar changes happened in the restaurants. After 1954 "we could eat downtown then. They had some little shops. We would go down there and eat" without encountering hostility or indifference from restaurant employees. In short, some white owners quickly recognized there was more economic opportunity in serving African American customers than in snubbing them.[71]

But on Route 31 in Maryland, it was still hard for African Americans to find hospitable places to eat. Lewis recalls that, in her junior year, she began to carpool back and forth between Westchester and Durham with two male students from Peekskill who had cars. In 1955 "we got so we could stop in some parts of Maryland, [but] not too much." But by the time Lewis graduated from NCCU in 1957, she says, "we could ride up and down and you could do what you wanted to do."[72] In other parts of the country, jim crow died at a much slower pace. Speaking of her experience in the South, Motown superstar Diana Ross writes, "Segregation did not stop in the 1950s but continued well into the sixties and, in some areas, even the seventies."[73] In urban centers on the East and West Coasts, the black spaces that were a consequence of jim crow segregation helped assimilate black immigrants from various regions of the South and the rest of the Americas into an urban African American identity. In many instances, these social spaces helped push many into a veritable African American melting pot of native blacks and blacks from the South and the Caribbean. And so it was that African Americans developed the worldview they called soul. Soul became very popular, and many blacks used it to counteract the painful realities of racism on both coasts.

THE CHITLIN CIRCUIT

The Origins and Meanings of
Soul and Soul Food

Born and raised in Augusta, Georgia, singer, songwriter, and choreographer James Brown is considered the undisputed father of soul. In his autobiography, he writes that by 1962 soul "meant a lot of things—in music and out. It was about the roots of black music, and it was kind of a pride thing, too, being proud of yourself and your people." He adds, "Soul music and the civil rights movement went hand in hand, sort of grew up together."[1] Before the civil rights movement, black entertainers like Brown, B.B. King, Ray Charles, Al Green, Gladys Knight, Nina Simone, and Aretha Franklin made their living on the "chitlin circuit," a string of black-owned honky-tonks, nightclubs, and theaters. The circuit wove throughout the Southeast and Midwest, stretching from Nashville to Chicago and into New York. Performers would often do consecutive one-night stands, frequently more than eight hundred miles apart. The routine went: drive for hours, stop, set up the bandstand, play for five hours, break down the bandstand, and drive for several more hours. On the road, performers often settled for sandwiches from the colored window of segregated restaurants until they arrived at the next venue.[2]

On the circuit were the New Era in Nashville; Evan's Bar and Grill in Forestville, Maryland (just outside of the District of Columbia); the Royal in Baltimore; Pittsburgh's Westray Plaza, the Hurricane, and Crawford Grill; and New York's Club Harlem and Small's Paradise, to name just a few venues. The chitlin circuit was crucial to black artists like James Brown and B.B. King because it offered the only way for them to perform for their fans during a period when the white media did not cover and

FIGURE 7.1 Negro bunkhouse, Childersburg, Ala., May 1942. Farm Security Administration, Office of War Information, Library of Congress, Prints and Photographs Division, LC-USF34-082813-C.

mainstream venues did not book black artists. The entertainers called it the chitlin circuit because club owners sold chitlins and other soul food dishes out of their kitchens. Early in her career, Gladys Knight performed in a house band on the circuit, playing at "roadside joints and honky-tonks across the South," she recalled. "No menus. No kitchens. Just a grizzly old guy selling catfish nuggets, corn fritters, or pig ear sandwiches in a corner."[3] The circuit went beyond small hole-in-the-wall clubs, however. Elaborate African American–operated theaters like the Regent in Washington, D.C., the Uptown in Philadelphia, the Apollo in New York, the Fox in Detroit, and the Regal in Chicago were big-time venues considered part of the circuit.[4] These theaters did not have kitchens that sold food, but savvy African American entrepreneurs established places nearby where you could purchase good-tasting meals.

Various soul food traditions cropped up in connection with the circuit. In New York, for example, soul food was eating fried chicken and waffles—perhaps early on a Sunday morning after spending all night listening to bebop jazz musicians such as Miles Davis and Thelonius Monk. The legend goes that this northern soul food tradition began when artists in New York ordered chicken for breakfast after missing dinner on Saturday

FIGURE 7.2 Negro café, Washington, D.C., July–November 1937. Farm Security Administration, Office of War Information, Library of Congress, Prints and Photographs Division, LC-USF34-008544-D.

night because they were performing and ordered waffles as the hot bread to eat with the fried chicken. Similarly, at Kelly's restaurant in Atlantic City, the queen of soul, Aretha Franklin, remembered after-hours meals of "hot sauced wings and grits for days." Franklin also recalled that near Chicago's Regal Theater there was a "food stand, tucked a few doors away from the theater, that served greasy burgers made with a spicy sausage in the meat, topped with crispy fries, Lord, have mercy. The artists couldn't wait to get offstage to wolf down those burgers."[5] When performing in northwest Washington, D.C., African American entertainers ate at Cecilia's Restaurant, conveniently located across the street from the Howard Theater. Harlem, the site of New York's Odeon and the Apollo theaters, had a bunch of restaurants: Grits 'n' Eggs, Well's Waffle House, the Bon Goo Barbecue, the Red Rooster, and Tillie's Chicken Shack, among others. Most of these restaurants had been open since the 1930s and 1940s. But nobody called them soul food restaurants then.

It was in the 1960s that African American urban dwellers, first in the Southeast and then in the Northeast, gradually made the transition from talking about rock music (rhythm and blues) and southern food to calling it soul music and soul food. In the face of the increasing ethnic diversity of urban centers, soul became associated with African American culture and ethnicity. People with soul had a down-home style that migrants from the rural South could unite around. For this working class, composed predominantly of underemployed urban dwellers, soul made them members of an exclusive group of cultural critics. Soul gave them insider status in a racist society that treated them like outsiders, and it emerged as an alternative culture that undermined white definitions of acceptability.[6]

Beginning with discussions in the 1960s and 1970s, soul was considered the cultural component of black power, the most visible black nationalist idea of the twentieth century. At its heart, soul is the ability to survive and keep on keeping on despite racist obstacles to obtaining life's necessities. In the language of soul, the more you have been through and survived, the more soul you have. Soul roots go back to the 1920s and the Harlem Renaissance movement.

THE POLITICAL ORIGINS OF SOUL

The 1920s movement began after democratic struggles in Europe during the post-World War I era failed to carry over and improve conditions for blacks in the United States. Similarly, the black power and soul movements of the post-World War II era were, among other things, a response to the limited gains made after the 1954 Supreme Court decision in *Brown vs. the Board of Education*, the outlawing of school segregation, and the civil rights movement that followed. Black power and soul in their various manifestations, depending on the group, were rooted in the black revivalism of Malcolm X, the direct action protests as well as the political and economic organizing campaigns of the Student Nonviolent Coordinating Committee (SNCC), and the armed resistance to police brutality of the Black Panther Party for Self-Defense. In addition, militant African independence movements in the 1950s and 1960s stirred African Americans to action, producing a new and "brilliant generation" of angry black intellectuals that rivaled those of the Harlem Renaissance.[7]

Both the urban riots that followed the assassinations of Medger Evers, Martin Luther King, Jr., and several other important figures within the civil rights movement in the 1960s and the failure of American liberalism shaped the development of soul. In *Report from Black America*, published in 1969, activist and civil rights strategist Bayard Rustin observed that African Americans in the early 1960s "began to get Blackenized." Black power and soul proponents such as Stokely Carmichael (Kwame Ture), H. Rap Brown, Amiri Baraka, and others called for "thinking black" and moving beyond the double consciousness outlined in W. E. B. Du Bois's classic book *The Souls of Black Folk* to a new, independent, proud black identity. Rustin argues that soul was the cultural arm of the black power movement that called for, among other actions, singing, talking, and eating according to the African heritage of black people in America.[8]

In a 1967 article entitled "African Negritude—Black American Soul," published in the journal *Africa Today*, W. A. Jeanpierre argues that soul is the same as African negritude. Both negritude and soul were political and cultural concepts rooted in the values that informed black Americans about African civilizations, black genius, and the things that made black people across the globe unique. The difference between negritude and soul was in their origins: elite African intellectuals, many of them living in Europe, created the idea of negritude; northern working-class urban African Americans with southern roots created soul ideology, which subsequently spread to more affluent northern black communities. From Jeanpierre's article, one can conclude that there is a class and regional formula to soul: poor black folks have more soul than wealthier ones; urban black folks have more soul than suburban black folks. In this formula, the more black, poor, and urban you are, the more soul you have.[9]

Soul and soul food, according to one scholar, developed out of a larger black power project that called for creating black cultural expressions different from white society.[10] Oral interviews conducted with those who lived through the civil rights and black power movements illustrate this point. For example, Lamenta Crouch, a longtime educator in Prince George's County, Maryland, associates the term "soul food" with the black power movement of the 1960s and 1970s. Crouch graduated from an HBCU in Virginia in the 1960s and moved to Washington, D.C. She remembers black power in the metropolitan Washington area largely as a black identity movement. Crouch says, "I can't remember exactly the first time that I heard it, but it was in the same era of black power, soul brother, and all that business of having an identity that was uniquely ours." She adds, "It was during that era that the soul food term came up and I think it was kind of like, ok this is ours. This is something we can claim is ours that identifies us as a people and we [have] some value and we have something to contribute."[11]

Clara Pittman observed that black power in northern California inspired black people finally to stand up for their rights and "speak for themselves," openly expressing a pride in their unique African heritage and an awareness of the contributions they made to American society. During the 1960s and 1970s, she was in her early twenties, just out of the Marine Corps, and living in northern California (not far from Oakland where Bobby Seal and Huey P. Newton started the Black Panther Party in 1966).[12]

In Westchester County, New York, black power did not have the kind of popularity or influence it had in the District of Columbia and northern California. Westchester residents born before the Depression had little to no experience with black power. For example, Ella Barnett, born in 1915, claimed "black power didn't mean anything to me. It really didn't make a difference."[13] Margaret Opie and Sundiata Sadique, however, both Westchester activists born in the 1930s, had a very different interpretation of the influence of black power in the county. Starting in the 1960s, Opie became very involved in local, county, and national politics. She held positions such as membership chair of the Ossining NAACP and director of the Center for Peace in Justice, which was started in Ossining and is now a countywide organization located in the county seat in the city of White Plains. She also held the position of director of the Ossining Economic Opportunity Center (one of President Lyndon B. Johnson's War on Poverty programs) and was a 1972 delegate to the Democratic National Convention in Miami representing Westchester County.[14]

Sundiata Sadique, formerly Walter Brooks, moved to Westchester County in 1963 from just across the Hudson River in nearby Rockland County. After high school, he joined the U.S. Army, where he was a paratrooper in the 101st Airborne. After his tour was up, Sadique spent a brief period in Chicago, where the message of the Nation of Islam's Elijah Muhammad and the Fruit of Islam (all the adult male members of the Nation who were trained in self-defense) attracted his attention. Before returning to Rockland County, he became a member of both the Nation and the Fruit of Islam. In Rockland, he served first as secretary of the Congress of Racial Equality (CORE) and later became the chairman of the CORE chapter there. He came to Ossining in 1967 with Bill Scott, the chairman of Rockland County's CORE chapter. When Sadique first arrived in Ossining, he took a job cutting hair at George Watson's barbershop. From the town's only black barbershop he started recruiting and organizing blacks for both the Nation and CORE, selling copies of the newspaper Malcolm X started while he was a member of the Nation, *Muhammad Speaks*. (The photographer for the Nation of Islam, Bernard Jenkins, also lived in Ossining.)[15]

During the 1960s and 1970s, the Nation, CORE, and the Black Panthers all launched organizing efforts in Westchester County. The Nation, an exclusively alternative black nationalist religious organization, had better results than the overtly political organizing efforts of CORE and the Black Panthers. Sadique and other members of the Nation living in

Westchester County made the thirty-minute car or train trip to Harlem to attend Malcolm X's Temple No. 7. Elijah Muhammad assigned Malcolm to New York to recruit the large number of blacks that lived in Harlem and the greater New York area.[16]

In his early days, Malcolm and his lieutenants carried out their proselytizing efforts in front of the Theresa Hotel located next to the Chock Full o' Nuts Café at Seventh Avenue and 125th Street. Malcolm, a tall, handsome redhead, delivered his charismatic Black Nationalist critique of the problems of black society and the solutions offered by Elijah Muhammad standing on top of a wooden soapbox. In addition to his street-corner oratory, Malcolm and his followers at Temple No. 7 operated several restaurants in Harlem and a black nationalist newspaper with a distribution network that extended as far as the city of Peekskill in northern Westchester County. As Malcolm's popularity increased, African Americans in and around Harlem flocked to hear him preach. Malcolm remained the minister in charge in Harlem until he left the Nation in 1964. Recruiting efforts continued to go very well after Malcolm's departure, however, as evidenced by the establishment of a Nation of Islam temple and restaurant in the lower Westchester County city of Mount Vernon.[17]

In contrast to the Nation, CORE first came to northern Westchester to address problems within the local fire departments. In Peekskill, racist members of the city's full-time professional fire department denied African American firemen the right to ride on city fire trucks, forcing the men to take taxis to fires. Similarly, racist members of the Ossining Volunteer Fire Department practiced a policy of blackballing that shut out African American volunteers. Despite its valiant efforts, CORE was unable to establish a local chapter in Ossining. The Black Panthers had similar organizing difficulties in northern Westchester.[18]

In the 1970s the Black Panthers established chapters in Chicago and New York City. They also attempted to make inroads into Westchester County with breakfast programs in poor black neighborhoods. In Ossining, however, where Sing Sing Prison was located, most African Americans viewed outsiders like CORE and the Black Panther organizers with contempt, fear, and suspicion.[19]

The older generation of African Americans, most of them southern migrants like Ella Barnett, were politically very conservative and disagreed with black power and black nationalism. Younger black folk feared law enforcement officials. Sundiata Sadique recalls that when he moved to Ossining, fear of the police paralyzed many black residents. Young activists like Margaret Opie, who became politically mobilized as members of the

NAACP in Westchester, simply did not trust outside political operatives representing CORE and the Panthers. Maybe they suspected that they might really be undercover agents.[20]

Back in the 1940s, Westchester County had become an unfriendly place for black activists and the message of black power. The county had become like a police state, perhaps in response to the Peekskill Riots of 1949 and the communist hysteria surrounding the Rosenbergs' execution at Sing Sing Prison in1953. "This was like a prison town and a police state to me when I started living here," says Sundiata Sadique. "Black people were very afraid of law enforcement. So I think it had something to do with the prison, you know if you go back to the Rosenbergs when they saw that, when they were electrocuted in Sing Sing and the kind of turnout of the racist ... so it took a while" to get black folks organized. Basically, all they had in African American communities in the county was the NAACP.[21] For many African Americans in the county, then, black power never made significant inroads.

In general, black power never gained the popularity and mass appeal of soul. Black power advanced soul ideology because it championed the study of African culture and the development of a black consciousness. It also encouraged African Americans to imitate the black power movement's example of adopting Africanisms: African dress, natural hairstyles, soul music, and soul food. Black power proponents argued that for too long white society had been declaring that African American culture was not worthy of respect. In reaction, African Americans sought to develop a new cultural identity through soul that would unite and guide the black power movement. Before the country could be changed, however, the African American community had to redefine its cultural values and reject white acculturation. Like wearing African attire or sporting an Afro, eating soul food in the 1960s and 1970s represented a political statement for those with a new black consciousness, "a declaration of the right," writes Rustin, "and the necessity to be different."[22]

SOUL

In the 1960s and 1970s soul became the requirement for entrance and acceptance in African American communities. At the same time, soul helped upwardly mobile and assimilated African Americans stay connected with their roots after their migration to largely white suburban communities. Civil rights activist Bayard Rustin argues that the "soul renaissance" challenged college-educated African Americans with mobility to "say no" to the impulse to assimilate into white society and thus forfeit their black-ness. It deified black church culture, natural hair, ghetto life, black music, and soul food. In Rustin's words, it was the sudden discovery that "black is beautiful and that white is not necessarily right; it was a card of identity, a pass key to a private club, a membership in a mystical body to which Negroes belonged by birthright and from which whites for a change were excluded by the color of the their skins."[23]

Soul ideology from the 1960s also maintained that African Americans had hard-earned experiential wisdom that came from growing up black in America. That is, through years of surviving racism in the Americas, people of African descent had developed a natural instinct and intuitive understanding of how to make something wonderful out of the simple or out of what wealthier folks claimed had no apparent value. In the same vein, soul intuition informed African American cultural productions such as dress, music, and food. Soul is a hunch about what is good in a racist so-ciety that defines most cultural productions associated with black folk as inferior. Soul intuition is an African American trait that developed as Af-ricans negotiated the Atlantic slave trade, slavery, and jim crow. It served black people as a necessary collective consciousness developed largely out of the limited resources that white society granted African American peo-ple who were forced to adapt to ghetto environments.[24]

In the early 1960s business owners in northern black communities like Harlem utilized soul vocabulary to attract black customers. But soul was not just a commercial creation. African Americans in northern inner-city neighborhoods started identifying with the poor man's music and food that they enjoyed and reminded them of their southern roots according to "race rather than region," writes one sociologist.[25]

Alton Hornsby, Jr., grew up in southeast Atlanta in the 1940s and 1950s. Back then, black people didn't talk about soul food. "They would just say chitlins, pigs' feet, southern fried chicken, etc., [and] barbecue, just things that black folk ate and some white folk." He goes on to say, "I don't re-member the term 'soul food' coming into such popularity until about the same time as the early phases of the civil right movement. . . . Then it was being referred to as soul food and also soul music. We used to call it rock and roll. Then about that time the names 'soul food' and 'soul music' began to be used more commonly."[26]

Thus, starting with the 1960s, urban dwellers in cities like Atlanta gradually made the transition from talking about rock music (rhythm and blues) and southern food to calling it soul music and soul food. In the face of the ethnic diversity of northern cities, soul became associated with

African American culture and ethnicity. People with soul had a down-home style that migrants from the rural South could unite around. For this working class, composed predominantly of underemployed urban dwellers, soul made them members of a special group of cultural experts. Soul gave them privileges in a racist society that denied them opportunities, and it emerged as a counterculture that undermined white authority.

African Americans took the common knowledge about how to cook and eat soul food as a source of collective identity. Soul food, like soul music, represented another example of the subculture that served as an exclusive African American club, off limits to those who did not live the black experience. The use of soul food as part of the black experience becomes difficult, because there is no single black experience, just as there is no one type of soul food. Descriptions of soul food from the 1960s and 1970s illustrate this point.[27]

SOUL FOOD DEFINED

Some argue that soul food is basically southern food. "I don't know any of those so-called soul food items that southern Euro-Americans particularly did not eat," says Alton Hornsby, Jr., who has spent his life in Atlanta, Georgia, with the exception of short stints in Nashville, Tennessee, and Austin, Texas.[28] Natives of the black belt region of Alabama and South Carolina (born in 1933 and 1928, respectively) make similar observations.[29] Interviews reveal that differences in cuisine are more regional than ethnic; black and white folk in the South ate according to essentially African American–shaped culinary traditions formed over hundreds of years. The differences in eating habits are greater between northerners and southerners of any race than between white and black southerners.[30]

Ella Barnett, for example, a professional caterer for over fifty years in Westchester County, observed that the food requests from white and black clients were very different.[31] According to the 1930 census records, however, at that time most of the county's African American population had been born in the South or raised by one or more parents born in the South. In contrast, most of the white population had been born in the North, born in Europe (Italy, Ireland, Eastern Europe), or raised by one or more parents that were European.[32]

Over the years, Barnett found that her white clients "didn't know nothing about soul food" and "never had anything like that." It was her African American clients that wanted a "little bit different" kind of cooking: "Black folks want pigs' fit [sic] and chitlins and stuff like that." Soul food, says Barnett, is "black folk's food, that's what I call it."[33] Reginald T. Ward, Joseph "Mac" Johnson, and Clara Pittman all define soul food as the "food that you were brought up on."[34]

A part-time caterer and superb cook of southern cuisine, Reginald T. Ward left Robinsonville in Martin County, North Carolina, the day after graduating from high school in 1962. "In my hometown there was no work," he said. "I graduated from high school on a Wednesday, and on Thursday I was gone." He first migrated to California to attend UCLA. After completing school, he migrated to the southern Westchester city of Mount Vernon, where his brother lived. His brother had left for New York years before, taking a room in a boardinghouse owned by women who had previously lived seven miles from the Wards' home in North Carolina. "We all had friends that lived in our town that migrated to Mount Vernon," says Ward. "Some of the kids that I grew up with were living there at the time." He asserts that soul food was food that they had all enjoyed as children in North Carolina. It was food that had "flavor and taste."[35]

Joseph "Mac" Johnson was born in Banks, Alabama, in Pike's County, in 1933. He is a retired professional cook and restaurateur living in Poughkeepsie, in Dutchess County, New York. During World War II, his father had migrated to Poughkeepsie to work in an elevator factory and sent money home to his family, who were tenants on a dairy farm. Mac went into the military after high school and worked as a cook. After his tour, he took a job as a dishwasher for the state of New York at the Hudson River Psychiatric Center in Poughkeepsie. By 1952 he was the head cook at the center. He went to school and advanced to a position at the Bureau of Nutrition Services, among other jobs for the state of New York. From 1966 to the 1980s he operated a very profitable take-out-only venue, simply called Joe's Barbecue, that specialized in chopped barbecue and other southern soul food dishes. Posting only professionally made signs and menus, requiring his employees to wear uniforms, and keeping the barbecue stand spotless, Johnson successfully marketed southern food to both black and white customers.[36]

According to Johnson, soul food is inexpensive food that is "seasoned so good that it fascinates you." He adds, "I am seventy-two years old, the things that they sell now you could go to the slaughter house [in urban areas of Alabama] and they would give them to you. Pigs' feet, they would give to you, spare ribs," and chitlins. "So you had to learn to cook those things."[37] Interestingly, when the food industry started marketing southern African American cookery such as soul food in the 1960s, supermarkets started putting "their soul food on display in frozen packages, cellophane-wrapped bags, and instant-mix boxes," writes an author in a 1969 article published in the African American magazine *Sepia*. In the late 1960s whites in the food industry began making money off soul food after years of laughing at the black women who collected the hogs' ears and pigs' feet that slaughterhouses and butcher shops discarded. "Your corner A&P right now may be stocking boxes and bags and cans of prepared soul food," says the article in *Sepia*, "guaranteed authentic, no doubt, by a Soul Housekeeping seal-of-approval."[38]

Clara Pittman, who grew up in Pinehurst, Georgia, and St. Petersburg, Florida, agrees with Ward and Johnson's definition of soul food. She says that before soul food became profitable for grocers, when she was growing up in the 1950s, it "was basically all the food that blacks had to eat. It was the least expensive and the only food they could afford to buy." She adds, "I would say on average of three or four days a week you had either necks, bones, or chitlins, or pigs' feet, with some greens, or some type of corn bread or biscuits or whatever."[39]

In the city of Mount Vernon, New York, North Carolinian Reginald Ward remembers that in the 1960s he and fellow southerner Eugene Watts survived on similar kinds of inexpensive meals prepared at a restaurant called Green's Royal Palm. According to Ward, that place "kept me and Gene alive!" Like Gene Watts, the owner of Green's Royal Palm was a migrant from Virginia. "We went there every morning, every day, because it was what we could afford," says Ward. "Everything he had was affordable. He had fatback and biscuits, with a cup of coffee would have cost you about sixty-five cents." Ward adds, "The biscuit was huge! Then he made chicken gizzards and chicken necks in a stew over rice." A large serving of the stew and rice filled you up, and it only cost about $1.50.[40] Alton Hornsby of Atlanta argues that economics reasons might have caused black southerners to eat more of what today we call soul food items in larger quantities than did white southerners, but every poor person struggling to survive ate soul food on a regular basis.[41]

It was during the civil rights and black power movements of the 1960s that the survival food of black southerners became the revolutionary high cuisine of bourgeoisie African Americans. Writing in 1968, Eldridge Cleaver said "ghetto blacks" ate soul food out of necessity while the black bourgeoisie ate chitlins and such as a "counter-revolutionary" act that mocked white definitions of fine dining.[42] For example, in 1969 a writer for the Chicago *Defender*, a black newspaper, described soul food as high cuisine, a "blend of the best traditional cookery of Africa, Spain, France, and the American colonies to which Negroes added their knowledge of culinary herbs."[43] Cleaver scoffed at the glorification of soul food. Black folks in the ghetto "want steaks. *Beef steaks.*"[44]

BLACK INTELLECTUAL PROPERTY RIGHTS

The black power movement and the glorification of distinctively black culture inspired the emergence of the black arts movement of the 1960s. One of the leading figures in the black arts movement, Amiri Baraka, formerly LeRoi Jones, wrote about soul food in 1966 in his book *Home: Social Essays*. In an essay on soul food, he presented a rebuttal to critics who argued that African Americans had no language or characteristic cuisine. He insisted that hog maws, chitlins, sweet potato pie, pork sausage and gravy, fried chicken or chicken in the basket, barbecued ribs, hopping John, hush puppies, fried fish, hoe cakes, biscuits, salt pork, dumplings, and gumbo all came directly out of the black belt region of the South and represented the best of African American cookery. "No characteristic food? Oh, man, come on.... Maws are things ofays [whites] seldom get to peck [eat], nor are you likely ever to hear about Charlie eating a chitterling. Sweet potato pies, a good friend of mine asked recently, 'Do they taste anything like pumpkin?' Negative. They taste more like memory, if you're not uptown."[45]

In response to the black power and black arts movements, the first soul food cookbooks began to appear in progressive bookstores in the 1960s. Before then, largely white southerners had published cookbooks with instructions on how to make "southern dishes" like those Baraka described. These southern cookbooks, however, angered black chefs such as Verta Mae Grosvenor. An African American cook and writer originally from South Carolina, Grosvenor used her considerable cooking talents to raise money for organizations like SNCC. After she migrated to New York, she made a name for herself as a Harlem caterer and author during the black power movement.[46]

What bothered Grosvenor were white women like Henrietta Stanley Dull (home economics editor of the *Atlanta Journal*) who called themselves in their cookbooks "experts of southern cuisine." The back cover of Dull's *Southern Cooking* describes her as the "first lady of Georgia and the outstanding culinary expert in the South." In response to the claim, Grosvenor argues that Dull's book "ain't nothing but a soul food cookbook with the exception that Mrs. Dull is a white lady and it is a $5.95 hardbook by a big publishing house." Grosvenor was angry because white authors and publishers were profiting from an African American invention without compensating or acknowledging African Americans. "Cookbooks ain't nothing but a racist hustle." She adds, "It's all about some money, honey, and if that ain't so, how come it ain't Carver Chunky Peanut Butter?" Grosvenor goes on to say, "We cooked our way to freedom, and outside of a few soul food cookbooks there has been no reference to our participation in, and contribution to, the culinary arts."[47]

A few of the earliest contributions to the literature of soul food cookery provide insights into the black power roots of soul food. In the introductions to their cookbooks, several black culinary artists carefully describe, in distinctly black nationalist terms, what soul food is and what it most definitely is not, apparently in an attempt to patent and protect their intellectual property rights from the likes of the Dulls of the world. In his 1969 soul food cookbook, for example, southern-born African American Bob Jeffries emphasizes that soul food is not southern food in general. "When people ask me about soul food, I tell them that I have been cooking 'soul' for over forty years—only we did not call it that back home. We just called it real good cooking, southern style. However . . . not all southern food is 'soul.'" He goes on to explain, "Soul food cooking is an example of how really good southern Negro cooks cooked with what they had available to them"; it's about knowing how to season food to perfection. Jeffries argues that southern African American cooks "have always had an understanding and knowledge of herbs, spices, and seasonings and have known how to use them."[48]

Returning to the theme of black invention and property rights, he goes on to say that "what makes soul food unique—and more indigenous to this country than any other so-called American cooking style—is that it was created and evolved almost without European influence."[49] In earlier chapters in this book, I argue against Jeffries's black nationalist interpretation of soul food. Instead I argue that soul food is distinctively African American but was influenced by Europeans, who introduced corn to African foodways and then provided cornmeal, meat, fish, and other ingredients as rations to the first enslaved Africans in southern North America. In 1971 culinary writer Helen Mendes seconded Jeffries's Afrocentric view of soul food in her book *The African Heritage Cookbook*. Soul food unites black Americans "with each other, and provides an unbroken link to their African past." She adds, "At the heart of Soul cooking lay many elements of African cooking."[50]

In *A Pinch of Soul in Book Form*, published in 1969, Pearl Bowser uses the words "our" and "us" throughout her description of soul food. I interpret this choice as signifying her belief that soul food is the intellectual invention and property of southern-born African Americans. It's about how we somehow transformed "such things as animal fodder into rich peanut soup or wild plants into some of our favorite and tastiest vegetables dishes," and it "represents a legacy of good eating bequeathed to us by *our parents and grandparents*," who as slaves and later as sharecroppers "broke their backs but not their spirits."[51]

According to Bowser, "Soul food is also food rich in taste. What is bland becomes exciting by the addition of *our spices*—garlic, pepper, bay leaf—and the other condiments which are always on the table along with the salt and pepper—hot pepper sauce, either from the West Indies or Louisiana, and vinegar to go on many meats and vegetables." In another section of her book, she writes, "Our main meat source is still pork—fried, barbecued, roasted, smoked, pickled, spicy and hot."[52]

RESTAURANTS AND SOUL FOOD IN THE LATE 1960S

Bowser and others writing in the late 1960s and early 1970s observed that the black power movement made soul food both fashionable and popular in urban restaurants. Bowser argues that it was the black power movement that gave black people a sense of pride about their food. In addition, the message of black power inspired people like her to write soul food cookbooks: "There was a time when soul food could be had only at home or when provided by the church sisters. It certainly never appeared in print and was seldom referred to with pride, however much it was enjoyed. Its emerging popularity is due not only to its significance as a remembrance of things past but also as an affirmation that black is beautiful."[53]

Black power also inspired restaurateurs to put soul food on their menus. An article in *Sepia* confirms the growing popularity of soul food. Published in 1969, the article says, "Soul Food is so 'in' these days that restaurants all over the right neighborhoods are featuring it. But now restaurants in many of the wrong neighborhoods are opening up to serve soul food too.... Soul food is 'in' and wouldn't you know it, the price has gone up as the demand has soared." The article goes on to say, "Four bits used to get you a meal in lots of restaurants if you didn't mind a cracked plate and no tablecloth. The menu was scratched fresh everyday onto a blackboard and your choice was typically either chicken or ox-tail served up with greens and rice. For an extra dime you could have a piece of fresh homemade sweet potato pie. Now that such substantial eating has been dubbed 'soul food' it's started moving downtown—and the prices are moving up."[54]

Notable African American celebrities in the 1960s invested in short-lived attempts to sell soul food restaurant franchises. Starting in 1968, gospel recording artist Mahalia Jackson sold a Chicken Store franchise that sold "mouth-watering southern fried chicken along with catfish, sweet potato pie and hot biscuits." James Brown entered into a similar venture franchising Gold Platter soul food restaurants all over the country. The "menu at the look-alike chain outlets will feature chicken with French fries, cole slaw and cornbread; catfish with hush puppies; or less cultured hamburgers and cheeseburgers. Everything is to be served up, of course, on a gold platter just like the sign out front." Muhammad Ali got into the act too, with a franchise of restaurants that featured what he called the "Champburger." Starting in Miami, Ali hoped to start a chain of black-owned-and-operated Champburger Palaces in black neighborhoods. "In addition to the Champburger, the establishments also will sell hot dogs, fried chicken, fried fish, boiled fish, other food products and soft drinks." Southern-born blacks, however, argued that Ali's Chamburger palaces were not serving soul food.[55]

REAL SOUL FOOD

Debates over soul food were common on the streets of New York City and other cities. Northerners and southerners just did not agree on the definition of soul food. Southerners complained that much of the food advertised as soul food by restaurants was not soul food at all or was "more Southern than soul." "To people who just do not know better," wrote Bob Jeffries, it means "only chicken and ribs, corn pone, collards, and 'sweet-taters,' but nothing could be more authentically soul than a supper of freshly caught fish, a fish stew, or an outdoor fish fry."[56] Southerners in New York argued that, for real soul food, you had to stand in line at Harlem restaurants like the Red Rooster, Jock's Place, and Obie's, where they sold trotters, neck bones, pigs' tails, smothered pork chops, black-eyed peas, candied yams, and "grits 'n' eggs."

For many, soul food was difficult to describe because it was all wrapped up in feelings. "Soul food takes its name from a feeling of kinship among Blacks," wrote Jim Harwood and Ed Callahan, who coauthored a soul food cookbook. It is "impossible to define but recognizable among those who have it." Similarly, Harlem restaurant owner and cook Obie Green, who, like James Brown, was a native of Augusta, Georgia, insisted that soul is cooking with love. "And I cook with soul and feeling." Bob Jeffries, also a southerner, argued that soul food was down-home food "cooked with care and love—with soul."[57] South Carolina-born culinary writer and cook Verta Mae Grosvenor also makes the argument that the right feelings are essential to making soul food, "and you can't it get [them] from no recipe book (mine included)." She insists that a good cookbook does not make a good cook. "How a book gon tell you how to cook." It's what you "put in the cooking and I don't mean spices either." Jeffries also agreed that soul food was made without recipes; it was made with inexpensive ingredients that "any fool would know how to cook" if they grew up eating it.[58]

Soul food, then, according to black cooks, is an art form that comes from immersion in a black community and an intimate relationship with the southern experience. Soul food originated in the quarters of enslaved Africans in the sixteenth to nineteenth centuries. It is a blend, or creolization, of many cooking traditions that Africans across the Americas seasoned to their own definition of perfection with their knowledge of culinary herbs gained from their ancestors. Soul food was spiritual food because some dishes were served only on Sundays and other special days during slavery and thereafter.

It was simple food, yet it was often complex in its preparation. Soul food required a cook with a good sense of timing of when to season, how long to stir, mix, fry, boil, sauté, bake, grill, dry, or smoke an ingredient and how to cut, skin, dip, batter, or barbecue. Without timing and skill, a cook had no soul worth talking about. Soul food was nitty-gritty food that tasted good and helped African Americans survive during difficult times. For a long time, none of its ingredients came in a can or box, and thus soul food was free of artificial preservatives. Oral history based on African folkways ensured that cooks passed on recipes from one generation to the next, and recipes and cooking techniques developed out of a common black experience and struggle with racism. Summing up reflections and commentaries on soul from the black power era, I have been able to formulate six statements about and working definitions for soul food:

> *Soul is* a cultural mixture of various African tribes and kingdoms
> *Soul is* adaptations and values developed during slavery and
>   emancipation
> *Soul is* the style of rural folk culture
> *Soul is* the values and styles of planter elites in the Americas
> *Soul is* spirituality and experiential wisdom that make black folk
>   unique
> *Soul is* putting a premium on suffering, endurance, and surviving with
>   dignity

During the 1960s and 1970s a somewhat heated debated developed between three camps within the African American community: African

American intellectuals who argued that soul food was uniquely part of black culture and therefore the intellectual capital of black folk; white intellectuals who insisted that soul food was a southern regional food that belonged to southerners; and members of the Nation of Islam, advocates of natural food diets, and college- and university-educated African Americans who argued that soul food was nothing to be celebrated or guarded as their own because it was killing black folks. I discuss the last school of thought in the final chapter, when I turn to critics of soul food and movements advocating natural food diets. But before that, in the next chapter, I turn to a look at the history of Caribbean influences on soul food and urban identity.

THE DECLINING INFLUENCE OF SOUL FOOD

The Growth of Caribbean Cuisine in Urban Areas

In the summer of 2005, while combing through the 1930 census records for Westchester County, New York, to locate southern black migrants for research I was doing on the Great Migration and the Great Depression, I noticed that African Americans and Latinos (Chileans, Puerto Ricans, Iberians, Mexicans, and Argentines) tended to reside in the same lower-income neighborhoods in the villages of North Tarrytown (now Sleepy Hollow) and Tarrytown. Earlier, I had also noticed that WPA records described blacks and Latinos in 1930s eating in the same restaurants, frequenting the same nightclubs and theaters, and intermarrying in Harlem, thirty-five miles to the south of the Tarrytowns. These descriptions struck me as odd when contrasted to contemporary Tarrytown and Sleepy Hollow, where Latinos now far outnumber African Americans residents and mostly Ecuadorian-, Dominican-, Puerto Rican-, Colombian and Brazilian-owned bodegas, restaurants, and luncheonettes are part of the uptown culinary landscape of both towns. What is even more interesting is the fact that there is not one black-owned soul food restaurant in either town, although there are three black churches. Similar descriptions fit the current situation in the surrounding urban centers in the Hudson Valley that also attracted black southern migrants in the 1920s and 1930s. The changes in urban centers of New York encouraged me to use interviews and written sources to explore the declining influence of soul food and the growing influence of Caribbean cuisines on African American foodways in different times and places.

My findings, though they concentrate only on New York City and Westchester County, nonetheless suggest a tentative framework for explaining where and why the Caribbeanization of soul food has emerged in urban New York. Caribbean influence on black foodways has been the strongest within the ethnic subgroups in which blacks and Caribbean migrants felt the most comfortable. While the nature and location of these subgroups shifted over time, interethnic relationships tended to be strongest between those who shared a common language, passion, or employer, as well as among younger African Americans and Caribbean migrants who shared the same class status and ethnic group identity. This understanding of the conditions that fostered connections among African Americans and Caribbean migrants in New York emerged from my examination of a wave of migrants who came to New York between 1930 and 1970, particularly Cubans, Afro-Panamanians, and African Americans in Harlem and Brooklyn in the 1950s and 1960s and in the smaller suburban setting of Westchester County, where Tarrytown and North Tarrytown experienced an influx of Puerto Ricans and Cubans.

THE 1930s AND 1940s
MIGRATION AND SETTLEMENT PATTERNS
IN THE FIRST WAVE

Because motives for and patterns of immigration influence to a large extent migrants' subsequent experiences and relationships with other groups, it is difficult to understand the influence of Caribbean cultures on urban identities. Some of the earliest examples of Cuban immigration to New York, for example, were rooted in a long history of colonialism, racism, and classism in the Caribbean basin. Political persecution, poverty, hunger, and lack of opportunity under Spanish colonialism motivated Cubans to start emigrating to the United States beginning in the 1860s. Cuban oligarchs and foreign investors continued to dominate the best land, occupations, and opportunities on the island following Cuba's independence from Spain in 1898, prompting Cuban immigrants to arrive in the United States in a slow but steady stream. Until the 1930s, Tampa was the center of the Cuban American expatriate community and a thriving cigar industry. After 1930, however, new arrivals of Afro-Cubans, many of them musicians, baseball players, and cigar makers, tended to settle in New York City. Because of restrictive racist housing practices, the majority of black immigrants from the Caribbean who settled in New York in the early twentieth century, whether Puerto Rico, Cuban, or Panamanian, found lodging in existing African American neighborhoods. Most of New York's early Afro-Cuban immigrants settled in Harlem. Much smaller and whiter Cuban communities developed in Brooklyn (near the Navy Yard), Queens, the Bronx, and Staten Island. The small number of Cuban immigrants in New York City—they account for only a fraction of the eighteen thousand or so Cubans in the United States in 1940—prevented the development of distinctive Cuban communities there before 1950.[1]

Puerto Rican immigration to New York was similarly fueled by poverty, unemployment, and hunger, but factors specific to the Puerto Rican context meant that Puerto Ricans formed tight-knit, distinctive communities in the city. The mass migration of Puerto Ricans to New York City began during World War I, when wartime restrictions on European migration caused labor shortages in the city and manufacturers and employers in the service industries recruited Puerto Ricans to meet their labor demands.[2] The first Puerto Rican diaspora in New York City consisted of three hundred individuals who settled on the Lower West Side of Manhattan along Eighth Avenue between Fourteenth and Thirtieth Streets in 1910. The largest influx of Puerto Ricans to Harlem came directly from Puerto Rico after 1917, when the U.S. Congress passed a bill granting citizenship to all native-born Puerto Ricans. Three regiments of Puerto Rican soldiers settled in Harlem between 1918 and 1919, for instance, bringing their families with them.[3] The Puerto Rican population of the United States swelled from 1,513 in 1910 to almost 53,000 in 1930. As the number of Puerto Ricans in East Harlem increased, the area gained the popular names "Spanish Harlem" and "El Barrio." By 1935 the Puerto Rican diaspora in New York, consisting of three communities throughout the city, had swelled to approximately 75,000 people. Some 35,000 of them lived in Spanish Harlem. The others were in South Brooklyn, where 30,000 Puerto Ricans lived, and on the West Side between Broadway and Amsterdam in the vicinity of Columbia University, the home of the most elite immigrants: merchants, restaurant operators, and barbers.[4] Although the number of African Puerto Ricans who migrated to New York is unknown, one historian argues that "black and brown Puerto Ricans were a significant and conspicuous presence" in Harlem in the 1920s and 1930s.[5]

RELATIONSHIPS FORGED THROUGH MUSIC AND FOOD

According to one WPA report, African Americans and Latinos frequented the same social clubs, informal hangouts, theaters, and ballrooms during the 1930s. Some of these clubs included orchestras featuring Afro-Cuban artists fresh from the club scene in Havana. Such artists came to the United States because racism in Cuba hampered their careers artistically and financially, but they chose to settle in New York rather than Florida, where the racial climate drove a wedge between black and white Latin musicians.[6] After Cubop began to catch on in 1947, it became even more common to see Latino and African Americans playing together in traditionally African American venues and afterward enjoying traditional southern and Caribbean food. Latin Americans, West Indians, and African Americans often frequented the same restaurants in Harlem and the Upper West Side.[7]

Caribbean and African American artists developed relationships because they shared common interests: cutting-edge jazz and, to a lesser degree, good, inexpensive food. Language barriers did not prevent blacks and Latinos like the charismatic conga drummer and brilliant composer Afro-Cuban Chano Pozo and South Carolinian trumpeter Dizzy Gillespie from communicating. In the words of Dizzy, they spoke to each other in the universal language of music and the "bebop language." The hip lingo of jazz artists bridged the customary gap between native English and Spanish speakers and allowed them to communicate with each other. "Most bebop language came about because some guy said something and it stuck. Another guy started using it, then another one, and before you knew it, we had a whole language," writes Dizzy.[8] An ethnic subgroup of crossover artists interested in combining the best of Latin and North American jazz emulated each other's music, language, and food in urban New York. This subgroup was most comfortable at the jazz clubs and multiethnic eateries that were located primarily in Harlem and Spanish Harlem before the 1950s.

THE 1950s AND THE 1960s
MIGRATION AND SETTLEMENT PATTERNS
IN THE SECOND WAVE

A second wave of African American and Hispanic migrants arrived in New York in the 1950s and 1960s. The number of Hispanic migrants, particularly Puerto Ricans, far outweighed the number of African Americans from the South. This was in part because beginning in the late 1950s San Juan, Puerto Rico, served as the "international training ground" of the U.S. government's Point Four Program, which promoted a U.S. capitalist model of development for the third world as an alternative to Communism. In order for the program to work, the Harry S Truman administration and the Puerto

Rican colonial government under Luis Muñoz Marín negotiated the emptying out of the island's poorest sectors during the late 1940s, encouraging these areas' inhabitants, "many of them mulattos," to migrate to urban centers in the United States, including New York, Chicago, and Philadelphia. The poor received reduced airfare between the island and the mainland. Some six hundred thousand "mostly rural unskilled" Puerto Ricans filled the demand for cheap labor in U.S. manufacturing. The migration of the poorest sector of the island permitted social mobility among those who remained, seemingly proving the government's capitalist model of third world development superior to the Soviet Union's socialist model.[9]

Among these second-wave Puerto Rican migrants were Eddie Cruz and his family, who joined relatives in the United States and settled in a largely Puerto Rican, Spanish-speaking community. Born in 1941 in Yauco, Puerto Rico, Cruz arrived with his family in New York in 1947, settling in East Harlem around 107th Street. Cruz's parents were just starting a family, and they wanted their children to have a better quality of life than was available to them in Puerto Rico. They moved to East Harlem because Eddie's uncle lived there; he helped Eddie's father find a factory job. The family lived at several different addresses in El Barrio before moving to the projects in Brooklyn in 1956. In the 1950s the "suburbs" of Brooklyn, to use Cruz's term, were very diverse: "The projects were mixed back then, but I would say mostly Puerto Ricans and blacks."[10]

In the 1950s and 1960s Brooklyn was also a destination (sometimes a transfer station) for working-class African American migrants from the South, working-class Afro-Panamanians (from the Canal Zone region of Panama City), Afro-Cubans from Havana, and middle-class Cubans, most of them white, from provincial cities. "Just like in every other part of Latin America and many parts of the world, the dream was to come to the United States," remembers Cuban migrant Francisco Corona.[11] Corona was born in 1933 in Guayos, Las Villas Province (later renamed Sancti Spíritus), Cuba. During the military dictatorship of General Fulgencio Batista y Zaldívar (1952–1959), members of about six extended families in Guayos responded to the corruption and repression of Batista's regime by immigrating to the Borough Hall section of Brooklyn.[12] As life got tougher under the Batista dictatorship, Cuban expatriates from Guayos "began to sponsor friends and families who also wanted to come to New York," Corona remembers.[13]

"Shortly thereafter," Corona says, "some of the families from Guayos started to relocate to Tarrytown." The first Cuban to settle in Tarrytown was Angelo Hernandez, who had arrived in Brooklyn from Guayos around

1953.[14] Hernandez and a Cuban named Aurelio Garcia went to Tarrytown to do a survey for a Puerto Rican–owned radio station in New York City whose management wanted to learn about the taste of the town's Hispanic residents: what programs they listened to and what products they consumed. Hernandez asked the people he was surveying about job opportunities and learned of an opening at the upscale Tappan Hill Restaurant in Tarrytown. In the 1950s job opportunities, many of them at nurseries and factories, including General Motors (and later Union Carbide), were abundant in the Tarrytowns and the surrounding area. Hernandez took the job at Tappan Hill because it offered free room and board and a uniform, perks that significantly reduced his living expenses. The first Hispanic to work at the Tappan Hill had been the Ecuadorian Miguel Lopez, who was sent there by an employment agency in New York City around 1951. Lopez left Tappan Hill and was replaced by his brother. Then Cubans, following Hernandez, began to fill job openings at the restaurant. Hernandez secured jobs for Ralph Hernandez (no relation), Francisco Corona, and Oliverio Ojito Fardales, all from Guayos.

One of the first Guayos-owned homes in Brooklyn on Harry Street became the receiving station where fresh arrivals got their footing. New migrants to Tarrytown went to Harry Street "to get news about family members back home and to learn about job [opportunities]," among other things. Unlike earlier Afro-Cuban immigrants to New York City, the Guayos Cubans who immigrated to the Tarrytowns tended to be white and economically better off.[15]

Panamanian immigrants to Brooklyn in the 1960s offer an interesting contrast to the Tarrytown Cubans. George Priestly, an Afro-Panamanian sociologist who conducted about sixty interviews with Panamanian immigrants to the United States, was born in 1941 and raised in a working-class community in Panama City, Panama. His father was a native-born Afro-Panamanian, and his mother was a second-generation Afro-Panamanian of Caribbean descent who was bilingual but preferred to speak English. Most Afro-Panamanians of Priestly's generation were raised speaking English with at least one parent in the home while attending a Hispanic public school system. There were also English-language schools in Panama City that many Afro-Panamanian children attended in evenings or over summer vacation. On weekend nights, African American GIs frequented black bars in Panama City, and many Afro-Panamanians were exposed to aspects of American culture through them. "You would see black folks hanging out, some speaking English, some speaking Spanish, some speaking Spanglish," Priestly recalled. His older brother operated the first black-owned men's boutique in Panama in the 1950s in the working-class community of Panama City. "Eighty percent of his customers were African American GIs," Priestly says. This meant that his family, like many other Panamanian immigrants, was "pre-sensitized to African American culture" before migrating to New York.[16]

Afro-Panamanians began immigrating to the Bushwick section of Brooklyn in the early 1960s. Priestly moved there in 1961 at the age of twenty. The Panamanian community at the time was quite small. Most of the earliest arrivals were Afro-Panamanians of West Indian descent. Over time, Franklin Avenue in Brooklyn became the center of New York's Panamanian community. In part because of Panamanians' familiarity with English and their exposure to American culture, the members of this community tended to interact with African Americans to a considerable degree. "There were two or three Panamanian families in Bushwick who introduced me to their African American and Puerto Rican friends," Priestly recalls. "They would take me to clubs in Bed-Stuy [Bedford-Stuyvesant] and Crown Heights. And the clubs that they used to take us to were largely African American clubs."[17]

In the 1960s some of the African Americans in Brooklyn were also newcomers to New York, just having arrived from the South. But there were many fewer black southern migrants to the North in the post–World War II period than in the period following World War I. In the 1950s and 1960s New York City's and Westchester County's African American population consisted largely of folks born in the South, as well as the children and grandchildren of southerners. Metropolitan New York's Latino community included old-timers with very rudimentary English language skills who had arrived before the Second World War and their bilingual children and grandchildren born in the Big Apple and its surrounding suburbs, but it also included a much larger group of more recent migrants from the Caribbean basin who tended to speak only Spanish.

SEPARATE AND SHARED AMUSEMENTS
OF SECOND-WAVE IMMIGRANTS

The first Cubans who came to Westchester County in the 1950s were all single men. They tended to keep to themselves or to eat, drink, and dance with Puerto Ricans, going to their bars, clubs, and ballrooms in the Tarrytowns and Manhattan.[18] By 1977, however, there were about three thousand Cubans living in the Tarrytowns, along with "a scattering of Dominicans, Venezuelans, and Puerto Ricans," in all enough Spanish-speaking

migrants to support two cocktail lounges on Cortland Street, La Emba-
jada and La Teresa, and a Venezuelan bar and disco called La Arriba at 11
Beekman Avenue.[19] The Latin cocktail lounges on Cortland Street were
a stone's throw from three African American bar and grills: De Carlo's,
the Upper-Class Men, and the Wonderful Bar. Cubans also founded their
own social club in uptown North Tarrytown on Beekman Avenue. As the
nature of these institutions makes clear, Latino immigrants and African
Americans remained socially segregated in the Tarrytowns. "You would
not see Hispanics in these [black-owned] bars back then," says Alice Conqueran, as "there were not that many of them, and they stuck together" in
their own shops and restaurants.[20]

The exception to this pattern of social segregation in the Tarrytowns
occurred among GM workers, who belonged to a comfortable shared subgroup as fellow workers and union members. On the GM assembly line,
there was a leveling of the language and ethnic divisions that segregated
older Hispanics and African Americans in the villages. The auto union to
which all blue-collar workers at the plant belonged created a multiethnic working-class solidarity between African American and Hispanics that
made them feel comfortable together.[21]

Just as Hispanics and African Americans tended to enjoy separate entertainment in the Tarrytowns (with the exception of GM workers in certain contexts), they also frequented separate eateries. There were no black-
owned- and -operated restaurants or luncheonettes in the Tarrytowns.
(In fact, there are none today.) The only African Americans eateries were
the bar and grills in town: Club Six, the Upper Class Men, the Wonderful
Bar, and De Carlo's. In addition, for religious African Americans, the black
churches in the villages served not only as spiritual filling stations but,
to some extent, as eateries.[22] In contrast, Latin Americans had their own
eateries. In North Tarrytown, there were already Puerto Rican–run Bodegas on Cortland Street, which by the late 1950s had become the center of
the Puerto Rican community. Hispanic bodegas were small shops where
drinks and food were sold for consumption on or off the premises.[23] In
addition to Puerto Rican shops and restaurants, there were also other Latino immigrant–owned establishments. In the 1970s there was the Cuban-
owned Corona's Luncheonette (discussed below) and Renaldo Barrios's
Nite and Day Delicatessen. Both of these Cuban eateries were located on
Beekman Avenue in North Tarrytown, not far from the GM plant. The Nite
and Day sold inexpensive Latin soul food takeout such as Cuban fritas
(Cuban-style hamburgers), Cuban empanadas (a pastry filled with ground
beef seasoned with cumin, garlic, green peppers, and raisins), and a tra-

ditional Cuban sandwich (a wedge of ham, roast pork, and Swiss cheese dressed with a blend of butter, mayonnaise, and mustard and grilled until the bread is crusty). North Tarrytown had a Dominican restaurant at 109 Beekman Avenue called El Jaravi. Signature Dominican soul food include dishes like *mangu* (a dish reminiscent of mashed potatoes made from plantains and other ingredients), octopus salad, *arroz con pollo* (rice and chicken), and *arroz con camarones* (rice and shrimp characteristically seasoned with cilantro in addition to other herbs and spices).[24]

DOMINICAN MANGU

(for six servings)
3 large green plantains
1½ oz. salt
1 cup reserved plantain boiling liquid
6 oz. sliced onion (white)
6 oz sliced Cuban or Anaheim peppers
2 oz. olive oil

Wash the plantains then boil for about twenty minutes, depending on their size and age. Be sure they are fully cooked. Let cool, remove pulp from skins, and place in a bowl with the salt. Mash with the indicated amount of boiling liquid. Sauté onions and peppers in the olive oil. Put the mash in a serving dish and top with the sautéed onions and peppers, including the oil. Typically served with bacon and cheese.

In Tarrytown, Guayos Cubans Jorge Pozas and Juan González ran bodegas on Main Street, while Pozas and Orestes Suarez operated the Lucky Seven Grocery at 31 Main Street. In addition to their bodegas, both Pozas and González operated restaurants. González ran the La Via, a bar and restaurant on Orchard Street, and Pozas (and later Orestes Suarez) ran the Lucky Seven, a luncheonette next door to his bodega.[25] Cuban men milled around the Lucky Seven smoking, sipping café pico (a traditional Cuban coffee), eating plantain soup, yellow rice, black beans, and *ropa vieja* (shredded beef), and "discussing in Spanish the burning issues of the day." Orestes Suarez explains, "This is the way of life in the old country.... When work is done it is the custom to gather around and talk."[26]

As in the bars and social clubs, the language barrier in most of the area eateries inhibited the formation of friendships between Spanish-speaking immigrants and English-speaking African Americans. But African Ameri-

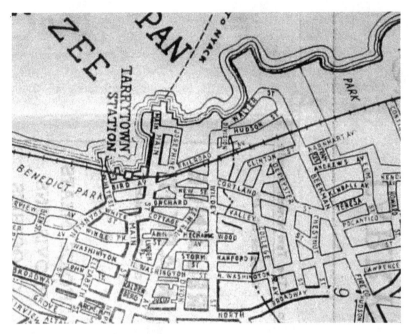

FIGURE 8.1 1950 map of the streets occupied by blacks and Latinos in the Tarrytowns.
Courtesy Tarrytown Historical Society.

cans did acquire a taste for Latin soul food and become regular takeout customers. The exception to this rule was Corona's Luncheonette on Beekman Avenue, one block from the GM plant in North Tarrytown. Corona's became an important space where five or more days a week blacks and Hispanics socialized over a good Cuban lunch. The owner, Francisco Corona, worked at GM for a brief period before opening his luncheonette. Corona's became a designated restaurant for GM plant workers and the only eatery in the two villages where African American and Hispanic coworkers mingled. But, again, the customers at Corona's shared a multiethnic class identity as unionized auto workers at the local GM plant. "I had customers from all parts of the world, Cubans, Venezuelans, all kinds of Hispanics" and "a lot of African Americans," Corona recalls. He estimates that he had more African American customers than Hispanics because perhaps twice as many of them worked at the plant in the 1960s. The African American workers, recalls Francisco Corona, "really like our kind of food."[27]

A fascinating contrast to the situation in the Tarrytowns is the relationships that developed between African Americans and Afro-Panamanians at informal eateries in Brooklyn. In the 1960s family dinners were a "big deal" in Brooklyn, recalls George Priestly. But there were also African American and Afro-Panamanian women who would cook out of their own homes, throwing "paid parties" to earn rent money. Priestly says that, as newcomers to New York, Afro-Panamanian emigrants loved paid parties because they "enlarged [their] contact with other folk" who showed them the ropes. The concept of going from one house to another eating and partying was "something we learned from African Americans," Priestly remembers. He used to attend paid parties with an Afro-Panamanian friend nicknamed Charlie Boogaloo, who knew all the best spots and all the people that ran them. "When you went with Charlie, you could go in and eat or drink and then split," Priestly says. "He would know about seven different places and we would just go from house to house paying a couple of dollars, eating, and then go back to our party or stay there."[28] Different house parties had different kinds of food. African American homes usually served up southern food. At an Afro-Panamanian home, there would be West Indian meat patties and rice and peas, chicken, fried plantains, potato salad, and Central American tamales.

In the late 1960s and early 1970s in Brooklyn, Panamanians started opening small formal eateries in and around Franklin Avenue. "In these restaurants," says Priestly, "you would find a range of food—those with origins in the English-speaking Caribbean, those with origins strictly in Panama, and those adopted from African Americans here." The "so-called Panamanian restaurants" sold soul food, "food [with a cornmeal base] that you would think is completely South American," and West Indian food, "rice and peas and all that stuff . . . referred to as Afro-Panamanian food."[29] These small Brooklyn restaurants drew crowds of working-class West Indian, Latin American, and African American customers. The diverse menu at such restaurants made their multiethnic working-class customers feel as though they were staying within their own culinary environment.

In the absence of a language barrier, then—and perhaps also in part because of the small size of the Afro-Panamanian community in New York City—African Americans and Afro-Latinos in the city shared food and attended parties together in 1950s and 1960s Brooklyn. In Westchester County, as I discuss in the next section, schools, eateries, and community centers were important meeting places where African American and bilingual Latino youth developed long-lasting friendships. Older Hispanic immigrants with elementary English skills, by contrast, spent the majority of their time in Spanish-speaking barbershops, bars, bodegas, churches, and clubs maintaining friendships with other Hispanic immigrants. Except for GM workers, moreover, most Tarrytown Cubans worked on jobs and in departments with Latino personnel. As a result, Latin American immigrants with very little English fluency largely remained separated from African Americans in the Tarrytowns, cloistered in pockets of Hispanic public spaces.

YOUTH CULTURE AND CARIBBEAN INFLUENCE
ON AFRICAN AMERICANS

Young people, in particular, tend to travel outside their ethnic safety zones. As studies of rapping and deejaying in New York have shown, youth culture is one of the sites where cultural interaction and hybridization between African Americans and Caribbeans has been most intense. In the words of one study, this is because the lives of youth of different ethnicities "are structured by similar conditions and result in similar understandings of themselves and the world."[30] The mambo, Motown, and salsa mania that influenced youth culture in the 1950s and 1960s did a great deal to erase the invisible line that sometimes separated African Americans and Hispanics in metropolitan New York and suburban Westchester County. Mambo mania coincided with the diminishing cultural and language barriers to African American and Latino relations in New York. Like food, music drew bilingual Hispanic youth to spaces that also attracted African American youth. Latino youth growing up in New York developed a multiethnic consciousness that acknowledged their African heritage rather than denying it, as many of their parents' generation did.[31] By the time Motown mania hit the city in the 1960s, the divide between African American and Puerto Rican youth had virtually vanished. For example, born in 1940, bilingual Sonya Cruz remembers growing up in El Barrio in the 1960s. There was a local luncheonette/soda fountain frequented by Puerto Rican and African American youth. The proprietor of the store had a jukebox that played both "Latin American hits and popular Motown artists."[32] Similar cultural sharing was happening in the Bronx.

In 1940 the Bronx had a black and Puerto Rican population of about 83,500. Historian Evelyn Gonzalez argues that "after War II, the most important change in the Bronx was the coming of thousands of Southern blacks and Spanish speaking Puerto Ricans" like Harold Jones and Sonya Sanchez.[33] The number of African Americans and Puerto Ricans in the Bronx had increased from 160,000 in 1950 to more than 350,000 in 1960, with the majority residing in the South Bronx.[34] Bubba Dukes's father took a job in a furniture factory and relocated his family to the newly opened Patterson House. "And when the projects open up, I guess it's a big thing for people to move into the projects and move away from the tenement, the tenement housing."[35] In the 1950s Patterson House had a mixture of residents from South Carolina, Virginia, Tennessee, Barbados, Jamaica, and Puerto Rico. African American Victoria Archibald-Good also grew up in the Patterson House. She recalled growing up with Puerto Ricans neighbors on all sides of her family's apartment: "The Perez family lived right across the hall from us on the fourth floor. There were the Bonitas too, on the fourth floor, but on the other side."[36] The halls of the Paterson House smelt like an international food court at a mall.

Nathan Dukes recalls growing up to the smell of chitlins, rice and beans, turkey, and ham being prepared. "You had a lot of vegetables, collard greens, turnips; spinach was one of the main courses that a lot of the moms would prepare. . . . All up and down the hallways" you would smell the different ethnic dishes being prepared, especially on holidays like Thanksgiving, Christmas, and Easter.[37] Some of Victoria Archibald-Good's fondest childhood memories were of the food of Puerto Rican neighbors. "I remember Mr. Bonita used to make donuts for everybody. And he had this big pot of oil and we would just like to sit on the stoop, because we could smell them from the stoop. And he would call us up and everybody would have a freshly made donut. It was a lot of fun."[38] Puerto Ricans in the Patterson House were "our buddies" and "very good" friends, says Dukes. Many of these friendships would later develop into multiethnic marriages.[39] As a result of New York City residential patterns in buildings like the Patterson House, familiar friendships developed between the African American and Caribbean children. Starting in the 1960s, if not much earlier, as this chapter argues, African Americans in New York developed a more diasporic conceptualization of soul food than the exclusionary down-home Southern one that the black power partisans of the soul ideology championed. For African American and Caribbean residents in urban New York, soul food was far more inclusive, encompassing the African-influenced cuisines of South Carolinians, Cubans, Puerto Ricans, Panamanians, West Indians, and Dominicans that proliferated in multiethnic communities of color in New York in the 1960s through 1980s.

In addition to public housing projects, other important spaces for black encounters with Caribbean cultures in New York included rent parties, house parties, and clubs. In these spaces, it was quite common for black and Latino youth to become bilingual in their choice of music, language, and food. Afro-Cuban GM worker Freddy Pino married an African American from North Tarrytown named Barbara Ann Cardwell. The two met in

1965 at a cocktail lounge called the White Birch Inn across the Hudson River in nearby Spring Valley, New York. Neither of Barbara's parents objected to her having an Afro-Cuban suitor; her entire family accepted him from the beginning. Pino taught his African American wife of over forty years about Cuban traditions, such as "little Christmas." She also learned how to cook rice and beans, Cuban-style pork, and turkey Cuban style. Her husband died in 2006, but to this day she continues the traditions to which he introduced.[40]

CONCLUSION

Describing the culinary influence of Caribbeans on African Americans in New York City and Westchester County from the 1930s through the 1960s requires understanding the complexity of the factors that influenced their interaction, from the initial social and economic conditions that acted as an impetus for various groups' migrations and shaped their settlement patterns to the constraining and catalyzing roles played by employment, racism, music, entertainment, language, food, and love. Latin American and African Americans musicians in the 1930s shared bandstands, restaurants, hotels, and boardinghouse rooms as they traveled the famed chitlin circuit.

When a second wave of immigrants came to New York in the 1950s and 1960s, some of them traveling north to Westchester County, language barriers and cultural differences kept African American and Latinos over twenty segregated from each other. As a result, Caribbean influence on African American culinary taste happened at a far slower speed there than in Brooklyn, Manhattan, and the Bronx. The exception to this rule were African Americans and Latino GM workers in the Tarrytowns who belonged to the same unions: they frequented the same eatery during their lunch hour, and thus black GM workers (who lived in various parts of metropolitan New York) were far more influenced by Caribbean cultures than were nonemployees. In contrast, black and Latino youth shared a common ethnic subculture: mambo and Motown music. As a consequence, they broke bread far more often in each others homes and at Caribbean-run restaurants in the Tarrytowns. Luncheonettes with mambo- and Motown-playing jukeboxes played an important role in shaping the urban ethnic identity of black and Latino youth.

Tentatively, then, one can conclude that Caribbeans influenced black culinary taste more often within ethnic subgroups in which they felt the most comfortable. In the 1930s and 1940s it was the jazz subculture of black and Hispanic Harlem. For Tarrytown adults of the 1950s, it was the male-dominated subculture of GM's multiethnic auto workers' union. And among immigrant and migrant youth, the mambo subculture of the 1950s and the Motown and Latin jazz culture of Harlem, Brooklyn, and the Bronx were particularly significant in fostering shared cultural identities across the racial divide. In the absence of further study, of course, these conclusions remain only tentative, but they offer a useful starting point for organizing and explaining the declining influence of southern culture in northern urban centers.

FOOD REBELS

*African American Critics and
Opponents of Soul Food*

During the 1960s and 1970s several debates developed over soul food. Some African American intellectuals such as Amiri Baraka and Verta Mae Grosvenor argued that soul food was a unique part of black culture and therefore the intellectual capital of black folk. European American food critics like Craig Claiborne insisted that soul food was a southern regional food that belonged to southerners. And three groups of African Americans I call "food rebels" argued that soul food is nothing to be celebrated or guarded as our own because it was killing us. I argue that black Muslims, advocates of natural food diets, and university-educated African Americans have filled an important role neglected by medical professionals in influencing many African Americans to question the wisdom of eating traditional soul food.

Alternative diets to soul food, such as vegetarianism, have their roots in the dietary teachings of the Nation of Islam and advocates of natural food diets such as Alvenia M. Fulton and Dick Gregory. African Americans saw how the diets advocated by the Nation and naturalists improved people's health and began investigating the role of nutrition in health. Some, like Marcellas Barksdale and Yemaja Jubilee, reduced or completely stopped their consumption of soul food. Barksdale says that he only eats it on special occasions because his doctor warned him that his heart and blood pressure could no longer take such rich food on a regular basis. Jubilee explains, "I had a lot of medical problems and used to weigh 238 lbs." She argues it was because of the soul food: "I cooked it myself, just the way my mama taught me to cook it. I had clogged arteries, high blood pressure, high cholesterol, and the doctor said I had to make a change!"[1]

Before the 1970s most medical associations did not talk at any length about the health effects of the traditional American diet. Dr. Elijah Saunders, who was head of cardiology at Providence Hospital in Baltimore, insists, "The medical profession as a whole has not done very well at teaching doctors and medical students in training about nutrition." Historically, nutrition has been one of the "most undertaught subjects" in medical school. In many places, the medical school curriculum still crowds out content on nutrition. It has only been since the late 1970s that the health care professions have realized "how important nutrition is."[2] This coincides with the experiences of several people interviewed for this book. They stated that few medical professionals talked about the relationship between nutrition and health until the 1970s.

Joan B. Lewis is a member of the American Dietitian Association and a registered dietitian with more than forty years of experience. She has worked in hospitals in metropolitan New York and the District of Columbia, predominately with African American clients. She observed that before the 1970s most people paid little attention to what they ate unless physicians spoke to them about it.[3] Clara Bullard Pittman says recommendations to exercise, watch what you eat, stop eating pork, and reduce your intake of sugar and salt, "you didn't hear any of that in the 1960s and 1970s." She adds that you also did not hear medical professionals talking about the alarming rates of high blood pressure and diabetes among African Americans.[4] Lewis, born in 1935, says that, growing up, "We didn't have a whole lot of sodas, we drank water or milk." In addition, "everybody walked everywhere." But in the 1970s it seemed like "everybody got a car," and walking became the exception, not the rule. Many people drastically increased their portion sizes at the table while decreasing their daily physical activity. Before the 1990s doctors rarely talked about the need for more fiber in people's diets or referred to childhood obesity as a national problem. "Schools took out the physical ed. programs, and everybody needed to do some exercise," recalls Lewis.[5]

Dr. Rodney Ellis, who specializes in cases of obesity, agrees. African American southerners who have lived past the age of one hundred generally ate pesticide-free foods, walked a lot more, and did regular physical activity that kept their blood pressure low and their high-density lipoproteins (favorable cholesterol levels) up. Moreover, before World War II, people drove less and depended less on power tools to do manual labor like cutting wood, brush, and grass. In the rural societies that most southerners lived in, people did more physical activity, which reduced incidents of obesity, hypertension, and diabetes. In contrast, in post-1960s North America, in both urban and rural settings, Americans started getting much less physical activity. Classic soul food contributed to poor health because the consumption of animal fats clogged arteries. Foods high in saturated fats like lard-fried chicken "are just not good for you," says Ellis. In addition, "classic soul food has a fair amount of salt in it. And chronic high amounts can cause hypertension."[6]

Over the years, Joan B. Lewis has observed that "predominately black people have high blood pressure and hypertension, that's the salt involved. And large numbers of African Americans have diabetes," passed on to them genetically. "Remember now, high blood pressure leads to strokes and heart attacks. Diabetes leads to high blood pressure, high cholesterol, and strokes and heart attacks. . . . And now we have a lot of black people that have what we call renal or kidney failure and my father had that, because his blood pressure was so high that it destroyed the kidney." North Americans are historically more overweight than residents of any other nation in the world; African American eating habits are just as problematic as the eating habits of other ethnic groups within the United States. According to Lewis, historically the eating patterns that you see among most Americans including consuming "sugar, salt, fat, you know fatty products, a whole lot of fried stuff, a whole lot of pork products, a whole lot of fast food, no vegetables, no fruit, [and generally] no good wholesome things." Lewis goes on to say that, over the last eight to ten years, the younger generation has "leaned heavily" on "vegetarian items. It was a blessing in disguise" because those that do are consuming less fat and reducing their chance of obesity and risk factors for high blood pressure and diabetes.[7]

In the 1970s there were a few African American physicians who spoke out against the soul food diet by publishing articles in *Ebony* magazine that called for food reform. For instance, Dr. Therman E. Evans was way ahead of his time in his understanding of the relationship between food and health. In March 1972 he wrote that, as African Americans, "We cannot continue to disregard what we eat as if our diet has no effect on our health status. In fact, what we eat is both directly and indirectly related to every major illness we know of, including heart disease, high blood pressure, cancer, diabetes, and infectious diseases." Evans observed that African Americans needed both more nutritious food and exercise.[8] Five years later, *Ebony* published the article "Good Health Is a Family Affair: Good Nutrition, Exercise, Sleep, Physical Examinations, Etc.," in its May 1977 issue.[9] In this article, Dr. Keith W. Sehnert recommended the increased consumption of "raw fruits and vegetables because they add necessary vitamins and minerals and valuable bulk to your diet." Moreover, Sehnert wanted African Americans to cook and bake with "polyunsaturated vegetable oils" instead of high-cholesterol saturated fats like butter and lard. He also championed the replacement of whole milk products with skimmed milk products and advised the consumption of only three eggs per week. As for meat, Sehnert believe it was much wiser to consume more fish, fowl, "beans, nuts, and new soya-meat extenders and substitutes … because they are lower in calories and fat than beef, lamb or pork."[10] A year after that, a Dr. Lemah of Meharry Medical College, an HBCU in Nashville, was interviewed for an article in *Ebony* that said African Americans needed to reduce the amount of refined carbohydrates in their diets. In different ways, all three physicians were calling for radical food reforms, or the transition to what Dr. Elijah Saunders of the University of Maryland Medical School calls "heart-healthy meals."[11]

Yet these reforms would not be easy. Dr. Saunders found that it was far easier to suggest changes than to implement them. For example, during his tenure as head of cardiology at Providence Hospital in Baltimore, Saunders remembers the battle he faced in getting the food service department to serve heart-healthy meals to his African American patients who were hospitalized for heart attacks and strokes. Moreover, Saunders could not persuade the hospital's cafeteria to move beyond a typical soul food menu: "they voted me down," he says. In contrast to the four doctors quoted, historically African American physicians have been resistant to reform the soul food diet because of the belief that to do so would make African Americans into "somebody else," says Saunders.[12]

The silence of black doctors on nutrition left an opening filled by the Nation of Islam, college students exposed to alternative views of eating, and advocates of natural food diets. For almost twenty years, these three groups were the only ones within African American communities talking about the importance of diet and exercise. The Nation of Islam, for example, had no concerns about African Americans becoming something they were not. They argued that that had already happened during slavery: "Peas, collard greens, turnip greens, sweet potatoes and white potatoes are very cheaply raised foods [boldfaced in the original text]," said Elijah Muhammad. "The Southern slave masters used them to feed the slaves, and still advise the consumption of them."[13] Elijah Muhammad argued that African Americans learned a destructive culture from an oppressive white Christian power structure during slavery and that this included their traditional diet. The change of the African American diet was one of the first radical changes a person made after joining the Nation of Islam.

THE NATION OF ISLAM

In the 1960s the Nation's training program for new converts at its Mount Vernon temple in Westchester County included extensive teaching on nutrition, with particular emphasis on not eating pork. Convert Eugene Watts recalled receiving about eight weeks of diet and nutritional instruction, much of it in the form of taped lectures given by Elijah Muhammad on the subject.[14] For many non-Muslims, the introduction to Nation's teachings on eating came from Elijah Muhammad's two-volume book *How to Eat to Live*, published in 1967 and 1972.

Despite the popularity of soul food in the 1960s and 1970s, food rebels like Elijah Muhammad had an impact in black communities. Yet there were no problems between food rebels like the members of the Nation of Islam and black nationalists like Amiri Baraka who advocated soul food as black folk's cuisine. "I mean, look at Elijah Muhammad, there were a whole lot of Baptists that would never be Muslim, but they stopped eating pork," says Dick Gregory.[15]

Many were familiar with the Nation's swine restrictions, but Muhammad was also a staunch proponent of eating whole grains and opposed the consumption of processed foods like white rice, bread, and sugar. "Eat wheat—never white flour, which has been robbed of all its natural vitamins and proteins sold separately as cereals," says Muhammad. "You know as well as I that the white race is a commercializing people and they do not worry about the lives they jeopardize so long as the dollar is safe. You might find yourself eating death if you follow them."[16] Muhammad theorized that blue-eyed white devils had conspired to use deadly white eating habits to eliminate blacks. Whites, he explained, promoted the consumption of unhealthy processed food and spicy and greasy food in order to weaken and eventually wear out black folk. "Muslim lore," as one historian puts it, maintained that years of following white foodways were ultimately responsible for multiplying sickness and disease and severely lowering life expectancy in African American communities. The Nation argued that the white's food conspiracy worked both to eradicate black people and to make white medical doctors and undertakers rich.[17]

Most likely, members of the Nation sold copies of *How to Eat to Live* the same way they sold the Nation of Islam's paper *The Final Call* and its delicious and nutritious bean pies: by direct marketing on street corners and in businesses operated by its members. In African American communities in metropolitan New York as well as in other parts of the country, the Nation operated its own supermarkets, fish markets, and restaurants. Male members of the Nation also hawked merchandise at busy intersections. Some street vendors were sympathetic to the message of the Nation and contributed by selling literature and the recorded lectures of Elijah Muhammad and Malcolm X.

BEAN PIE RECIPE

2 cups navy beans (cooked)
1 stick butter
1 14-oz. can evaporated milk
4 eggs
1 tsp. nutmeg
1 tsp. cinnamon
2 tbsp. flour
2 cups sugar
2 tbsp. vanilla

Preheat oven to 350 degrees. In electric blender, blend together beans, butter, milk, eggs, nutmeg, cinnamon, and flour for around two minutes on medium speed. Put mixture in a large mixing bowl. Mix in sugar and vanilla. Stir well. Pour into pie shells. Bake for around an hour until golden brown. Yields two to three pies.

Adapted from www.muhammadspeaks.com/Pie.html

Starting in 1954, Malcolm X and the members of Temple 7 were the face of the Nation of Islam's message about food in metropolitan New York.[18] The only African Americans he knew of "who had any sense of being very disciplined nutritionally would probably be the Muslims," says Harlem native Roy Miller. "I think that Malcolm X personified that publicly," Miller maintains. On many occasions, "he spoke very vigilantly about, 'you don't eat that pig,' and all that sort of stuff." In what he said and how he lived, Malcolm, says Miller, "made a lot of people conscious about what they were eating and being very careful about what you were eating." Rudy Bradshaw, another Harlem native, had a brother who was very close to Malcolm. He said that if you went to a place to eat and ordered pork,

FIGURE 9.1 World heavyweight boxing champion Muhammad Ali, *right*, with Black Muslim leader Malcolm X, New York City, March 1, 1964. AP Image Collection.

"Malcolm would ridicule you in a joking way ... he did that with [Harlem intellectuals] John Hendrik Clarke and Dr. Benyohagen [aka Dr. Ben]." He would remind them that the pig is the dirtiest animal on the farm and subsequently over time persuaded them and others to reform their eating traditions. In contrast to soul food restaurants, Black Muslim restaurants served beef and fish meals with brown rice, fresh vegetables, bean soup, and bean pies.[19]

The earliest challenges to soul food traditions in Westchester came from members of the Nation of Islam in the 1960s. Reginald Ward became a permanent fixture in Mount Vernon's African American community. Speaking of the influence of the Nation in the city, he recalls that a number of people he knew became Muslims and reformed their eating habits. In fact, Louis Farrakhan, who assumed most of Malcolm's responsibilities in metropolitan New York after Malcolm left the Nation in 1965, came to speak in Mount Vernon in the 1970s. Eugene Watts from Virginia was one of Ward's friends who converted to Islam.[20]

During the 1960s Eugene Watts operated a barbershop on Third Street in Mount Vernon. Next to his shop was a restaurant called Philly's Bake and Take owned by a member of the Nation of Islam. The restaurant "did really really good" business, says Watts. "I still hear people, and this has been over fifteen years, talk about how they miss that restaurant." The restaurant's cook at one time was a "Sister Lana." She also cooked for the Muslim convert and heavy-weight champion Muhammad Ali and "would go down to Harlem to Temple 7 and help them prepare food, and then come up here to Mount Vernon." Her specialty, recalls Watts, was bean soup. "That was an important staple for Muslims, the great northern bean. And [Sister Lana] would fix it in such a way that people would be lined up out the door to get a cup of this soup. . . . These were regular [non-Muslim customers]." When people heard that Sister Lana was in town, they quickly made their way over to Third Street. After a while, Watts began attending the Nation's Mount Vernon temple and eventually converted.[21]

After his conversion, Watts regularly played Nation of Islam audiocassette "tapes on how to eat" in his barbershop as a way of disseminating the teachings on food to his male customers. Watts recalls that in the 1960s the Nation had a major impact on black Mount Vernon, particularly on young African American males. There were also those who never converted but agreed with the Nation's message on food reform. He insists there were plenty of sympathizers who would say, "I admire what you are doing and I have your back. I just can't give up too much like you're giving it up." Watts goes on to say that, back then, if you went down to the Temple and showed an inability to sit still or sweated profusely, "the brothers would take you to the side and tell you that you were not eating the right stuff."[22]

Watts decided to become a vegetarian for health reasons shortly after converting to the Nation of Islam. "Afterwards I found out that my family had a history of high cholesterol and high blood pressure, a lot of medical problems associated with rich food." Watts's mother died at age thirty-seven of an aneurysm brought on by high blood pressure when he was a senior in high school.[23] Hypertension specialist Dr. Elijah Saunders confirms that the consumption of foods high in cholesterol and saturated fats leads to atherosclerosis, or cardiovascular disease, which is what causes heart attacks and brain aneurysms, both particularly prevalent among African Americans. Cholesterol and fat levels in the blood are directly related to diet and lifestyle. Saunders argues that "pork organs and extremities" such as chitlins and pigs' feet are also very high in saturated fat and increase one's risk factors for an aneurysm or heart attack.[24] Two nights before Eugene Watts's mother died, she ate a large bowl of chitlins. Watts says his mother "loved chitlins, and she was not supposed to eat them, and a neighbor brought them over, saying 'Ms. Watts, I fixed them just for you, you are going to love these chitlins.'" Once on the Nation's eating regimen, Eugene Watts stopped eating beef and fish as well as the pork so beloved by his mother.[25]

In 1962 the Nation of Islam claimed a membership of over a quarter of a million people. Elijah Muhammad sent Malcolm X, perhaps the Nation's best evangelist in the 1950s, to organize new temples in Boston, Philadelphia, New York, and Atlanta. In New York, Malcolm and his assistants sought to draw in possible converts to the Nation of Islam by "'fishing' on those Harlem corners—on the fringe of the Nationalist meetings." Of this activity, Malcolm X recalled that "everyone who was listening was interested in the revolution of the black race." He also fished at "little evangelical storefront churches. . . . These congregations were usually Southern migrant people, usually older, who would go anywhere to hear what they called 'good preaching.'" Yet there was also the offer of a soul food dinner. There were always members of the church "who were always putting out little signs announcing that inside they were selling fried chicken and chitlin' dinners to raise some money."[26]

The Nation also fished among the black working class and underclass. Particular efforts were made to fish incarcerated African American men, and indeed many who converted to Islam did so while in prison. Malcolm found that most of the people he preached to believed what he had to say about racism in America and immorality and ignorance among African Americans. But in the words of Malcolm, "our strict moral code and discipline was what repelled them most." He would explain to potential converts that, among other requirements, giving up "eating of the filthy pork or other injurious or unhealthful foods" was necessary if blacks were to move beyond the white man's goal of keeping them "immoral, unclean, and ignorant."[27] It was a lot easier to give up eating pork economically when you were in an institution and state officials provided you with three free meals a day. The economic reality for meat-eating African Americans living outside the controlled environment of prison walls was very different. Bobby Seale (originally from Texas) was the cofounder and designated cook of the "shotgun, rifle, and pistol-packing" Black Panther Party for Self-Defense of Oakland, California. He cooked affordable meals for the organization's meetings in the early days of the party. "I cooked our meals of piles of spaghetti or [pork] neckbones and greens, and while we ate, sucking and shining our neckbones, I raised jokes about the Muslim's organization not eating pork," says Seale. He goes on say, "Our grudge was against the racist white power-structure," not against ham hocks. It was a whole lot cheaper to buy a ham hock than other cuts of meat.[28] The Nation's antiswine message hit people's pocketbooks, but, more important, it challenged their traditions. Many met it with contempt, believing it to be foolishness because they had been raised on pork. For this reason, the Nation's antiswine message had its greatest influence among younger folk without well-established traditions of their own.

Clara Bullard Pittman, born in 1948, observed that in the 1970s the Nation's food reform message made virtually no impact on her older relatives who relocated from Pinehurst, Georgia, to St. Petersburg, Florida. "That age group, they were like, 'No! We grew up on soul food, that's our diet, and we are not going to stop. Pork has not killed me yet so I am going to keep eating it.'" In contrast, during the same period, Clara Bullard Pittman observed, "A lot of the young brothers" in northern California joining the Nation and reforming their eating habits, including no longer eating pork.[29]

Joan B. Lewis made similar observations about metropolitan Washington, D.C., in the 1960s and 1970s. She remembered quite a few African American men who had been incarcerated and returned from prison as non-pork-eating members of the Nation. She and others living in the District of Columbia described a scene in which the presence of the Nation of Islam was very strong.[30] Dr. Rodney Ellis, a native Washingtonian, was a Howard University undergraduate in northwest Washington, D.C., between 1966 and 1970. Ellis, too, argues that a change in African American attitudes toward some soul food can be traced back to the 1960s and to activists like Dick Gregory and the antiswine teachings of Elijah Muhammad and the members of the Nation of Islam. For example, Ellis recalls, "I will never forget Muhammad Ali coming to campus about 1966, 1967, and making fun of black folks eating pigs' feet. ... You know everybody was enthralled by him, and he must have had a sellout crowd of people. ... I remember him on two occasions talking about 'sticky pigs' feet, it sticks to your hands, it gets stuck together. You know what that is, that is pus, you're eating pus!' Man, that turned a whole lot of people, I think ... to having some concerns." Ellis goes on to say that, though many African American students at Howard may not have given up "bacon and ribs" after hearing Ali, they did leave the lecture reevaluating their eating habits and the wisdom of continuing to eat pigs' feet and chitlins.[31]

ADVOCATES OF NATURAL FOOD DIETS

Exposure to food rebels like Muhammad Ali and other members of the Nation of Islam led some African American undergraduates and graduate students to consider a radical break from traditional soul food, but others broke away after hearing a lecture on natural living from Dr. Alvenia M. Fulton (1907–1999) or Dick Gregory. Gregory says, "I don't know anybody, other than Elijah Muhammad, and his was an organization, that had the ear of African Americans like [Dr. Fulton] did. [Elijah Muhammad] had it on a national level, she had it beginning in Chicago, then [her message] started reaching out more toward white folk when she would go to the conferences." He adds, Dr. Fulton was "at the forefront" of what has became a trillion-dollar health and fitness movement. "She was very well respected by that whole white movement because they knew about her fasting knowledge, and in the black community" because her knowledge of herbs and nutrition was making sick people well.[32]

In the 1960s the Playboy Club was the most famous in the country. Hefner caught Gregory's show and in 1961 signed him to a three-year contract worth $250 a week. "After Hefner hired me, all kinds of things started to happen," recalls Gregory. "I started to get press notices, the newspapers sent people by to review my act, and the columnists started quoting my jokes." Meeting Martin Luther King, Jr., changed Gregory from a comedian to a civil rights activist. It was during the civil rights movement and Vietnam War that Gregory became one of the country's leading nightclub comics, political satirists, and activists.[33]

In an interview, I asked him how he became a vegetarian. He explained that one day, possibly during a civil rights march in the South, a sheriff kicked his wife, and he didn't come to her defense. "I had to convince myself," says Gregory, "that the reason that I didn't do anything about it was because I was nonviolent." He adds, "Then I said, 'If thou shalt not kill,' that should mean animals, too. So in 1963 I just decided I wasn't going to eat anything else that had to be killed," he explains. "I still drank a fifth of scotch a day and smoked four packs of cigarettes. So my becoming a vegetarian didn't have anything to do with health reasons. And I didn't even know how to spell it; I didn't know what a vegetarian was." But, after about eighteen months of being a vegetarian, his sinus trouble disappeared, and about six months after so did his ulcers. That "was the first time I realized that there was something about the food that they didn't tell us about."[34] Starting in 1967, even more enlightenment came when Gregory met Dr. Alvenia M. Fulton.

Fulton migrated to Chicago from Pulaski, Tennessee. In the 1950s she opened Fultonia's, a combination health food store, restaurant, and herbal pharmacy at 65th and Eberhardt on Chicago's South Side. When Fultonia's started, it was a real oddity; it was only later that people embraced the message of natural living in the United States, especially in African American communities where soul food constituted a large part of local cultural traditions.[35] Fulton's restaurant had a full menu that included soups, vegetarian chili, brown rice, vegetables, all varieties of fruit and vegetable juices, and whole grain breads and cakes. Fulton called her food, "soul food with a mission, and the mission is good health."[36]

Gregory met Fulton during his 1967 campaign for mayor of Chicago against the incumbent, Richard Daley. Fulton came by campaign headquarters and dropped off some salad for Gregory and his staff. "I had been a vegetarian," says Gregory, "so I said if you are running against Mayor Daley, you cannot eat anything anybody brings you!" He told his staff that if anybody should bring anything by, they were to take their name down and he would stop by and thank them later. Someone at the headquarters informed him that a really nice black woman "'brought all these salads here for you,'" says Gregory. "I went by one day to thank her," and the 1967 encounter with Fulton turned "my whole life around." As they sat and talked, Gregory told Fulton that he was going to go on a forty-day fast in protest of the war in Vietnam. "And she thought I knew something about fasting, which I didn't! And she taught me from day one to day forty what was going to go on in my body."[37] During the fast, Gregory went from 350 to 98 pounds and ran twenty-five miles a day. After the fast, his weight rose to 148 pounds, he was totally healthy, and he began to fast on a regular basis.

Over the next several years, Gregory and Fulton became close friends, and they collaborated in sharing their knowledge about fasting, herbs, and nutrition with anybody who would listen. There were plenty of African Americans who had eaten soul food all of their lives and had diabetes, hypertension, and heart disease in part because of it. They went to Fulton with the express purpose of breaking away from this diet. She offered an alternative that improved their health and energy levels; they in turn told their relatives and friends. Fulton's diet worked so well that it also attracted a lot of black celebrities such as actor Godfrey Cambridge, singers Eartha Kitt and Roberta Flack, gospel artist Mahalia Jackson, and comedian Redd Foxx.[38]

Fulton collaborated with Gregory on a cookbook entitled *Dick Gregory's Natural Diet for Folks Who Eat: Cookin' with Mother Nature*. The book,

FIGURE 9.2 Comedian Dick Gregory speaking to about two thousand students at the University of South Florida, April 14, 1971. AP Image Collection.

published in 1973, is the most compelling evidence that Fulton's work was an important influence on Gregory. In it, Gregory, with assistance from Fulton, denounces soul food for causing bloated stomachs, bald heads, varicose veins, swollen ankles, high blood pressure, heart trouble, and nervous tension in the black community. All these illnesses, he says, are the results of the soul food diet and its tradition of "heavy starch consumption, cooked food and greasy fried food consumption, and sugar and salt consumption." He argues, "One might say folks with all those difficulties are suffering from consumption!" Gregory also openly indicts African American political leaders and activists who advocated soul food by serving it at their meetings and events: "I personally would say that the quickest way to wipe out a group of people is to put them on a soul food diet. One of the tragedies is that the very folks in the black community who are most sophisticated in terms of the political realities in this country are nonetheless advocates of 'soul food.' They will lay down a heavy rap on genocide in America with regards to black folks, then walk into a soul food restaurant and help the genocide along."[39]

The same year he published the cookbook, Gregory also stopped doing his stand-up comedy routine at nightclubs. He explained to reporter Vernon Jarrett of the *Chicago Tribune* that "he had a problem in doing anything that would encourage people to consume alcohol or do anything that might be damaging to one's personal health." During the interview, Gregory informed Jarrett that soul food is "the worst food that you can eat. Nothing but garbage." Gregory felt that once African Americans started eating properly, their bodies and minds would change, and they would stop permitting other people to commit injustices against them. In short, starting around 1973, Gregory, influenced largely by Fulton, dedicated increasing amounts of time and energy to food reform. Writing in 1973, reporter Vernon Jarrett reported, "Dick's near full-time commitment today is to the human body and what is done to it and with it. And there is nothing funny about this commitment."[40]

Gregory's strategy of raising public awareness about world hunger and starvation by running marathons fueled only by water, fresh fruit juice, and a powdered supplement he created called Formula X ("a combination of kelp—that little green seaweed you see growing in the ocean—and a few other ingredients") gained him notoriety throughout the black community.[41] "He was a real activist" and "he would be on all the stations," says Fred Opie, Jr. In addition to radio appearances, Gregory lectured extensively on college campuses.[42]

"UPPER-CLASS FOLK"

Dick Gregory estimates that, at one time, he did 250 lectures a year at universities across the country. Gregory says he would "talk about vegetarianism and why you should buy into it." Those lectures "had a lot of influence on both black folks and white folks in America."[43] Edward Williamson attended Morgan State University, an HBCU located in the heart of Baltimore. He remembered attending lectures given by Gregory, Stokely Carmichael (Kwame Ture), and H. Rap Brown.[44]

Carmichael was a Howard University undergraduate and member of the Student Nonviolent Coordinating Committee and later the Black Panthers. In 1966 he coined the term "black power" at a freedom rally in Greenwood, Mississippi. Like Carmichael, H. Rap Brown was first a member of the SNCC and later the Black Panthers. Both Carmichael and Brown gave lectures on college campuses in the late 1960s and early 1970s in which they mentioned food within a black nationalist context.[45] Lamenta Crouch, a graduate of Virginia State College, an HBCU, remembers Carmichael talking about eating in a radically different way. Rejecting the argument that soul food was authentically African American cuisine, he suggested that African Americans should embrace food and cooking styles with African origins. Carmichael insisted that "if we are going to go all the way and claim who we are, then we should be eating as we did indigenously," recalls Crouch. Yet Crouch had doubts as to the motives of Carmichael's argument. "I don't know if his [message] was from a health standpoint as much as from" a black power perspective that "soul food is not really African food."[46] Similarly, Edward Williamson remembers hearing the message "anything that is white is not good for you." Carmichael especially emphasized that processed and refined white foods "were evil." His message was "don't eat white bread, don't eat sugar, don't eat potatoes, and don't eat white rice."[47]

Joan B. Lewis, who taught food safety courses on the campus of the University of the District of Columbia, noticed that vegetarianism became much more fashionable in the Washington metropolitan area around the 1970s. This was particularly true near the Howard University campus, where several vegetarian restaurants opened. Most of the vegetarians in the Washington metro area were African American college students, says Lewis. In addition, she saw vegetarians among the ranks of the area's college-educated African American professionals and the hard-working black people they worked and socialized with.[48] It was in Alexandria, Virginia, in Fairfax County, a suburb of Washington, D.C., that Clara Bullard Pittman first heard African American youth advocating a radical conversion to vegetarianism. In the 1970s "we used to call them 'upper-class black folk,'" says Pittman. "Those were the ones who could go away to college and educate themselves. . . . That's where I heard that stuff from."[49]

By the late 1970s African American students at colleges across the country were attending classes, rooming, and sometimes eating with food rebels of various stripes: Muslims in the Nation of Islam, Five Percenters, members of the Moorish Science Temple of America, those in the US Organization, African Hebrew Israelites, and the children of advocates of natural food diets. Among this very small but diverse population of college students 1 percent were full-fledged vegetarians, while others had dietary restrictions against pork and/or highly processed white sugar and flour. A smaller fraction became aware that the meat and dairy industries were using growth hormones to shorten the maturation periods of livestock and poultry. As a result, a tiny percentage became vegans, meaning that they stopped eating dairy as well as meat. Others students became what I call reformed soul food eaters: they gave up pork, for example, but otherwise ate standard African American, Caribbean-influenced cuisine. Sun-diata Sadique recalls that he had friends at Temple University in Philadel-phia who took up natural food cooking. When they returned to New York, they opened "soulless restaurants" in the city that specialized in meatless cooking using fruits, nuts, and vegetables. "So we had all these educated blacks coming back from college sharing this information with us," says Sadique.[50]

Perhaps it was a lecture by Gregory or Carmichael that inspired Ralph Johnson and Patricia Reed to write an article denouncing traditional soul food made with beef and pork in a 1981 edition of the *Black Collegian*, an academic journal dedicated to African American topics. In an Afrocentric article entitled "What's Wrong with Soul Food?" Johnson and Reed in-sisted that before the African slave trade West Africans ate a very healthy diet consisting of fresh fruits, vegetables, grains, and wild game. It was European slave traders who introduced inferior foods to West Africa and to African captives. Like Elijah Muhammad, Johnson and Reed insisted that slave owners only provided the cheapest foods to their slaves, such as "white refined rice, cornmeal, potatoes, pig fat, salt pork, grits, and sweet potatoes." They went on to say that African Americans continued to con-sume the same foods because they believed that it was the Africans' "na-tive food, but it is nothing more than slave food. Add to this slave food the chemicalized, refined sugary, fast, convenience foods of our modern soci-ety and you have quite a deadly combination."[51] Soul food, they insisted, was responsible for causing in blacks higher percentages of hypertension, strokes, and cancer than in whites. They concluded, "Black Americans can start to reverse those health statistics and gain back their health by utiliz-ing the West African diet, which is rightfully ours to begin with! Black Americans should unchain their dietary habits and let the 'soul food' diet die along with the concept of slavery!"[52]

It wasn't only upper-class and college-educated African Americans who moved away from soul food. Religious conversion rather than lectures by Dick Gregory or Stokely Carmichael reformed the eating habits of work-ing blacks like Louisiana-born Mary Keyes Burgess. First in Louisiana and later in Texas, Burgess learned at her mother's side how to cook whatever the family garden produced. Later in life she apparently became a Seven-Day-Adventist and "skillfully adapted a lacto-ovo-vegetarian" dietary re-gime to her black Louisiana and Texas roots to create vegetarian soul food recipes. As an adult, Burgess migrated to California, where she first began to cook professionally, at the Family Education Center in a black and His-panic section of San Bernardino. She became well-known for her vegetarian dishes where she lived and worked, and her fame led to the publication in 1976 of a book, *Soul to Soul: A Soul Food Vegetarian Cookbook*. "Soul food," she wrote, "can be more appealing than ever without meat—if you know what to use in its place.... Fortunately, modern food research has given us delicious and wholesome substitutes for meat."[53]

FRIED VEGETABLE CHICKEN

Batter
1 cup all-purpose flour
2 teaspoons chicken seasoning (salt, pepper, paprika)
1 egg
1 cup milk
½ teaspoon salt

Combine all ingredients and mix well.

Seasoning flour
½ cup all-purpose flour
2 teaspoon chicken seasoning
1 teaspoon garlic powder

Rinse one 19-oz. can Worthington's Soyameat or La Loma Terkettes. Add 1 teaspoon garlic powder. Let stand for one to two hours. Drain. Dip in batter and then dredge in seasoned flour. Deep-fry until golden brown.

Adapted from Mary Keyes Burgess, *Soul to Soul: A Soul Food Vegetarian Cookbook* (Santa Barbara, Calif.: Woodbridge, 1976), 50.

Alternative voices from the Nation of Islam, the university-trained, and advocates of natural food made important contributions to black folks' reconsidering the health and nutritional merits of soul food and the culinary legacy of their southern ancestors. Before the 1980s, the Nation of Islam, more than any other African American organization, raised the food consciousness of black people in the United States. In addition to the Nation, college students exposed to natural food activists and natural food advocates on the radio were the most progressive health educators in

African American communities in the absence of nutrition-minded physicians. Except for a few radicals, physicians refused to criticize traditional African American cookery.

Most of the people who became food rebels were exposed to alternative information about food during radio broadcasts, lectures, rallies, and Nation of Islam events or while incarcerated and surrounded with converts to the Nation of Islam. African Americans who left their communities to go to college or those in prison tended to be far more receptive to the message of food reform. The same was true for those who participated in black nationalist organizations in the 1960s and 1970s.

Yet food rebels did not have a mass influence on African Americans, although they did manage to persuade some younger generations of African Americans and those who spent time outside their traditional communities to reduce their consumption of pork, which was no small accomplishment. Perhaps the biggest challenge for alternative food restaurants like those of Muhammad Ali, Dr. Fulton, and the Nation of Islam was how to attract African American and Caribbean customers without having pork on their menu. A menu without fried pork chops, smothered pork chops, barbecued pork ribs, or greens seasoned with pork struck customers as unappealing. For most, it was incentive enough to leave an alternative restaurant and look for a "real" soul food joint with a traditional meat, meal, and molasses menu. In short, no-pork menus challenged the identity politics of African American and Caribbean customers. Because of their cultural allegiance to pork and pork-seasoned greens, many did not frequent swine-free restaurants like Ali's, Fulton's, and the Nation's even if the word on the street was that the food was good. The influence of food rebels on African American soul food in urban centers was thus limited to changing the eating habits of a very small percentage of African Americans and people of Caribbean descent.[54]

Many different factors led African Americans to break with soul food, including political, health, and cultural reasons. Some stopped eating soul food because they did not want to continue following the eating habits set by white slave owners (although, as this book has argued, soul food is the same general diet historically consumed by both black and white Southerners). Others stopped eating it because they were diagnosed with diabetes, hypertension, or cardiovascular disease. The more radical claimed serving soul food was an act of genocide because it was responsible for so many health problems in African American communities. Finally, some argued that breaking with soul food and eating like one's African ancestors was an expression of black cultural consciousness. During the civil rights and black power movements, breaking away from soul food became another way of resisting the white man's culture and returning to an idealized African culinary heritage. It was a return to a time when Africans ate darker whole grains, dark green leafy vegetables, and colorful fruits and nuts. In northern cities, politically rejecting soul food meant rejecting part of one's African diasporic urban identity. And perhaps that is the reason why so many food rebels tried to develop healthier food eateries. They understood the close association between soul food and people of African descent with southern and Caribbean roots. The people and the traditions of the cuisine were too interconnected simply to disengage black people completely from soul food; it would have to be adapted to the new circumstances. I have tried argue throughout this book that African peoples have always creatively adapted their food to their new realities. They learned to cook with new crops and animals before and after the Atlantic slave trade. As people of African descent today learn more about diet, obesity, and risk factors for high blood pressure and diabetes, they will adapt again. The masses of African Americans will continue to adapt soul food, as they have done for centuries, rather than yield to a call for complete abstinence.

EPILOGUE

Desegregation, urban renewal programs, poor business practices, and the death of the original owners of some restaurants caused the closing of some community soul food eateries. There are still barbecue rib and chicken shacks in large cities and smaller African American communities across the country. Older, larger, more established soul food restaurants like Sylvia Woods's in Harlem and Pascal's in southwest Atlanta have expanded over time.

Sylvia's renovated its Harlem facility near 125th Street and Malcolm X Boulevard and built a room for catered events. These additions allowed the restaurant to stay in competition with Amy Ruth's soul food restaurant, located south of Sylvia's on Malcolm X Boulevard. Amy Ruth's is an example of a newer upscale soul food restaurant opened in a gentrified section of Harlem catering to an ethnically mixed clientele. The restaurant's Website and word of mouth attract a long line of customers on Sundays. People patiently wait outside for a seat at its Sunday brunch. In the South, a new Pascal's opened in 2003 in an upscale building in the vicinity of the increasingly gentrified Atlanta University Center section of southwest Atlanta. Sylvia's opened a second restaurant in an upscale space near the Georgia government buildings in downtown Atlanta. Following the tradition of Well's in Harlem, recording artist Gladys Knight opened Gladys Knight's Chicken Waffle in midtown Atlanta. Atlanta, Washington, D.C., and New York also have relatively new alternative restaurants that specialize in health-conscious soul food. Many of these restaurants are responding to the war against trans fats raged by food activists in cities

FIGURE 10.1 A Sunday morning at M & G Diner on West 125th Street, Harlem, New York. Photo taken by the author.

like New York and Chicago. These activists have called for health departments to ban restaurants from using partially hydrogenated cooking oils, which contain trans fats that raise bad cholesterol levels and eventually cause clogged arteries and heart disease. The activists gained one of their greatest victories in the fall of 2006 when New York City mayor Michael Bloomberg announced the "nation's first major municipal ban on all but tiny amounts of artificial trans fats in restaurant cooking."[1]

When I was finishing this book, I came across a *Newsweek* article entitled "Saving Soul Food." The article reports that African American entrepreneurs, nutritionists, and pastors are "on a mission to improve African American diets, not by condemning their rich culinary heritage, but by reinventing time-honored recipes." Chefs like Lindsey Williams, Sylvia Woods's grandson, are publishing new health-conscious soul food cookbooks and opening up new restaurants with trendy healthy soul food menus.[2]

Chicago, St. Louis, Charleston, Tallahassee, Atlanta, and metropolitan Washington, D.C., have restaurants, juice bars, and delis run by Rabbi Ben Ammi, the spiritual leader of the African Hebrew Israelites of Jerusalem movement that started in 1966. The predominately African American members of the movement are vegan.[3] Their restaurants go by the name Soul Vegetarian, and they feature entrees made from nonmeat (mostly soy) and nondairy ingredients. They also sell fabulous nondairy ice cream in a variety of flavors. Another such vegetarian soul food restaurant is the Uptown Juice Bar, located on 125th Street in Harlem, just around the corner from Sylvia's. This unique restaurant and bakery serves delicious nonmeat, nondairy soul food as well as Caribbean dishes and baked goods made with soy, vegetables, fruits, and nuts.

It is not only eateries that have changed soul food; churches have as well. Progressive African American ministers are delivering sermons that challenge their parishioners to be better stewards over their bodies and are making an effort to serve healthier soul food at church-sponsored events. According to *Newsweek*, over two thousand churches have signed on to the National Cancer Institute's Body and Soul program. "Church leaders pledge to include more fruits and veggies in their meals and to preach healthy eating." The article goes on to say that the program in a sense champions "salvation, one fresh veggie at a time."[4]

FIGURE 10.2 Manna's Buffet and Catering Service, Harlem. Betty Parks and her family started Manna's Buffet and Catering Service in 1984. Today Manna's has two locations in Harlem and two in Brooklyn. This is a photo of the location at 2331 Street and Eighth Avenue in Harlem. Photo taken by the author.

The reform of soul food is happening on the home front as well. Admittedly, there is a greater concern with food reform in families exposed to information about healthy cooking and nutrition and where parents are college educated or well read. Still, many are making the change to a healthier form of soul food. I close with some personal stories of how some families have changed the way they prepare soul food to make it more heart healthy.

Yemaja Jubilee, originally from Charlotte County, Virginia, insists that her mother was obese because of her cooking style. Eventually, she died of complications commonly associated with obesity, such as diabetes. Jubilee's grandmother died of similar complications, and her father had a heart attack that motivated him to change his eating habits. Her two brothers also suffered heart attacks, one of them twice. Jubilee thus had plenty of motivation to "change my ways." Starting in the 1980s, she learned through trial and error in the kitchen that soul food could be reformed. "I really think soul food can be healthy because I have learned how to modify all of the recipes."[5]

While living in Nashville, she fell into catering when she covered a party for a girlfriend after a contracted caterer backed out on short notice. Those who came to the party were so impressed with her healthy soul food dishes that she went into business. She makes seasoned collard greens with turkey instead of pork and has perfected the art of seasoning other vegetables, like cabbage, with herbs, spices, and some powdered soup mixes instead of pork. She uses soy and vegetable dairy substitutes, along with egg and sugar substitutes, to make macaroni and cheese, rice pudding, and sweet potato pie, "and it still comes out good," argues Jubilee. In Virginia, she grew up eating pork and beans, cole slaw, and fried fish for dinner on Fridays. Now she sprays spots (a type of fish) and king fish with butter-flavored Pam, breads it with Jiffy corn bread mix, and then bakes in the oven; "it comes out crispy brown and you can't tell it from fried fish," she says. "My mother didn't believe that, or my uncles. What happened was I took my uncle some fish, and this was in the country. He said, 'Can't nobody fix no fish, I know you can't [without frying it].' And I said to him, 'Look and just wait.'" When he finally tasted the modified fish, she said that he couldn't tell the difference between it and a typical Virginia Friday night fish fry.[6]

In the 1980s Lamenta Crouch's husband was diagnosed with high blood pressure. As a result, the Prince Edward County, Virginia, native became very conscious of the foods she brought into the home and began to cook family meals low in both salt and animal fats. "We made some major changes and some subtle ones. For instance, we just took out all the red meat." In addition, Crouch perfected what she calls "healthy fried chicken": skinless chicken parts dipped in seasoned soy flour and then oven-baked with a little oil in a pan. After the chicken has browned, it is covered with aluminum foil and cooked for a few additional minutes. Crouch also learned how to make reformed collard greens by simmering them in a wok with olive oil, garlic, onion, and sea salt until they are tender. On the first Sunday of the month, however, when her family and friends come over, Crouch does "some down-home cooking."[7] Cardiologist Dr. Elijah Saunders recommends that people should enjoy soul food once in a while, the same way you would enjoy fine food when eating out. But the key is not to eat such rich food at home. Saunders says that he recognizes "that there is something special about [soul food] and that it is part of the cultural traditions of the South, and we [African American physicians] understand the emotional attachment to it. But you don't want to make it a regular part of how you eat."[8] Healthy limitations on soul food consumption include eating it sparingly when traveling or visiting away from home, modifying recipes using heart-healthy ingredients, and using one of the many new soy meat substitutes, including imitation chicken and ribs.

Other healthy cooking suggestions include measuring out what you are consuming. "It's more portion control than anything else," says nutritionist Joan B. Lewis. Before you sit down to eat, decide how much you should eat, measure out your desired portion, and stick to your decision. "If they would get to the point where they would regulate their portions, they would be fine. But what you see is a lot of young people that just totally overeat. [They] eat all day long, and nothing that is good for them ... a whole lot of fast food and a whole lot of junk food," says Lewis. Make a decision to move beyond what Yemaja Jubilee calls the "sit and gobble lane" of salty, fatty, greasy, and sweet fast food. Cook more often using wholesome food. Lewis suggests that people make several meals over the weekend and refrigerate or freeze them for consumption later in the week.[9]

The National Council of Negro Women has provided some excellent tips for cooking health-conscious soul food in *The Black Family Dinner Quilt Cookbook*. This cookbook suggests cooking and baking with margarine or liquid vegetable oils such as canola oil, safflower oil, or olive oil instead of lard. Other instructions for heart-healthy meals include avoiding deep-frying, cooking vegetables with animal fat, and baking with lard or butter. Avoid seasoning with salt or using seasonings containing sodium. Instead, try products like Wiley's Healthy Southern Classic soul food seasonings. Roast, bake, broil, grill, and stir-fry instead of deep-frying. Use smoked turkey, turkey bacon, and imitation soy meat products instead of ham hocks, fatback, and bacon to season greens. Remove most of the skin (which is primarily fat) from poultry before cooking. Eat more fiber-rich foods such as legumes, whole grain products, fruits and vegetables, brown rice, red potatoes, and whole wheat, spelt, or spinach pasta. Avoid organ meats as much as possible. Use olive oil and vinegar and vegetable-based mayonnaise dressings instead of dressings made with real mayonnaise. Eat soy or rice milk ice cream with zero cholesterol instead of high cholesterol ice cream.[10]

This book has attempted to explain how African American eating habits evolved before, during, and after slavery. It analyzed the world history of soul food, arguing that, like all cultures, African American culture is a hybrid. African American cookery originated in Africa, but Africans absorbed, in part, European, Asian, and Amerindian food cultures before their arrival in the Americas. Later, a hybridization of African foodways took place among the Africans that arrived in the Americas during the height of the slave trade (1701-1810). In the southern colonies of British North America, enslaved African cooks of various ethnicities gradually incorporated the food staples that were rationed to them by British, French, German, Scottish, and Irish masters. They also adapted their cookery to the food they could gather, grow, hunt, and fish in their new host regions. As two scholars have argued, "The history of any nation's diet is the history of the nation itself . . . mapping episodes of colonialism and migration, trade and exploration, cultural exchange and boundary-marking."[11] Throughout I have tried to show that the origins of soul food are rooted in world history, specifically, the European colonization of the Americas and the Atlantic slave trade. In addition, the origin of soul food is embedded in slavery in the South, jim crow segregation after the abolition of slavery, and black nationalism. Perhaps most interesting is the declining influence of southern-based soul food with the proliferation of African-influenced Caribbean-based soul food restaurants in northern urban centers like New York City. For example, the first company featuring African-influenced cuisine to franchise itself successfully has not been a soul food take-out company but the Brooklyn-based Golden Krust, which features Caribbean fast food such as jerked chicken, oxtail, curried goat, and an array of meat and nonmeat patties, including one made from soy.

I agree with culinary writers Jim Harwood and Ed Callahan, who wrote in 1969, "There's nothing secret or exclusive about Soul Food. . . . The Redman and poor White Southerner had an important share in its development, too. Not to mention any number of soldiers, explorers, settlers, traders and others of varied nationalities."[12] The central argument here is that the history of soul food is not quintessentially an African American history but a world history, with the contributions and creativity of Africans and African Americans at the center. You cannot talk about the origins of soul food without a discussion of the history of international travel within the Atlantic world and the cultural collaborations and clashes within that world. The second important point the book makes is that soul food took on many complex meanings in the 1960s, serving as a source of ethnic and family pride to some and as a reminder of slavery and nutritional miseducation to others. The health and fitness craze that started here in the United States has caused a minority of African Americans to move beyond soul food. Similar to the efforts of black power activists in the 1960s and 1970s, however, the message of critics of soul food and advocates of natural food diets has made few inroads in black communities. As I have discussed, soul food has been under attack but is still standing strong because it tastes good and is rooted deep in African American culture. Reforming soul food is in vogue, but not radical calls for its expulsion from African American restaurants, churches, and homes.

Notes

INTRODUCTION

1. Helen Mendes, *The African Heritage Cookbook* (New York: Macmillan, 1971); Verta Mae Smart-Grosvenor, "Soul Food," *McCall's*, (September 1970), p. 97; Sidney W. Mintz, *Tasting Food, Tasting Freedom: Excursions Into Eating, Culture, and the Past* (Boston: Beacon, 1996); Karen Hess, *The Carolina Rice Kitchen: The African Connection* (Columbia: University of South Carolina Press, 1992); Howard Paige, *Aspects of African-American Foodways* (Southfield, Mich.: Aspects of Publishing, 1999); Jessica B. Harris, *Iron Pots and Wooden Spoons: Africa's Gifts to New World Cooking* (New York: Atheneum, 1989); Psyche A. Williams-Forson, *Building Houses Out of Chicken Legs: Black Women, Food, and Power* (Chapel Hill: University of North Carolina Press, 2006).

2. All three scholars' essays on soul can be found in *Black Experience: Soul*, ed. Lee Rainwater (New Brunswick, N.J.: Transaction, 1973).

3. Doris Witt, *Black Hunger: Food and the Politics of U.S. Identity* (New York: Oxford University Press, 1999); William L. Van Deburg, *New Day in Babylon: The Black Power Movement and American Culture, 1965-1975* (Chicago: University of Chicago Press, 1992).

1. THE ATLANTIC SLAVE TRADE AND THE COLUMBIAN EXCHANGE

1. David Buisseret, introduction to *Creolization in the Americas*, ed. David Buisseret and Steven G. Reinhardt (College Station: Texas A&M Press for the University of Texas at Arlington, 2000), 4-8.

2. Helen Mendes, *The African Heritage Cookbook* (New York: Macmillan, 1971); Jessica B. Harris, *Iron Pots and Wooden Spoons: Africa's Gifts to New World Cooking*

(New York: Atheneum, 1989); Sophie D. Coe, *America's First Cuisines* (Austin: University of Texas Press, 1994); Jeffrey M. Pilcher, *¡Que Vivan los Tamales! Food and the Making of Mexican Identity* (Albuquerque: University of New Mexico Press, 1998); Diane M. Spivey, *Migration of African Cuisine* (Albany: State University of New York Press, 1999); Kenneth F. Kiple and Kriemhild Coneè Ornelas, eds., *The Cambridge World History of Food*, vol, 1, (Cambridge: Cambridge University Press, 2000).

3. Douglas Brent Chambers, "'He Gwine Sing He Country': Africans, Afro-Virginians, and the Development of Slave Culture in Virginia, 1690-1810" (Ph.D. diss., University of Virginia, 1996), 419, 423.

4. Pieter de Marees, *Description and Historical Account of the Gold Kingdom of Guinea (1602)*, trans. and ed. Albert van Dantzig and Adam Jones (New York: Oxford University Press, 1987), 130.

5. The Atlantic paradigm came from a reading of Fernand Braudel, *Capitalism and Material Life, 1400-1800*, trans. Miriam Kochan (New York: Harper and Row, 1973); Fernand Braudel, *Civilization and Capitalism, 15th-18th Century*, vol. 1, *The Structures of Everyday Life: The Limits of the Possible*, trans. Sian Reynolds (New York: Harper and Row, 1979); Paul Gilroy, *The Black Atlantic: Double Consciousness, and Modernity* (Cambridge: Harvard University Press, 1993); Jack P. Greene, "Beyond Power: Paradigm Subversion and Reformulation and the Re-creation of the Early Modern Atlantic World," in *Crossing Boundaries: Comparative History of Black People in Diaspora*, ed. Darlene Clark Hine and Jacqueline McLeod (Bloomington: Indiana University Press, 1999), 319-342; Alfred W. Crosby, Jr., *The Columbian Exchange: Biological and Cultural Consequences of 1492* (Westport, Conn.: Greenwood, 1973).

6. Xavier Domingo, "La Cocina Precolombiana en España," in *Conquista y Comida: Consecuencias del Encuentro de Dos Mundos*, ed. Janet Long (Mexico City: Universidad Nacional Autónoma de México, 1996), 19-24; Barbara Norman, *The Spanish Cook Book: Over 200 of the Best Recipes from the Kitchens of Spain* (New York: Bantam, 1966), 16; Teofilo F. Ruiz, *Spanish Society, 1400-1600* (New York: Pearson Education, 2001), 208-215, 221, 228-229.

7. Domingo, "La Cocina Precolombiana en España," 19-24; William W. Dunmire, *Gardens of New Spain: How Mediterranean Plants and Foods Changed America* (Austin: University of Texas Press, 2004), 12-24.

8. Richard Boyer and Geoffrey Spurling, eds., *Colonial Lives: Documents on Latin American History, 1550-1850* (New York: Oxford University Press, 2000), chaps. 4 and 5.

9. Robert Tomson, "Voyage to the West Indies and Mexico (1555-1558)," in *Colonial Travelers in Latin America*, ed. Irving A. Leonard (New York: Knopf, 1972), 58.

10. Robin Law and Kristin Mann, "West Africa in the Atlantic Community: The Case of the Slave Coast," *William and Mary Quarterly* 3d ser., 56, no. 2 (April 1999): 312.

11. Mendes, *The African Heritage Cookbook*, 14.

12. Robert W. July, *Precolonial Africa: An Economic and Social History* (New York: Scribner's, 1975), 66; de Marees, *Description of the Gold Kingdom*, 130.

13. Lamont Dehaven King, "State and Ethnicity in Precolonial Northern Nigeria," *Journal of African American Studies* 36, no. 4 (2001): 350; Chambers, "'He Gwine Sing He Country,'" 408.

14. De Marees, *Description of the Gold Kingdom*, 130.

15. Michel Adanson, *A voyage to Senegal, the isle of Goreé and the river Gambia* (London: J. Nourse, 1759), in John Pinkerton, *A General Collection of the Best and Most Interesting Voyages and Travels in all Parts of the World* ... (London: Longman, Hurst, Ross, Orme and Brown, 1813), 16:618; Mungo Park, *Travels in the Interior Districts of Africa: Performed in the Years 1795, 1796, and 1797, With an Account of a Subsequent Mission to that Country in 1805* (London: William Bulmer and Co., 1816; reprint, London: Dent: New York: Dutton, 1960), 7; Joseph Hawkins, *A History of a Voyage to the Coast of Africa and Travels into the Interior of that Country, Containing Particular Descriptions of the Climate and Inhabitants, and Interesting Particulars Concerning the Slave Trade* (1796; reprint, London: Cass, 1970), 12–15, 73, 77, 118–119; William Allen and T.R.H. Thomson, *A Narrative of the Expedition to the River Niger in 1841*, 2 vols. (London: Richard Bentley, 1848; reprint, London: Cass, 1968), 1:309, 318–319; Theodore Canot, *Captain Canot; or, Twenty Years of an African Slaver: Being an Account of His Career and Adventures on the Coast, in the Interior, on Shipboard, and in the West Indies, Written out and edited from the Captain's Journals, Memoranda and Conversations* (New York: D. Appleton, 1854), 177; de Marees, *Description of the Gold Kingdom*, 113; Crosby, *Columbian Exchange*, 185, 186; Sidney W. Mintz, *Tasting Food, Tasting Freedom: Excursions into Eating, Culture, and the Past* (Boston: Beacon, 1996), 38–39; Theresa Meléndez, "Corn," in *Rooted in America: Foodlore of Popular Fruits and Vegetables*, ed. David Scofield Wilson and Angus Kress Gillespie (Knoxville: University of Tennessee Press, 1999), 45.

16. De Marees, *Description of the Gold Kingdom*, 40.

17. Ibid., 40, 76, 113.

18. Karen Hess, *The Carolina Rice Kitchen: The African Connection* (Columbia: University of South Carolina Press, 1992), 13; Allen and Thomson, *A Narrative of the Expedition To The River Niger*, 1:397; Adanson, *A voyage to Senegal*, 635.

19. De Marees, *Description of the Gold Kingdom*, 40, 76, 113.

20. Linda M. Heywood, ed., *Central Africans and Cultural Transformation in the American Diaspora* (New York: Cambridge University Press, 2002), 93–94, 105; Mendes, *African Heritage Cookbook*, 38–39.

21. Frank J. Klinberg, ed., *The Carolina Chronicle of Dr. Francis Le Jau 1706–1717* (Berkeley: University of California Press, 1956), 7; see also Elizabeth Donnan, *Documents Illustrative of the History of the Slave Trade to America*, vol. 4 (New York: Octagon, 1969).

22. William Bosman [chief factor for the Dutch at the castle of St. George d'Elmina), *A New and Accurate Description of the Coast of Guinea, Divided into the Gold, the Slave, and the Ivory Coasts: A Geographical, Political, and Natural History of the*

Kingdoms and Countries: With a Particular Account of the Rise, Progress, and Present Condition of All the European Settlements Upon That Coast, and the Just Measures for Improving the Several Branches of the Guinea Trade (London, 1705), in Pinkerton, *A General Collection*, 16:392.

23. Hugh Thomas, *The Slave Trade: The History of the Atlantic Slave Trade, 1440-1870* (New York: Simon and Schuster, 1997), 353-356.

24. King, "State and Ethnicity in Precolonial Northern Nigeria," 354.

25. Mendes, *African Heritage Cookbook*, 22, 34-35

26. July, *Precolonial Africa*, 103.

27. Ibid., 38-40; Peter Lionel Wickins, *Economic History of Africa from the earliest times to partition* (New York: Oxford University Press, 1981), 94.

28. Mendes, *African Heritage Cookbook*, 24-27.

29. Femi J. Kolapo, "The Igbo and Their Neighbors During the Era of the Atlantic Slave Trade," *Slavery and Abolition* 25, no. 1 (April 2004): 116; Elizabeth Isichei, *The Igbo Peoples and the Europeans: Genesis of a Relationship—to 1906* (New York: St. Martin's, 1973).

30. Chambers, "'He Gwine Sing,'" 48, 51-52.

31. Allen and Thomson, *A Narrative of the Expedition To The River Niger*, 1:284-285, 388-389; de Marees, *Description of the Gold Kingdom*, 42, 122; Mendes, *African Heritage Cookbook*, 36; Abbé Proyart, *History of Loango, Kakongo, and Other Kingdoms*, in Pinkerton, *A General Collection*, 16:551, 554.

32. Hawkins, *A History of a Voyage to the Coast of Africa*, 73, 77, 101.

33. Ibid., 90-91.

34. Ibid., 135.

35. Hawkins, *A History of a Voyage to the Coast of Africa*, 201.

36. Ibid., 129-130.

37. July, *Precolonial Africa*, 74, 103.

38. Park, *Travels in the Interior Districts of Africa*, 215.

39. Ibid., 145.

40. Ibid., 215.

41. Ibid., 7-8.

42. Ibid., 8, 75.

43. Alex Haley, *Roots* (Garden City, N.Y.: Doubleday, 1976), 8; see also 14, 10, 21.

44. Canot, *Captain Canot*, 139-140.

45. Park, *Travels in the Interior Districts of Africa*, 214.

46. Ibid., 37-38.

47. Mendes, *African Heritage Cookbook*, 38-40.

48. Ibid., 215.

49. Hasia R. Diner, *Hungering For America: Italian, Irish, and Jewish Foodways in the Age of Migration* (Cambridge: Harvard University Press, 2001), 5.

50. De Marees, *Description of the Gold Kingdom*, 168.

51. Olaudah Equiano, "Traditional Igbo Religion and Culture" (1791), in *Afro-American Religious History: A Documentary Witness*, ed. Milton C. Sernett (Durham, N.C.: Duke University Press, 1985), 13-14.

52. Allen and Thomson, *A Narrative of the Expedition to The River Niger in 1841,* 1968), 2:201.

53. Ibid., 1:117.

54. De Marees, *Description of the Gold Kingdom,* 181.

55. [Africanus], "Remarks on the Slave Trade, and the Slavery of the Negroes," in *A Series of Letters* (London: J. Phillips, 1788), 47.

56. Hess, *The Carolina Rice Kitchen,* 5.

2. ADDING TO MY BREAD AND GREENS

1. Douglas Brent Chambers, "'He Gwine Sing He Country': Africans, Afro-Virginians, and the Development of Slave Culture in Virginia, 1690-1810" (Ph.D. diss., University of Virginia, 1996), 419.

2. Michael A. Gomez, *Exchanging Our Country Marks: The Transformation of African Identity in the Colonial and Antebellum South* (Chapel Hill: The University of North Carolina Press, 1998) 18, 20.

3. Daniel C. Littlefield, *Rice and Slaves: Ethnicity and the Slave Trade in Colonial South Carolina* (Baton Rouge: Louisiana State University Press, 1981), 20-21; Chambers, "'He Gwine Sing He Country,'" 410-412; Gomez, *Exchanging Our Country Marks,* 4.

4. Gomez, *Exchanging Our Country Marks,* 27.

5. Robin Law and Kristin Mann, "West Africa in the Atlantic Community: The Case of the Slave Coast," *William and Mary Quarterly,* 3d ser., 56, no. 2 (April 1999): 312.

6. Eugene D. Genovese, *Roll Jordan Roll: The World the Slaves Made* (1972; reprint, New York: Vintage, 1976), xv-xvii; Alfred W. Crosby, Jr., *The Columbian Exchange: Biological and Cultural Consequences of 1492* (Westport, Conn.: Greenwood, 1973), 66; Sidney W. Mintz, *Tasting Food, Tasting Freedom: Excursions Into Eating, Culture, and the Past* (Boston: Beacon, 1996), 44; Sam Bowers Hilliard, *Hog Meat and Hoecake: Food Supply in the Old South, 1840-1860* (Carbondale: Southern Illinois University Press, 1972); Joe Gray Taylor, *Eating, Drinking, and Visiting in the South: An Informal History* (Baton Rouge: Louisiana State University Press, 1982); Damon Lee Fowler, *Classical Southern Cooking: A Celebration of the Cuisine of the Old South* (New York: Crown, 1995); Helen Mendes, introduction to *The African Heritage Cookbook* (New York: Macmillan, 1971).

7. *Voyage of Don Manoel Gonzales (Late Merchant) of the City of Lisbon in Portugal, to Great Britain, about 1788,* in John Pinkerton, *A General Collection of the Best and Most Interesting Voyages and Travels in all Parts of the World . . .* (London: Longman, Hurst, Ross, Orme and Brown, 1813), 2:86-87, 145.

8. Louis Hughes, *Thirty Years a Slave from Bondage to Freedom: The Institution of Slavery as Seen on the Plantation and in the Home of the Planter* (Milwaukee, Wisc.: South Side Printing, 1897), 49.

9. Ibid., 144-145.

10. The term "parochial food-traditions" comes from Uma Narayan, "Eating Cultures: Incorporation, Identity, and Indian food," *Social Identities* 1, no. 1 (1995): 14.

11. Hughes, *Thirty Years a Slave*, 144-145.

12. *Voyage of Don Manoel Gonzales*, in Pinkerton, *A General Collection*, 2:144-145; Young, *A Tour of Ireland*, in Pinkerton, *A General Collection*, 4:39.

13. Stephen Mennell, *All Manners of Food: Eating and Taste in England and France from the Middle Ages to the Present* (Urbana: University of Illinois Press, 1996), 46; Fernand Braudel, *Capitalism and Material Life, 1400-1800*, trans. Miriam Kochan (New York: Harper and Row, 1973), 124, 125, 128-129; Molly Harrison, *The Kitchen in History* (New York: Scribner's, 1972), 32.

14. John Smith, "Descriptions of Virginia and Proceedings of the Colonie by Captain John Smith, 1612," in *Narratives of Early Virginia 1606-1625*, ed. Lyon Gardiner Tyler, vol. 5 of *Original Narratives of Early American History*, ed. J. Franklin Jameson (New York: Scribner's, 1907), 102; Donna R. Gabaccia, *We Are What We Eat: Food and the Making of Americans*, (Cambridge: Harvard University Press, 1998), 14-15; Harold E. Driver, *Indians of North America*, 2d ed. (1961; reprint, Chicago: University of Chicago Press, 1969), 91, 93; Sophie D. Coe, *America's First Cuisines* (Austin: University of Texas Press, 1994), 36, 133, 149-150, 158.

15. Coe, *America's First Cuisines*, 7-8; Gabaccia, *We Are What We Eat*, 14-15; John Edgerton, *Southern Food: At Home, on the Road, in History* (New York: Knopf, 1987), 248-249; Maryellen Spencer, "Food in Seventeenth-Century Tidewater Virginia: A Method for Studying Historical Cuisines" (Ph.D. diss., Virginia Polytechnic Institute and State University, 1982), 92.

16. Spencer, "Food in Seventeenth-Century Tidewater Virginia," 94-95.

17. Driver, *Indians of North America*, 89-94, 91, 93, 94; Smith, "Descriptions of Virginia," 96-97; Howard H. Peckham, ed., *Narratives of Colonial America, 1704-1765*, Lakeside Classics Series (Chicago: Donnelley and Sons, 1971), 92, 97, 99-101; Arthur Barlowe, "Captain Arthur Barlowe's Narrative of the First Voyage to The Coasts of America," in *Early English and French Voyages Chiefly from Hakluyt, 1534-1608*, ed. Henry S. Burrage, vol. 3 of *Original Narratives of Early American History*, ed. J. Franklin Jameson (New York: Scribner's, 1906), 235-236.

18. Spencer, "Food in Seventeenth-Century Tidewater Virginia," 94-95.

19. Chambers, "'He Gwine Sing,'" 424-425.

20. Alden Vaughn, *America Before the Revolution, 1725-1775* (Englewood Cliffs, New Jersey: Prentice-Hall, 1967), 19-20.

21. Charles Ball, *Slavery in the United States: A Narrative of the Life and Adventures of Charles Ball, a Black Man, Who Lived Forty Years in Maryland, South Carolina and Georgia, as a Slave* ... (Pittsburgh: J.T. Shryock, 1854), 20, 144-145.

22. Ibid., 20, 177, 181,

23. Hughes, *Thirty Years a Slave*, 49.

24. Mendes, *African Heritage Cookbook*, 23.

25. Brenda E. Stevenson, *Life in Black and White: Family and Community in the Slave South* (New York: Oxford University Press, 1996), x.

26. William Byrd, *The London Diary, 1717-1721, and Other Writings*, ed. Louis B. Wright and Marion Tinling (New York: Oxford University Press, 1958), 16-17.

27. Narayan, "Eating Cultures," 14.

28. Genovese, *Roll Jordan Roll*, 541, 543. See Elizabeth Fox-Genovese, *Within the Plantation Household: Black and White Women in the Old South* (Chapel Hill: University of North Carolina Press, 1988), 160-161; Gilberto Freyre, *The Mansions and the Shanties (Sobrados e Mucambos): The Making of Modern Brazil*, trans. and ed. Harriet de Onís (New York: Knopf, 1963), 185-192.

29. Byrd, *The London Diary*, 417-419; Chambers, "'He Gwine Sing,'" 421.

30. Byrd, *The London Diary*, 439, 444, 484-485, 490.

31. Peter H. Wood, *Black Majority: Negroes in Colonial South Carolina from 1670 through the Stono Rebellion* (New York: Norton, 1974), 6-8.

32. Winthrop D. Jordan, *White Over Black: American Attitudes Toward the Negro, 1550-1812* (Baltimore: Penguin, 1969), 47-48.

33. Richard Ligon, *A True and Exact History of the Island of Barbadoes* (London, 1673), reprinted in *After Africa: Extracts from British Travel Accounts and Journals of the Seventeenth, Eighteenth, and Nineteenth Centuries Concerning the Slaves, Their Manners, and Customs in the British West Indies*, ed. Roger D. Abrahams and John F. Szwed, with Leslie Baker and Adrian Stackhouse (New Haven: Yale University Press, 1983), 51-52.

34. James E. McWilliams, *A Revolution in Eating: How the Quest for Food Shaped America,* (New York: Columbia University Press, 2005), 129.

35. Littlefield, *Rice and Slaves*, 20. See Karen Hess, *The Carolina Rice Kitchen: The African Connection* (Columbia: University of South Carolina Press, 1992), 96.

36. Charles Leslie, *A New and Exact Account of Jamaica*, 3d ed. (London, 1740), reprinted in *After Africa*, 329. See John J. Stewart, *Account of Jamaica, and Its Inhabitants: By a Gentleman, a Long Resident in the West Indies* (London: Longman, Hurst, Rees, and Orme, 1808), 231-232.

37. Hilliard, *Hog Meat and Hoecake*, 62.

38. J. B. Moreton, "Manners and Customs in the West India Islands" (London, 1790), reprinted in *After Africa*, 290.

39. F. W. Bayley, *Four Years' Residence in the West Indies*, 3d ed. (London, 1833), 69-71, 437-438, reprinted in *After Africa*, 305.

40. Cynric Williams, *A Tour Through the Island of Jamaica* ... (London, 1826), 21-27, 62-64, reprinted in *After Africa*, 251-252.

41. Hess, *The Carolina Rice Kitchen*, 6.

42. Littlefield, *Rice and Slaves*, 29.

43. [Africanus], "Remarks on the Slave Trade, and the Slavery of the Negroes," in *A Series of Letters* (London: J. Phillips, 1788), 47.

44. Frank J. Klinberg, ed., *The Carolina Chronicle of Dr. Francis Le Jau 1706-1717*, University of California Publications in History, vol. 53, ed. J.S. Galbraith, R.N.

Burr, Brainerd Dyer, and J.C. King (Berkeley: University of California Press, 1956), 7.

45. Karen Hess, *The Carolina Rice Kitchen: The African Connection* (Columbia: University of South Carolina Press, 1992), 7; see also 96.

46. Larry Jean Ancelet, Jay D. Edwards, and Glen Pitre, with additional material by Carl Brasseux, *Cajun Country* (Jackson: University Press of Mississippi, 1991), 141-142.

47. Eliza Lucas Pinckney, *The Letterbook of Eliza Lucas Pinckney, 1739-1762*, ed. Elise Pinckney, with Marvin R. Zahniser (Chapel Hill: University of North Carolina Press, 1972), 28.

48. This interpretation was first suggested by Jessica B. Harris in *Iron Pots and Wooden Spoons: Africa's Gifts to New World Cooking* (New York: Atheneum, 1989), xvi; [Africanus], *Remarks on the Slave Trade*, 47.

49. Jen Schaw, *Journal of a Lady of Quality: Being the Narrative of a Journey from Scotland to the West Indies, North Carolina, and Portugal in the Years 1774 to 1776*, ed. Evangeline Walker Andrews, with Charles McLean Andrews (New Haven: Yale University Press, 1934), 296-297.

50. Littlefield, *Rice and Slaves*, 20-21.

51. Schaw, *Journal of a Lady of Quality*, 177.

52. McWilliams, *A Revolution in Eating*, 129.

53. Ibid.

3. HOG AND HOMINY

1. Eugene D. Genovese, *Roll Jordan Roll: The World the Slaves Made* (1972; reprint, New York: Vintage, 1976), 543.

2. Frederick Law Olmsted, *A Journey in the Seaboard Slave States In the Years 1853-1854* (1856; reprint, New York: Knickerbockers, 1904).

3. Adam Hodgson, *Remarks During a Journey Through North America In the Years 1819, 1820, and 1821 in a Series of Letters* (Westport, Connecticut: Negro Universities Press, 1970, first edition, New York: Seymour, Printer, 1823), 117.

4. Fredrika Bremer, *America of the Fifties: Letters of Fredrika Bremer*, ed. Adolph B. Benson (New York: The American-Scandinavian Foundation, 1924), 107-108.

5. Frederick Law Olmsted, *The Cotton Kingdom: A Traveler's Observations on Cotton and Slavery in the American Slave States. Based Upon Three Former Volumes of Journeys and Investigations by the Same Author*, ed. Arthur M. Schlesinger, Sr. (New York: Modern Library, 1984), 80.

6. Damon Lee Fowler, *Classical Southern Cooking: A Celebration of the Cuisine of the Old South* (New York: Crown, 1995), 140.

7. Olmsted, *A Journey in the Seaboard Slave States*, 143-144.

8. McWilliams, *A Revolution in Eating*, 90.

9. Peter Randolph, "Plantation Churches: Visible and Invisible" (1893), in *Afro-American Religious History: A Documentary Witness*, ed. Milton C. Sernett (Durham, N.C.: Duke University Press, 1985), 67.

10. Albert J. Raboteau, *Slave Religion: The "Invisible Institution" in the Antebellum South* (New York: Oxford University Press, 1978), 177, 219.

11. John Edgerton, *Southern Food: At Home, on the Road, in History* (New York: Knopf, 1987), 37.

12. Raboteau, *Slave Religion*, 212.

13. Bremer, *America of the Fifties*, 114-115.

14. Ibid., 120-123.

15. Raboteau, *Slave Religion*, 224-225.

16. Solomon Northup, *Twelve Years a Slave*, ed. Sue Eakin and Joseph Logsdon (Baton Rouge: Louisiana State University Press, 1968), 163-164; Susan Dabney Smedes, *Memorials of a Southern Planter*, ed. Fletcher M. Green (1887; reprint, New York: Knopf, 1965), 151.

17. Helen Mendes, *The African Heritage Cookbook* (New York: Macmillan, 1971), 60, 72.

18. John W. Blassingame, *The Slave Community: Plantation Life in the Antebellum South*, rev, ed, (New York: Oxford University Press, 1979), 101.

19. Elizabeth Fox-Genovese, *Within the Plantation Household: Black and White Women in the Old South* (Chapel Hill: University of North Carolina Press, 1988), 160-161; Gilberto Freyre, *The Mansions and the Shanties (Sobrados e Mucambos): The Making of Modern Brazil*, trans. and ed. Harriet de Onís (New York: Knopf, 1963), 185-192; Gilberto Freyre, *The Masters and the Slaves (Casa-grande & senzala): A Study in the Development of Brazilian Civilization*, trans. Samuel Putnam (New York: Knopf, 1956), 128-129; Genovese, *Roll Jordan Roll*, 541, 543; Matthew Gregory Lewis, *Journal of a West India Proprietor, 1815-1817*, ed. Mona Wilson (London: George Routledge, 1929), 92, 196-197; John Stewart, *A View of the Past and Present State of the Island of Jamaica; with Remarks on the Moral and Physical Condition of the slaves, and on the Abolition of Slavery in the Colonies.* (New York, Negro Universities Press, 1969 [first edition, 1823]), 268; Richard Robert Madden, *A Twelve Month's Residence in the West Indies, During the Transition from Slavery to Apprenticeship: With Incidental Notices of the State of Society, Prospects, and Natural Resources of Jamaica and Other Islands* (Philadelphia: Carey, Lea and Blanchard, 1835; reprint, West Port, Conn.: Negro Universities Press, 1970), 70.

20. Genovese, *Roll Jordan Roll*, xvi, xvii.

21. Olmsted, *The Cotton Kingdom*, 71; see Olmsted, *A Journey in the Seaboard Slave States*, 112.

22. Henry Louis Gates, Jr., ed., *The Classic Slave Narratives* (New York: Penguin, 1987), 299-300.

23. Olmsted, *The Cotton Kingdom*, 71.

24. Genovese, *Roll Jordan Roll*, 549; see 543.

25. Olmsted, *A Journey in the Seaboard Slave States*, 143.

26. Adèle Toussaint-Samson, *A Parisian in Brazil: A Travel Account of a Frenchwoman in Nineteenth-Century Rio De Janeiro*, ed. Emma Toussaint (Wilmington, Del.: Scholarly Resources, 2001), 30; Margarette Sheehan de Andrade, *Brazil-*

ian Cookery: Traditional and Modern (Rio de Janeiro: A Casa Do Livro Eldorado, 1978), 54, 62-63.

27. Richard Henry Dana, *To Cuba and Back*, ed. C. Harvey Gardiner (Carbondale: Southern Illinois University Press, 1966), 51, 69; James W. Steele, *Cuban Sketches* (New York: Putnam's, 1881), 191-193.

28. Olmsted, *A Journey in the Seaboard Slave States*, 208-209.

29. Ibid., 209.

30. Abraham Oakey Hall, *The Manhattaner in New Orleans; or, Phases of "Crescent City" Life* (New York: J. S. Redfield, 1851), 10.

31. Vera Kelsey, *Brazil in Capitals* (New York: Harper, 1942), 76; Andrade, *Brazilian Cookery*, 50, 56; Toussaint-Samson, *A Parisian in Brazil*, 30; Maria Graham, *Journal of a Voyage to Brazil, and the Residence There, During Part of the Years 1821, 1822, 1823* (London: Longman, Hurst, Rees, Orme, Brown, and Green, 1824; reprint, New York: Praeger, 1969), 113, 122; *Nieuhoff's Brazil* (1813) in John Pinkerton, *A General Collection of the Best and Most Interesting Voyages and Travels in all Parts of the World* . . . (London: Longman, Hurst, Ross, Orme and Brown, 1813), 14:868.

32. Karen Hess, *The Carolina Rice Kitchen: The African Connection* (Columbia: University of South Carolina Press, 1992), 103-104; Toussaint-Samson, *A Parisian in Brazil*, 30; John Mawe, *John Mawe's Journey into the Interior of Brazil* (1809), reprinted in *Colonial Travelers in Latin America*, ed. Irving A. Leonard (New York: Knopf, 1972), 212; *Nieuhoff's Brazil*, 14:868; James C. Fletcher and D. P. Kidder, *Brazil and the Brazilians Portrayed in Historical and Descriptive Sketches* (Boston: Little Brown, and Company: London: Sampson, Low, Son, & Co, 1866), 125; Theodore Canot, *Captain Canot; or, Twenty Years of an African Slaver: Being an Account of His Career and Adventures on the Coast, in the Interior, on Shipboard, and in the West Indies, Written out and edited from the Captain's Journals, Memoranda and Conversations* (New York: D. Appleton, 1854), 33, 38.

33. Louis Agassiz and Elizabeth Agassiz, *A Journey in Brazil* (Boston: Ticknor and Fields, 1868; reprint, New York: Praeger, 1969), 73. See Toussaint-Samson, *A Parisian in Brazil*, 55, 80; Graham, *Journal of a Voyage to Brazil*, 166, 280.

34. Olmsted, *A Journey in the Seaboard Slave States*, 143-144; Hilliard, *Hog Meat and Hoecake*, 43, 47, 55; Genovese, Roll Jordan Roll, 543, 548-549; Mendes, *The African heritage Cookbook*, 67, 69;

35. Ira Berlin, Joseph P. Reidy, and Leslie S. Rowland, eds., *Freedom's Soldiers: The Black Military Experience in the Civil War* (Cambridge: Cambridge University Press, 1998), 89; see 2-3. See also Edwin S. Redkey, ed., *A Grand Army of Black Men: Letters from African-American Soldiers in the Union Army, 1861-1865* (Cambridge: Cambridge University Press, 1992), 260-261.

36. Samuel H. Sprott, *Cush: A Civil War Memoir*, ed. Louis R. Smith, Jr., and Andrew Quist (Livingston: University of West Alabama, Livingston Press, 1999), 124; Alex Haley, *Roots* (Garden City, N.Y.: Doubleday, 1976), 534.

37. Berlin, Reidy, and Rowland, *Freedom's Soldiers*, 36.

38. Wiley, *The Life of Johnny Reb*, 104-105; Sprott, *Cush*, 16, 114; Haley, *Roots*, 542, 547.

39. Lee, J. Edward Lee and Ron Chepesiuk, eds., *South Carolina in the Civil War: The Confederate Experience in Letters and Diaries* (Jefferson, N.C.: McFarland, 2000), 89-91, 141; Bell Irvin Wiley, *The Life of Johnny Reb: The Common Soldier of the Confederacy*, (Garden City, N.Y.: Doubleday, 1971), 101, 103.

40. Harvey A. Levenstein, *Revolution at the Table: The Transformation of the American Diet* (New York: Oxford University Press, 1988), 27. See Eliza McHatton-Ripley, *From Flag to Flag; a Woman's Adventures and Experiences in the South During the War, in Mexico, and in Cuba* (New York, D. Appleton, 1889), 247-248.

41. Samuel H. Lockett, *Louisiana as It Is: A Geographical and Topographical Description of the State* (Baton Rouge: Louisiana State University Press, 1969), 48.

42. Wilbur O. Atwater and Charles D. Woods, *Dietary Studies with Reference to the Food of the Negro in Alabama in 1895 and 1896*, U.S. Department of Agriculture, Office of Experiment Stations, bulletin no. 38 (Washington, D.C.: U.S. Government Printing Office, 1897), 7.

43. Emma Speed Sampson, *Miss Minerva's Cook Book. De Way to a Man's Heart* (Chicago, 1931), 99.

44. Ibid.

45. Ibid., 268. See Atwater and Woods, *Dietary Studies*, 11.

46. Margaret Cussler and Mary L. de Give, *'Twixt the Cup and the Lip: Psychological and Socio-Cultural Factors Affecting Food Habits* (Washington, D.C.: Consortium, 1952), 248-249.

47. Joyce White, *Soul Food: Recipes and Reflections from African-American Churches* (New York: HarperCollins, 1998), 252.

48. Atwater and Woods, *Dietary Studies*, 19 (see also 16-17); H.D. Frissel and Isabel Bevier, *Dietary Studies of Negroes in Eastern Virginia in 1897 and 1898*, U.S. Department of Agriculture, Office of Experiment Stations, bulletin no. 71, (Washington, D.C.: Government Printing Office, 1899), 8.

49. Atwater and Woods, *Dietary Studies*, 20, 26; Sampson, *Miss Minerva's Cook Book*, 33.

50. Bennett Marshall and Gertha Couric, "Alabama Barbecue," p. 1-3, WPA State Records, "America Eats" Collection, Alabama, Box A 18, file entitled "Alabama Cuisine."

51. Frissel and Bevier, *Dietary Studies of Negroes in Eastern Virginia*, 8, 11.

52. Atwater and Woods, *Dietary Studies*, 20.

53. John Smith, "Descriptions of Virginia and Proceedings of the Colonie by Captain John Smith, 1612," in *Narratives of Early Virginia 1606-1625*, ed. Lyon Gardiner Tyler, vol. 5 of *Original Narratives of Early American History*, ed. J. Franklin Jameson (New York: Scribner's, 1907), 96-97; Northup, *Twelve Years a Slave*, 128; Fletcher Douglas Srygley, *Seventy Years in Dixie: Recollections and Sayings of T.W. Caskey and Others* (Nashville, Tenn.: Gospel Advocate, 1893), 86.

54. Atwater and Woods, *Dietary Studies*, 21.

55. Wendell B. Brooks Phillips, "Hog Killing," p. 1, box A 397, file, South Carolina Cuisine, WPA State Records Related, "America Eats" Collection; Atwater and Woods, *Dietary Studies*, 21.

56. Atwater and Woods, *Dietary Studies*, 64; Frissel and Bevier, *Dietary Studies of Negroes in Eastern Virginia*, 40; A.L.Tommie Bass, *Plain Southern Eating from the Reminiscences of A.L. Tommie Bass, Herbalist*, ed. John K. Crellin (Durham, N.C.: Duke University Press, 1988), 66.

57. Karen Iacobbo and Michael Iacobbo, *Vegetarian America: A History* (Westport, Conn.: Praeger, 2004); Colin Spencer, *Heretic's Feast: A History of Vegetarianism* (Hanover, N.H.: University Press of New England, 1996).

58. Joe Gray Taylor, *Eating, Drinking, and Visiting in the South: An Informal History* (Baton Rouge: Louisiana State University Press, 1982), 47-48, 109.

59. Floris Barnett Cash, *African American Women and Social Action: The Clubwomen and Volunteerism from Jim Crow to the New Deal, 1896-1936* (Westport, Conn.: Greenwood, 2001), 67-72; Cynthia Neverdon-Morton, "Self-Help Programs as Educative Activities of Black Women in the South, 1895-1925: Focus on Four Key Areas," *Journal of Negro Education* 51, no. 3 (Summer 1982): 210-216; Gerda Lerner, "Early Community Work of Black Club Women," *Journal of Negro History* 59, no. 2 (April 1974): 159-160.

60. Jacqueline Anne Rouse, "Out of the Shadow of Tuskegee: Margaret Murray Washington, Social Activism, and Race Vindication," *Journal of Negro History* 81, no. 1/4 (Winter-Autumn 1996): 35-37; Deborah Gray White, *Too Heavy a Load: Black Women in Defense of Themselves, 1894-1994* (New York: Norton, 1999), 24-30.

61. Rouse, "Out of the Shadow of Tuskegee," 33; Anne Firor Scott, "The Most Invisible of Them All: Black Women's Voluntary Associations," *Journal of Southern History* 56, no. 1 (February 1990): 16-22.

62. Rouse, "Out of the Shadow of Tuskegee," 34, 41-43.

63. *The Booker T. Washington papers*, vol. 5, *1899-1900*, ed. Louis R. Harlan, Raymond W. Smock, and Barbara S. Kraft (Urbana: University of Illinois Press, 1976), 270.

64. *The Booker T. Washington Papers*, vol. 4, *1895-98*, ed. Louis R. Harlan, Stuart B. Kaufman, Barbara S. Kraft, and Raymond W. Smock (Urbana: University of Illinois Press, 1975), 64.

65. James Weldon Johnson, *Along This Way: The Autobiography of James Weldon Johnson* (New York: Viking, 1933), 107-109.

66. Clifton Johnson, *Highways and Byways of the South* (New York: Macmillan, 1904), 46. See Srygley, *Seventy Years in Dixie*, 330-331; Johnson, *Along This Way*, 76-77, 330-331.

67. Johnson, *Along This Way*, 33, 54, 64-65.

68. Ibid., 54.

69. Taylor, *Eating, Drinking, and Visiting in the South*, 116-117.

70. Ibid., 117-118.

71. This concept is gleaned from David D. Hall, ed., *Lived Religion in America: Toward a History of Practice* (Princeton, N.J.: Princeton University Press, 1997).

72. For an overview of themes in African American religious history, see Timothy F. Fulop and Albert J. Raboteau, eds., *African-American Religion: Interpretive Essays in History and Culture* (New York: Routledge, 1997).

73. Atwater and Woods, *Dietary Studies*, 18.

74. W. E.B. Du Bois, *W.E.B. Du Bois, Writings: The Suppression of the African Slave-Trade, The Souls of Black Folk, Dusk of Dawn, Essays and Articles* (New York: Library of America, 1986), 496.

75. Michael Perman, *Struggle for Mastery: Disfranchisement in the South, 1888-1908*, (Chapel Hill: University of North Carolina Press, 2001), 244-247, 269; Jane Dailey, Glenda Elizabeth Gilmore, and Bryant Simon, eds., *Jumpin' Jim Crow: Southern Politics from Civil War to Civil Rights* (Princeton, N.J.: Princeton University Press, 2000), 3-4.

76. Ernest Von Hesse-Wartegg, *Travels on the Lower Mississippi, 1879-1880: A Memoir by Ernest Von Hesse-Wartegy*, trans. and ed. Frederic Trautman (Columbia: University of Missouri Press, 1990), 99.

77. *Weekly Louisianian* (New Orleans), January 8, 1881.

78. Race riots started in Atlanta, Georgia, in 1906; East St. Louis in May 1917; Houston, Texas, in August 1917; South Carolina on May 10, 1919; Longview, Texas, on July 11, 1919; Washington, D.C., on July 20, 1919; Chicago on July 27, 1919; Knoxville, Tennessee, on August 30, 1919; Omaha, Nebraska, on September 28, 1919; Elaine, Arkansas, on October 1, 1919; and Tulsa, Oklahoma, on May 1921. See Robert V. Haynes, *A Night of Violence: The Houston Riot of 1917* (Baton Rouge: Louisiana State University Press, 1976), 18-19; Lee E. Williams and Lee E. Williams II, *Anatomy of Four Race Riots: Racial Conflict in Knoxville, Elaine (Arkansas), Tulsa, and Chicago, 1919-1921* (Hattiesburg: University and College Press of Mississippi, 1972), 4; Elliott M. Rudwick, *Race Riot at East St. Louis, July 2, 1917* (Carbondale: Southern Illinois University Press, 1964), 4; Stephen A. Gura, "The Limits of Mob Law: The Elaine Race Riot of 1919" (honor thesis., Emory University, 1983), 31-32; Scott Ellsworth, *Death in a Promised Land: The Tulsa Race Riot of 1921* (Baton Rouge: Louisiana State University Press, 1982), 89.

79. Rudwick, *Race Riot*, 210-213, 221; Williams and Williams, *Anatomy of Four Race Riots*, 6-7.

80. *Topeka Plain* (Kansas), July 29, 1921, Tuskegee Institute News Clippings File, p. 0369 R 14.

4. THE GREAT MIGRATION

1. R. H. Leavell, T.R. Snavely, T.J. Woofter, Jr., W.T.B. Williams, and Francis D. Tyson, *Negro Migration in 1916-17* (Washington, D.C.: Government Printing Office, 1919), 27, 58-61, 78-79, 115.

2. Leavell et al., *Negro Migration in 1916-17*, 87, 104-105; Michael Perman, *Struggle for Mastery: Disfranchisement in the South, 1888-1908* (Chapel Hill: University of North Carolina Press, 2001), 269.

3. Leavell et al., *Negro Migration in 1916-17*, 101, 105, 107, 28-31. On the Great Migration in general, see Carole Marks, *Farewell—We're Good and Gone: The Great Black Migration* (Bloomington: Indiana University Press, 1989). On the migration to Chicago, see James Grossman, *Land of Hope: Chicago, Black Southerners, and the Great Migration* (Chicago: University of Chicago Press, 1989). On Westchester County, see Andrew Wiese, *Places of Their Own: African American Suburbanization in the Twentieth Century* (Chicago: University of Chicago Press, 2004), chap. 2. On Harlem, see Gilbert Osofsky, *Harlem: The Making of a Ghetto. Negro New York, 1890-1930* (New York: Harper Torchbooks, 1964). On Cleveland, see Kenneth L. Kusmer, *A Ghetto Takes Shape: Black Cleveland, 1870-1930* (Urbana: University of Illinois Press, 1976).

4. For more on the Harlem Renaissance, see Anne Elizabeth Carroll, *Word, Image, and the New Negro: Representation and Identity in the Harlem Renaissance* (Bloomington: Indiana University Press, 2005).

5. Sheila Ferguson, *Soul Food: Classic Cuisine From the Deep South* (New York: Grove Press, 1989), xiii-xiv; Langston Hughes, *The Langston Hughes Reader* (New York: Braziller, w31958), 368-371.

6. The term "freedom belt" comes from Gene Baro, "Soul Food," *Vogue* 155 (March 1970), 80.

7. James Weldon Johnson, *Along This Way: The Autobiography of James Weldon Johnson* (New York: Viking, 1933), 64-65. See Leavell et al., *Negro Migration*, 28; Louis Armstrong, *Satchmo: My Life in New Orleans* (New York: Da Capo, 1986), 189; Maya Angelou, *I Know Why the Caged Bird Sings* (1969; reprint, New York: Bantam, 1970), 4.

8. Angelou, *I Know Why the Caged Bird Sings*, 4.

9. Alexander Smalls, *Grace the Table: Stories and Recipes from My Southern Revival*, with Hattie Jones (New York: HarperCollins, 1997), 16-17.

10. Adam Clayton Powell, Jr., *Adam by Adam: The Autobiography of Adam Clayton Powell, Jr.* (New York: Dial, 1971), 1-8.

11. Ibid., 17-18.

12. Ibid., 16.

13. Ferguson, *Soul Food*, xxi-xxvi.

14. Smalls, *Grace the Table*, 18-20, 65-66; Joyce White, *Soul Food: Recipes and Reflections from African-American Churches* (New York: HarperCollins, 1998), 149.

15. St. Clair Drake and Horace R. Cayton, *Black Metropolis: A Study of Negro Life in a Northern City* (1945; reprint, Chicago: University of Chicago Press, 1993); Tracy N. Poe, "The Origins of Soul Food in Black Urban Identity: Chicago, 1915-1947," *American Studies International* 37, no. 1 (February 1999): 5-7.

16. Drake and Cayton, *Black Metropolis*, 608.

17. Ibid., 547.

18. Ibid., 578–579.
19. A. D.A. Moser, "Farm Family Diets in the Lower Coastal Plains of South Carolina," South Carolina Agricultural Experiment Station, Clemson Agricultural College, bulletin no. 319, June 1939; idem, "Food Habits of South Carolina Farm Families," South Carolina Agricultural Experiment Station, Clemson Agricultural College, bulletin no. 343, November 1942.
20. Moser, "Food Habits of South Carolina Farm Families," 25.
21. Moser, "Farm Family Diets in the Lower Coastal Plains of South Carolina," 42–44.
22. Dorothy Dickins, "A Nutrition Investigation of Negro Tenants in the Yazoo Mississippi Delta," Mississippi Agricultural Experiment Station, A & M College, bulletin no. 254, August 1928, 33.
23. Moser, "Farm Family Diets in the Lower Coastal Plains of South Carolina," 42–44.
24. Moser, "Lower Coastal Plains of South Carolina Farm Families," 44–45.
25. Moser, "Lower Coastal Plains of South Carolina Farm Families," 45.
26. Ibid., 42–45.
27. Dickins, "A Nutrition Investigation of Negro Tenants," 35.
28. Ibid., 45–47.
29. For more on Caribbean migration to New York, see Frederick Douglass Opie, "Eating, Dancing, and Courting in New York: Black and Latino Relations, 1930–1970," *Journal of Social History* (forthcoming).
30. Harvey Brett, "Report on Cuban Population in N.Y.C.," November 25, 1935, p. 3 (see also pp. 1, 4), "Feeding the City Project Collection," WPA Papers, New York City Municipal Archives, New York, N.Y. (hereafter FCWPA), roll 269; Strong, "Puerto Rican Colony in N.Y.," 1935(?), p. 2, FCWPA, roll 269.
31. Jose Pastrana, "Fuentes Restaurant 1326 Fifth Avenue," December 10, 1940, pp. 1–2, "Eating Out in Foreign Restaurants," FCWPA, roll 144.
32. Ibid., 3; "Central American, Spanish American," p. 11, "Eating Out in Foreign Restaurants," FCWPA, roll 153.
33. Jose Pastrana, "El Favorito Restaurant," pp. 1–2, FCWPA, roll 269.
34. Ibid., 2–4; Strong, "Puerto Rican Colony in N.Y.," pp. 3–4.
35. "Street Vendors," pp. 7–9, FCWPA, roll 153.
36. Sarah Chavez, "Harlem Restaurants," September 26, 1940, p. 2, FCWPA, roll 144.
37. Wiese, *Places of Their Own*, 26.
38. Margaret B. (Cooper) Opie, interview, summer 2005; Katie (White) Green, interview, summer 2005.
39. Green, interview.
40. Ella (Christopher) Barnett, interview, summer 2005.
41. Ibid.
42. Ibid.
43. Ibid.; Opie family bible, consulted in Cloverdale, Virginia.

44. 1930 federal census of the village of North Tarrytown.

45. Fred Opie, Jr., interview, summer 2005.

46. Ibid.

47. Dorothy Opie, interview, summer 2005.

48. Fred Opie, Jr., interview.

49. Barnett, interview.

50. For more on African-American migration to Harlem, see Osofsky, *Harlem*.

51. Nora White, interview, summer 2005.

52. Verta Mae Smart-Grosvenor, "Soul Food," *McCall's* 97 (September 1970): 72.

53. Pearl Bowser and Joan Eckstein, *A Pinch of Soul in Book Form* (New York: Avon, 1969), 13.

54. Smalls, *Grace the Table*, 6, 18–20.

55. Bowser and Eckstein, *A Pinch of Soul in Book Form*, 190.

56. Ibid., 13, 154.

57. Nettie C. Banks, interview, summer 2005.

58. Green, interview.

59. White, interview.

60. A.L. Tommie Bass, *Plain Southern Eating from the Reminiscences of A.L. Tommie Bass, Herbalist*, ed. John K. Crellin (Durham, N.C.: Duke University Press, 1988), 79–80; White, *Soul Food*, 297–298.

61. Ruth and Roy Miller, interview, 2005.

62. Clara Bullard Pittman, interview, summer 2005.

63. Outlaw, interview.

64. White, interview.

65. Yemaja Jubilee, interview, summer 2005

66. Banks, interview.

67. Reginald T. Ward, interview, summer 2005.

68. White, *Soul Food*, 293.

69. Stephen Erwin, "Collards," November 14, 1984, box 1, Autobiographical Writings, Rare Book, Manuscript, and Special Collections Library Duke University.

70. White, *Soul Food*, 293.

71. Ibid., 273.

72. Drake and Cayton, *Black Metropolis*, 613.

73. Ibid., 381.

74. Ibid., 418.

75. Ibid., 423.

76. Frances Warren and Jim Warren, interview, summer 2005.

77. Ward, interview.

78. Ibid.

79. Warren and Warren, interview.

80. Jubilee, interview.

81. This interpretation was first suggested by Jessica B. Harris in *Iron Pots and Wooden Spoons: Africa's Gifts to New World Cooking* (New York: Atheneum, 1989),

xvi; the dab-a-dab dish is mentioned on p. 47 of [Africanus, pseudo.], "Remarks on the Slave Trader, and the Slavery of the Negroes," in *A Series of Letters* (London: J. Phillips, 1788).

82. Lamenta Diane (Watkins) Crouch, interview, summer 2005.

83. Outlaw, interview.

84. White, *Soul Food*, 1–3.

85. Marcellas C.D. Barksdale, interview, summer 2005.

86. Mary A. Poole, "Alabama Deep Sea Fishing Rodeo," November 5, 1937, p. 1, box A 13, file Alabama Cities and Towns, Mobile Cuisine, Work Project Administration (State Records), Manuscript Division, Library of Congress, Washington, D.C. (hereafter WPA SR).

87. White, *Soul Food*, 1–3.

88. Ibid.

89. Smalls, *Grace the Table*, 73.

90. Banks, interview.

91. Gracilla, "Barboursville, Virginia," August 18, 1941, p. 1, box A 829 file, WPA SR.

5. THE BEANS AND GREENS OF NECESSITY

1. Theodore Kornweibel, Jr., "An Economic Profile of Black Life in the Twenties," *Journal of Black Studies* 6, no. 4. (June 1976): 311–313; William A. Sundstrom, "Last Hired, First Fired? Unemployment and Urban Black Workers During the Great Depression," *Journal of Economic History* 52, no. 2 (June 1992): 420–422.

2. St. Clair Drake and Horace R. Cayton, *Black Metropolis: A Study of Negro Life in a Northern City* (1945; reprint, Chicago: University of Chicago Press, 1993), 293–295.

3. Sundstrom, "Last Hired, First Fired," 417–418.

4. "Unemployed men in front of Al Capone's Soup Kitchen [Chicago]," February 1931, RG 306-N, Records of the United States Information Agency, box 677, file 1, U.S. National Archives II, College Park, Md.

5. Lorena Hickok quoted Malcolm J. Miller in a letter to Harry L. Hopkins (Federal Civil Works administrator), Athens, Ga., January 11, 1934, Georgia Field Reports, p. 4, Papers of Harry L. Hopkins, Franklin D. Roosevelt Presidential Library, Hyde Park, N.Y.; Hickok to Hopkins, Moultrie, Ga., January 23, 1934, Georgia Field Reports, Papers of Harry L. Hopkins, p. 4.

6. "Food Crisis in Cleveland," photo and caption, May 5, 1938, RG 306-N, Records of the United States Information Agency, box 677, file 1, 306-NT-677-2, National Archives II, College Park, Md.

7. Nina Simone, *The Autobiography of Nina Simone: I Put A Spell On You*, with Stephen Cleary (New York: Da Capo, 1993), 5, 6.

8. Hickok to Hopkins, Columbia, S.C., February 5, 1934, Florida Field Reports, pp. 4–5, Papers of Harry L. Hopkins.

9. Simone, *Autobiography*, 6.

10. Joe Gray Taylor, *Eating, Drinking, and Visiting in the South: An Informal History* (Baton Rouge: Louisiana State University Press, 1982), 142.

11. Hickok to Hopkins, Georgia, January 16, 1934, Georgia Field Reports, pp. 7–8, Papers of Harry L. Hopkins.

12. Nora (Burns) White, interview, summer 2005.

13. Ibid.

14. Ibid.

15. Frances Warren and Jim Warren, interview, summer 2005.

16. Simone, *Autobiography*, 8–9.

17. Ralph David Abernathy, *And the Walls Came Tumbling Down: An Autobiography* (New York: Harper and Row, 1989), 6; see also 8.

18. Ibid., 6; see also 12, 25–26.

19. Maya Angelou, *I Know Why the Caged Bird Sings* (1969; reprint, New York: Bantam, 1970), 19–20.

20. Ruth Miller, Roy Miller, and Rudolf Bradshaw, interview, summer 2005.

21. Cheryl Lynn Greenberg, *Or Does It Explode? Black Harlem in the Great Depression* (New York: Oxford University Press, 1991).

22. Langston Hughes, *The Langston Hughes Reader* (New York: Braziller, 1958), 372.

23. Ibid., 373.

24. Sheila Ferguson, *Soul Food: Classic Cuisine from the Deep South* (New York: Grove, 1989), xv.

25. Robert Weisbrot, *Father Divine: The Utopian Evangelist of the Depression Era Who Became an American Legend* (Boston: Beacon, 1983), 37–40.

26. Ibid., 9.

27. Carleton Maybee, interview, summer 2005.

28. Weisbrot, *Father Divine*, 11–12, 34–38, 40.

29. Miller, Miller, and Bradshaw, interview; and Dorothy M. Evelyn, interview, summer 2005.

30. Miller, Miller, and Bradshaw, interview.

31. Maybee, interview.

32. Miller, Miller, and Bradshaw, interview.

33. Ibid.

34. Evelyn, interview.

35. Ibid.

36. Ibid.

37. Fred Opie, Jr., and Dorothy Opie, interviews, summer 2005.

38. Margaret B. (Cooper) Opie, interview, summer 2005.

39. Ibid.; Katie Green (White), interview, summer 2005.

40. Margaret Opie, interview.

41. Psyche A. Williams-Forson, *Building Houses Out of Chicken Legs: Black Women, Food, and Power* (Chapel Hill: University of North Carolina Press, 2006), 145.

42. For an in-depth discussion of African Americans and chicken, see Williams-Forson's *Building Houses Out of Chicken Legs*

43. Gracilla, "Barboursville, Virginia," August 18, 1941, p. 1, box A 829 file, WPA SR," 1.

44. Nettie C. Banks, interview, summer 2005.

45. Yemaja Jubilee, interview, summer 2005.

46. Benjamin Outlaw, interview, summer 2005.

47. Joan B. Lewis, interview, summer 2005.

48. Stephen Erwin, "[Southern] Food," November 8, 1984, box 1, Autobiographical Writings: 1974-1990, Stephen Erwin Collection, Rare Book, Manuscript, and Special Collections Library, Duke University, Durham, N.C.

49. Abernathy, *And the Walls Came Tumbling Down*, 25-26.

50. Ibid., 25.

51. Joyce White, *Soul Food: Recipes and Reflections from African-American Churches* (New York: HarperCollins, 1998), 104.

52. The name of the town is in question.

53. Lamenta Diane (Watkins) Crouch, interview, summer 2005.

54. Alexander Smalls, *Grace the Table: Stories and Recipes from My Southern Revival*, with Hattie Jones (New York: HarperCollins, 1997), 3.

55. Nora White, interview.

56. Beryl Ellington, interview, summer 2005.

6. EATING JIM CROW

1. Robin D.G. Kelley, "'We Are Not What We Seem': Rethinking Black Working-Class Opposition in the Jim Crow South," in *The New African American Urban History*, ed. Kenneth W. Goings and Raymond A. Mohl (Thousand Oaks, Calif.: Sage, 1996), 192-197.

2. For more on jim crow, see Mark M. Smith, *How Race Is Made: Slavery, Segregation, and the Senses* (Chapel Hill: University of North Carolina Press, 2006); R. Douglas Hurt, ed., *African American Life in the Rural South, 1900-1950* (Columbia: University of Missouri Press, 2003); Leon F. Litwack, *Trouble in Mind: Black Southerners in the Age of Jim Crow* (New York: Knopf, 1998).

3. Eugene Watts, interview, summer 2005. This chapter is modeled after studies on black community formation such as Joe W. Trotter, Jr., *Black Milwaukee: The Making of an Industrial Proletariat, 1915-45* (Urbana: University of Illinois Press, 1985); and Kenneth L. Kusmer, *A Ghetto Takes Shape: Black Cleveland, 1870-1930* (Urbana: University of Illinois Press, 1976).

4. Joseph "Mac" Johnson, interview, summer 2005.

5. Diana Ross, *Secrets of a Sparrow: Memoirs* (New York: Villard, 1993), 82.

6. Joseph Johnson, interview.

7. Watts, interview.

8. Litwack, *Trouble in Mind*. Evelyn Brooks Higginbotham talks about the politics of respectability in *Righteous Discontent: The Women's Movement in the Black Baptist Church, 1880-1920* (Cambridge, MA: Harvard University Press, 1993).9.

James C. Scott, *Weapons of the Weak: Everyday Forms of Peasant Resistance* (New Haven, Conn.: Yale University Press, 1985); idem, *Domination and the Arts of Resistance: The Hidden Transcripts* (New Haven, Conn.: Yale University Press, 1990).

10. Kelley, "'We Are Not What We Seem,'" 190-191.

11. Lamenta Diane (Watkins) Crouch, interview, summer 2005; Reginald T. Ward, interview, summer 2005.

12. Margaret B. (Cooper) Opie, interview, summer 2005; Alice N. Conqueran, interview, summer 2005; and Joan B. Lewis, interview, summer 2005.

13. Lewis, interview.

14. Dr. Rodney Ellis, interview, summer 2005; Lewis, interview.

15. On the geography of Richmond's African-American business community and neighborhoods, see Elsa Barkley Brown and Gregg D. Kimball, "Mapping the Terrain of Black Richmond," in *The New African American Urban History*, ed. Kenneth W. Goings and Raymond A. Mohl (Thousand Oaks, Calif.: Sage, 1996).

16. Yemaja Jubilee, interview, summer 2005.

17. Andrew Wiese, *Places of Their Own: African American Suburbanization in the Twentieth Century* (Chicago: University of Chicago Press, 2004), 26-27. Langston Hughes uses the "Bottoms" to designate an African American community in his novel *Not Without Laughter* (1969; reprint, New York: Touchstone, 1995).

18. For more on black migration to and settlement in Cleveland, see Kusmer, *A Ghetto Takes Shape*; and Wiese, *Places of Their Own*, 70-90.

19. "Eugene 'Hot Sauce' Williams, Barbecue Operator of Cleveland, Ohio," *Ebony*, March 1950, 37-40.

20. Ibid., 37-38.

21. Joseph Johnson, interview.

22. Watts, interview; Betty Joyce Johnson, interview, summer 2005.

23. Betty Johnson, interview. See William H. Chafe, *Civilities and Civil Rights: Greensboro, North Carolina, and the Black Struggle for Freedom* (New York: Oxford University Press, 1981), 109-120.

24. Lewis, interview.

25. Sadie B. Hornsby, revised by Sarah H. Hall, "The Barbecue Stand," Georgia Folder, 2301A-2318, pp. 5-7, 3709, Federal Writers Project (WPA) Papers, University of North Carolina, Chapel Hill, Manuscript Department.

26. Ibid., 8-9.

27. Bennett Marshall and Gertha Couric, "Alabama Barbecue," pp. 1-3, U.S. Work Project Administration (State Records), Alabama, box A 18, file "Alabama Cuisine," 2, Library of Congress, Manuscript Division, Washington, D.C. See "Monroe, Louisiana Barbecue," p. 8, U.S. Work Project Administration (State Records), Louisiana, box A 160, file "Cuisine."

28. Hornsby, "The Barbecue Stand," 8-9.

29. Ibid., 9-11, 15.

30. Ibid., 12, 14, 15-16.

31. On the history of black Georgia and the southwest Atlanta area in particular, see John Dittmer, *Black Georgia in the Progressive Era, 1900-1920* (Urbana: University of Illinois Press, 1977); and Wiese, *Places of Their Own*, 174-196.

32. Stanlie M. James, interview, summer 2005.

33. Marcellas C. D. Barksdale, interview, summer 2005.

34. James, interview.

35. Alton Hornsby Jr., interview, summer 2005.

36. James, interview.

37. Ralph David Abernathy, *And the Walls Came Tumbling Down: An Autobiography* (New York: Harper and Row, 1989), 64-67.

38. Ibid., 64, 65, 67.

39. Crouch, interview.

40. Neely, interview.

41. Crouch, interview.

42. Neely, interview.

43. Crouch, interview.

44. Ross, *Secrets of a Sparrow*, 83.

45. Segregation and the desegregation of restaurants in New York are documented in Martha Biondi's *To Stand and Fight: The Struggle for Civil Rights in Postwar New York City* (Cambridge: Harvard University Press, 2003), 36-37, 79-82, 85, 89-90.

46. Sarah Chavez, "Harlem Restaurants," October 2, 1940, two different drafts available, FCWPA, roll 144.

47. Burton W. Peretti, *Jazz in American Culture* (Chicago: Dee, 1997), 126-136.

48. Carmen John Leggio, interview, summer 2005.

49. Rudolph Bradshaw, in Ruth Miller, Roy Miller, and Rudolf Bradshaw, interview, summer 2005.

50. Sarah Chavez, "Southern Cooking," p. 7, FCWPA, roll 153; idem, "Harlem Restaurants," September 26, 1940, p. 3, FCWPA, roll 144.

51. Sarah Chavez, "Harlem Restaurants," September 27, 1940, FCWPA, roll 144.

52. Irving Ripps "Specials Today—and Everyday," September 17, 1940, p. 10, FCWPA, roll 144; Macdougall, "Poor Men's Fare," p. 11, FCWPA, roll 153.

53. Evelyn Gonzalez, *The Bronx* (New York: Columbia University Press, 2004), 109-110.

54. Mark Naison and Maxine Gordon, interview with Kwame Brathwaite, May 17, 2002, pp. 2, 3, 6, 7, Bronx African American History Project, Bronx County Historical Society Archive Collection, Bronx, N.Y. (hereafter BAAHP).

55. Mark Naison, interview with Frank Belton, n.d. (ca. 2006), pp. 4-5, BAAHP.

56. Mark Naison, interview with Nathan "Bubba" Dukes, n.d. (ca. 2006), p. 1, BAAHP.

57. Paul Gilroy, *"There Ain't No Black in the Union Jack": The Cultural Politics of Race and Nation* (Chicago: University of Chicago Press, 1991), 158.

58. For more on black neighborhoods in Westchester, see Wiese, *Places of Their Own.*

59. Conqueran, interview, summer 2005.

60. Ibid.

61. Ibid.

62. Margaret Opie, interview.

63. Conqueran, interview, summer 2005; Christopher Boswell, interview, summer 2005.

64. Boswell, interview.

65. Ibid.

66. Conqueran, interview, summer 2005. See also Leggio, interview; Lewis, interview.

67. Conqueran, interview, summer 2005.

68. Margaret Opie, interview.

69. Ibid.; Lewis, interview.

70. Lewis, interview.

71. Ibid.

72. Ibid. See Robert E. Weems, Jr., *Desegregating the Dollar: African American Consumerism in the Twentieth Century* (New York: New York University Press, 1998).

73. Ross, *Secrets of a Sparrow*, 82.

7. THE CHITLIN CIRCUIT

1. James Brown and Bruce Tucker, *James Brown: The Godfather of Soul* (1986; reprint, New York: Thunder's Mouth, 1997), 173.

2. A good example of the chitlin circuit is portrayed in the first half of the movie *Ray*, starring Jamie Fox. Also see Oscar J. Jordan III, "Jimi Hendrix and Chitlin' Circuit," *P-Funk Review*, February 2004; Charles Sawyer, *The Arrival of B.B. King: The Authorized Biography* (Garden City, N.Y.: Doubleday, 1980), 73.

3. Gladys Knight, *Between Each Line of Pain and Glory: My Life Story* (New York: Hyperion, 1997), 125.

4. Information on venues gleaned from a recording of a radio feature on the chitlin circuit found at www.soul-patrol.com/soul/chitlin.htm.

5. Aretha Franklin and David Ritz, *From These Roots* (New York: Villard, 1999), 95, 106.

6. Monique Guillory and Richard C. Green, eds., *Soul: Black Power, Politics, and Pleasure* (New York: New York University Press, 1998), 3; Eddie S. Glaude, Jr., *Is It Nation Time? Contemporary Essays on Black Power and Black Nationalism* (Chicago: University of Chicago Press, 2002).

7. Bayard Rustin, "Black Folks, White Folks," in Peter Goldman, ed., *Report from Black America* (New York: Simon and Schuster, 1969), 144.

8. Ibid., 143; Stokely Carmichael and Charles V. Hamilton, *Black Power: The Politics of Liberation in America* (New York: Vintage Books, 1967), 37-38, 44, 46; Komozi

Woodard, *A Nation Within A Nation: Amiri Baraka (LeRoi Jones) and Black Power Politics* (Chapel Hill: University of New Carolina Press, 1999), 32, 86.

9. W. A. Jeanpierre, "African Negritude—Black American Soul," *Africa Today* 14, no. 6 (December 1967): 10-11.

10. Doris Witt, *Black Hunger: Food and the Politics of U.S. Identity* (New York: Oxford University Press. 1999), 97. See also Scott Brown, *Fighting for US: Maulana Karenga, the US Organization, and Black Cultural Nationalism* (New York: New York University Press, 2003); and Jeffrey O.G. Ogbar, *Black Power: Radical Politics and African American Identity* (Baltimore: Johns Hopkins University Press, 2004).

11. Lamenta Diane (Watkins) Crouch, interview, summer 2005.

12. Clara Bullard Pittman, interview, summer 2005.

13. Ella (Christopher) Barnett, interview, summer 2005.

14. Margaret B. (Cooper) Opie, interview, summer 2005.

15. Sundiata Sadique (formerly Walter Brooks), interview, summer 2005. For more on the Nation of Islam, see Ogbar, *Black Power*, chap. 1; William L. Van Deburg, *Hoodlums: Black Villains and Social Bandits in American Life* (Chicago: University of Chicago Press, 2004);and C. Eric Lincoln, *The Black Muslims in America* (Grand Rapids, Mich.: Eerdsmans, 1993).

16. Sadique, interview.

17. Ibid.; Margaret Opie, interview.

18. Ibid.

19. Ibid.

20. Ibid.

21. Ibid.

22. Rustin, "Black Folks, White Folks," 157. See William L. Van Deburg, *New Day in Babylon: The Black Power Movement and American Culture, 1965-1975* (Chicago: University of Chicago Press, 1992), 27-28.

23. Rustin, "Black Folks, White Folks," 152.

24. Robert Blauner, "Black Culture: Lower-Class Result or Ethnic Creation?" in *Black Experience: Soul*, ed. Lee Rainwater (New Brunswick, N.J.: Transaction, 1973), 153-161.

25. Ulf Hannerz, "The Significance of Soul," based on fieldwork in Washington, D.C., July/August 1968, in *Black Experience*, 19.

26. Alton Hornsby, Jr., interview, summer 2005.

27. Witt, *Black Hunger*, 97.

28. Hornsby, interview.

29. Joseph "Mac" Johnson, interview, summer 2005; and Nora (Burns) White, interview, summer 2005.

30. Joe Gray Taylor, *Eating, Drinking, and Visiting in the South: An Informal History* (Baton Rouge: Louisiana State University Press, 1982), 89.

31. Barnett, interview.

32. 1930 federal census of the villages of Tarrytown, North Tarrytown, Ossining, and the City of Mount Vernon.

33. Barnett, interview.
34. Reginald T. Ward, interview, summer 2005; Joseph Johnson, interview; and Pittman, interview.
35. Ward, interview.
36. Joseph Johnson, interview.
37. Ibid
38. "Soul Food Moves Down Town," *Sepia* (Fort Worth, Tex.) 18 (May 1969): 46, 48-49.
39. Pittman, interview.
40. Ward, interview.
41. Hornsby, interview.
42. Eldridge Cleaver, *Soul on Ice* (New York: McGraw-Hill, 1968), 29.
43. "Soul Cookery Described on TV Series," *Daily Defender* (Chicago), January 9, 1969, 24.
44. Cleaver, *Soul on Ice*, 29.
45. Amiri Baraka [LeRoi Jones], *Home: Social Essays* (New York: Morrow, 1966), 101-102.
46. Verta Mae Grosvenor, *Black Atlantic Cooking* (New York: Prentice-Hall, 1990). For more on SNCC, see Howard Zinn, *SNCC: The New Abolitionists* (Boston: Beacon, 1965).
47. Verta Mae Grosvenor, "Racism in the Kitchen," *Black World* 19 (October 1970): 26-26.
48. Bob Jeffries, *Soul Food Cook Book* (Indianapolis, N.Y.: Bobbs-Merrill, 1969), vii.
49. Ibid., ix.
50. Helen Mendes, *The African Heritage Cookbook* (New York: Macmillan, 1971), 11, 15.
51. Pearl Bowser and Joan Eckstein, *A Pinch of Soul in Book Form* (New York: Avon, 1969), 12.
52. Ibid., 12-13.
53. Ibid., 12.
54. "Soul Food Moves Down Town," 46, 49.
55. Ibid., 49.
56. Craig Claiborne, "Cooking with Soul," *New York Times Magazine*, November 3, 1968, 104; Jeffries, *Soul Food Cook Book*, 9.
57. Jim Harwood and Ed Callahan, *Soul Food Cook Book* (Concord, Calif.: Nitty Gritty, 1969), 1-2; Obie Green cited in Claiborne, "Cooking with Soul," 102; Jeffries, *Soul Food Cook Book*, ix.
58. Verta Mae Grosvenor, "Soul Food," *McCall's* 97 (September 1970): 72; Jeffries, *Soul Food Cook Book*, ix.

8. THE DECLINING INFLUENCE OF SOUL FOOD

1. Harvey Brett, "Report on Cuban Population in N.Y.C.," pp. 1, 3–4, November 25, 1935, FCWPA, roll 269; Strong, "Puerto Rican Colony in N.Y.," 1935(?), p. 2, FCWPA, roll 269; "Spanish American Restaurants," p. 2, FCWPA, "Eating Out in Foreign Restaurants" research folder, roll 144; Irma Watkins-Owens, *Blood Relations: Caribbean Immigrants and the Harlem Community, 1900–1930* (Bloomington: Indiana University Press, 1996), 4; Lisa Brock and Digna Castañeda Fuertes, eds., *Between Race and Empire: African-Americans and Cubans Before the Cuban Revolution* (Philadelphia: Temple University Press, 1998), 253.
2. Agustín Laó-Montes and Arlene Dávila, eds., *Mambo Montage: The Latinization of New York* (New York: Columbia University Press, 2001), 105.
3. Strong, "Puerto Rican Colony," pp. 1–2; Jose Pastrana, "El Favorito Restaurant," pp. 1, 4, FCWPA, "Eating Out Foreign Restaurants" research folder, roll 144.
4. Strong, "Puerto Rican Colony," pp. 1–2.
5. Winston James, *Holding Aloft the Banner of Ethiopia: Caribbean Radicalism in Early Twentieth-Century America* (London: Verso, 1998), 197.
6. Jairo Moreno, "Bauzá-Gillespie-Latin/Jazz: Difference, Modernity, and the Black Caribbean," *South Atlantic Quarterly* 103 no. 1 (Winter 2004): 83–85; Donald L. Maggin, *The Life and Times of John Birks Gillespie, Dizzy* (New York: HarperEntertainment, 2005), 216.
7. Harvey Brett, "Report on Cuban Population in N.Y.C.," pp. 1, 3–4, November 25, 1935, FCWPA, roll 269; Strong, "Puerto Rican Colony," p. 2; "Spanish American Restaurants," p. 2.
8. Dizzy Gillespie, *Dizzy: To Be or Not to Bop. The Autobiography of Dizzy Gillespie with Al Fraser* (New York: Doubleday, 1979), 317–319.
9. Laó-Montes and Dávila, *Mambo Montage*, 107.
10. Edwin Cruise, interview, December 2006.
11. Francisco Corona, interview, December 2006.
12. Ibid.; Louis A. Perez, Jr., *Cuba Between Reform and Revolution* (New York: Oxford University Press, 1995), 288–312.
13. Corona, interview.
14. Ibid.
15. Ibid.
16. George Priestly, interview, 2006.
17. Ibid.
18. Oliverio Ojito Fardales, interview, December 2006
19. "Tarry Town's Cuban Flavor," *New York Times*, March 20, 1977.
20. Alice N. Conqueran, interviews, summer 2005 and December 2006.
21. This insight was inspired by my interview with sociologist George Priestly and his comments on after-hours joints in Brooklyn and the leveling that took place between African Panamanians there.

22. Corona, interview.
23. Hugh Bradley, *Havana: Cinderella's City*, (Garden City, N.Y.: Doubleday, Doran, 1941), 352.
24. *New York Times*, March 20, 1977
25. Corona, interview; Mariano Meneses, interview, December 2006.
26. *New York Times*, March 20, 1977.
27. Corona, interview.
28. Priestly, interview.
29. Ibid.
30. Laó-Montes and Dávila, *Mambo Montage*, 239.
31. Ibid. 240-241.
32. Sonya (Cruz) Jones, interview, December 2006.
33. Evelyn Gonzalez, *The Bronx* (New York: Columbia University Press, 2004), 109.
34. Ibid., 109-110.
35. Mark Naison, interview with Nathan "Bubba" Dukes, n.d. (ca. 2006), pp. 1-3, BAAHP (hereafter Dukes, interview).
36. Mark Naison, "'It Take a Village to Raise a Child': Growing Up in the Patterson Houses in the 1950s and Early 1960s: An Interview with Victoria Archibald-Good," *Bronx County Historical Society Journal* 40, no. 1 (Spring 2003): 9.
37. Dukes, interview, 5.
38. Naison, "'It Take a Village to Raise a Child,'" 9.
39. Dukes, interview, 18.
40. Barbara (Cardwell) Pino, interview, December 2006.

9. FOOD REBELS

1. Marcellas C.D. Barksdale, interview, summer 2005; Yemaja Jubilee, interview, summer 2005.
2. Dr. Elijah Saunders, interview, summer 2005.
3. Joan B. Lewis, interview, summer 2005.
4. Clara Bullard Pittman, interview, summer 2005.
5. Lewis, interview.
6. Dr. Rodney Ellis, interview, summer 2005.
7. Lewis, interview.
8. Sherman E. Evans, "On the Health of Black Americans," *Ebony*, March 1977, 112.
9. "Good Health Is a Family Affair: Good Nutrition, Exercise, Sleep, Physical Examinations, Etc." [interview with Dr. Keith W. Sehnert], *Ebony*, May 1977, 107-114.
10. Ibid., 110, 112.
11. Saunders, interview. See Bill Rhoden, "The 10 Worst Things You Can Do to Your Health," *Ebony*, January 10, 1978, 30-35.

12. Saunders, interview.
13. Elijah Muhammad, *How to Eat to Live* (Chicago: Muhammad's Temple of Islam No. 2, 1967), 1:5, 6, 10.
14. Eugene Watts, interview, summer 2005.
15. Dick Gregory, interview, summer 2005.
16. Muhammad, *How to Eat to Live*, 1:6.
17. William L. Van Deburg, *Hoodlums: Black Villains and Social Bandits in American Life* (Chicago: University of Chicago Press, 2004), 97, 98.
18. Malcolm X, *The Autobiography of Malcolm X*, with Alex Haley (New York: Ballantine, 1964), 217-224.
19. Ruth Miller, Roy Miller, and Rudolf Bradshaw, interview, summer 2005.
20. Reginald T. Ward, interview, summer 2005; Watts, interview.
21. Watts, interview.
22. Ibid.
23. Ibid.
24. Saunders, interview.
25. Watts, interview.
26. Malcolm X, *Autobiography*, 215-225, esp. 219.
27. Ibid., 219, 221.
28. Bobby Seale, *A Lonely Rage: The Autobiography of Bobby Seale* (New York: Times Books, 1978), 159, 168.
29. Pittman, interview.
30. Lewis, interview.
31. Ellis, interview.
32. Gregory, interview.
33. Dick Gregory, *Nigger: An Autobiography*, with Robert Lipsyte (New York: Washington Square, 1964), 145.
34. Gregory, interview.
35. Alvenia Fulton, *Radiant Health Through Nutrition* (Chicago: Life Line, 1980); Gregory, *Nigger*, 17.
36. Alfred Duckett, "How to Eat and Love," *Sepia* 22, no. 5 (May 1973): 74-79, esp. 80.
37. Ibid.
38. Gregory, interview; Duckett, "How to Eat and Love," 80.
39. Dick Gregory, *Dick Gregory's Natural Diet for Folks Who Eat: Cookin' With Mother Nature*, ed. James R. McGraw, with Alvenia M. Fulton (1973; reprint, New York: Perennial-Harper, 1974), 80, 81.
40. Vernon Jarrett, "Dick Gregory's Health Advocacy," *Chicago Tribune*, May 23, 1973, 18.
41. Dick Gregory, *Callus on My Soul: A Memoir by Dick Gregory* (Atlanta: Longstreet Press, 2000), 176; see 174-178, 186-190.
42. Fred Opie, Jr., interview, summer 2005.
43. Gregory, interview.

44. Edward Williamson, interview, summer 2005.

45. Scott Brown, *Fighting for US: Maulana Karenga, the US Organization, and Black Cultural Nationalism* (New York: New York University Press, 2003), 78, 88; Howard Zinn, *SNCC: The New Abolitionists* (Boston: Beacon, 1965).

46. Lamenta Diane (Watkins) Crouch, interview, summer 2005.

47. Williamson, interview.

48. Lewis, interview.

49. Pittman, interview.

50. Sundiata Sadique (formerly Walter Brooks), interview, summer 2005.

51. Ralph Johnson and Patricia Reed, "What's Wrong with Soul Food?" *Black Collegian*, December 1980/January 1981, 21.

52. Ibid., 22.

53. Mary Keyes Burgess, *Soul to Soul: A Soul Food Vegetarian Cookbook* (Santa Barbara, Calif.: Woodbridge, 1976), 13, 19.

54. Margaret Opie, interview.

EPILOGUE

1. "New York Bans Most Trans Fats in Restaurants," *New York Times*, December 6, 2006, p. 1.

2. "Saving Soul Food," *Newsweek*, January 30, 2006.

3. Ben Ammi, *God, the Black Man and Truth*, 2d ed. (Washington, D.C.: Communicators, 1990).

4. "Saving Soul Food."

5. Yemaja Jubilee, interview, summer 2005.

6. Ibid.

7. Lamenta Diane (Watkins) Crouch, interview, summer 2005.

8. Dr. Elijah Saunders, interview, summer 2005.

9. Joan B. Lewis, interview, summer 2005; Yemaja Jubilee, interview, summer 2005.

10. Dorothy I. Height, *The Black Family Dinner Quilt Cookbook*, with the National Council of Negro Women (Memphis, Tenn.: Wimmer Companies, 1993), 213–214. Other examples of healthy soul food cook books include Mary Keyes Burgess, *Soul to Soul: A Soul Food Vegetarian Cookbook* (Santa Barbara, Calif.: Woodbridge, 1976); Jonell Nash, *Low-Fat Soul* (New York: Ballantine, 1996); and Fabiola Demps Gaines and Roniece Weaver, *The New Soul Food Cookbook for People with Diabetes*, 2d ed. (Alexandria, Va.: American Diabetes Association, 2006).

11. David Bell and Gill Valentine, *Consuming Geographies: We Are Where We Eat* (London: Routledge, 1997), 10, 116.

12. Jim Harwood and Ed Callahan, *Soul Food Cook Book* (Concord, Calif.: Nitty Gritty, 1969), 1–2.

Bibliography

ARCHIVAL SOURCES

Bronx African American History Project, Bronx County Historical Society Archive Collection, Bronx, N.Y. (BAAHP)

Oral History Transcripts

Franklin D. Roosevelt Presidential Library, Hyde Park, N.Y.

Papers of Harry L. Hopkins

Library of Congress, Manuscript Division, Washington, D.C.

U.S. Work Projects Administration (WPA) (Special Studies and Projects 1530–1942) "America Eats" Collection
WPA State Records (SR)
Slave Narratives

National Archives II, College Park, Md.

Records of the United States Information Agency
Office of the Secretary of Agriculture
Records of the Work Projects Administration
Gift Still Pictures in the National Archives, Harmon Foundation Collection, Prints: Art Works by Negro Artists, 1922–1967

New York City Municipal Archives, New York, N.Y.

WPA Papers, "Feeding the City Project Collection" (FCWPA)

New York City Public Library, New York, N.Y.	Photography Collection United States Public Documents Office Records Agricultural Experiment Station Bulletins
Opie Family Archive, Tarrytown, N.Y., Croton-Hudson, N.Y., Cloverdale, Va.	
Rare Book, Manuscript, and Special Collections Library, Duke University, Durham, N.C.	Information Folder Memoirs Autobiographical Writings
Schomburg Center for Research in Black Culture, Harlem, N.Y.	*Black Collegian* *Black Scholar* *Black World* *Ebony* *Freedomways* *Negro Digest* *Sepia*
Smithsonian American Art Museum, Washington, D.C.	Photography Collection
Tuskegee Institute News Clippings File	*Topeka Plain* (Kansas)
University of North Carolina, Chapel Hill, Manuscript Department	Federal Writers Project (WPA) Papers
Westchester County Archives, Elmsford, N.Y.	1930 Federal Census of the Villages of Tarrytown, North Tarrytown, Ossining, and the City of Mount Vernon

INTERVIEWS

Interviews are with the author.

Banks, Nettie C., *summer 2005*
Barksdale, Marcellas C.D., *summer 2005*
Barnett, Ella (Christopher), *summer 2005*
Boswell, Christopher, *summer 2005*
Conqueran, Alice N., *summer 2005, December 2006*
Corona, Francisco, *December 2006*
Crouch, Lamenta Diane (Watkins), *summer 2005*
Cruise, Edwin, *December 2006*
Ellington, Beryl, *summer 2005*

Ellis, Dr. Rodney, *summer 2005*

Evelyn, Dorothy M, *summer 2005*

Fardales, Oliverio Ojito, *December 2006*

Green, Katie (White), *summer 2005*

Gregory, Dick, *summer 2005*

Hornsby, Alton, Jr., *summer 2005*

James, Stanlie M., *summer 2005*

Johnson, Betty Joyce, *summer 2005*

Johnson, Joseph "Mac," *summer 2005*

Jones, Sonya (Cruz), *December 2006*

Jubilee, Yemaja, *summer 2005*

Leggio, Carmen John, *summer 2005*

Lewis, Joan B., *summer 2005*

Maybee, Carleton, *summer 2005*

Meneses, Mariano, *December 2006*

Miller, Ruth, Roy Miller, and Rudolf Bradshaw, *summer 2005*

Neely, Francis Ann (Watkins), *summer 2007*

Opie, Dorothy, *summer 2005*

Opie, Fred, Jr., *summer 2005*

Opie, Margaret B. (Cooper), *summer 2005*

Outlaw, Benjamin, *summer 2005*

Pino, Barbara (Cardwell), *December 2006*

Pittman, Clara Bullard, *summer 2005*

Priestly, George, *December 2006*

Sadique, Sundiata (formerly Walter Brooks), *summer 2005*

Saunders, Dr. Elijah, *summer 2005*

Ward, Reginald T., *summer 2005*

Warren, Frances and Jim Warren, *summer 2005*

Watts, Eugene, *summer 2005*

White, Nora (Burns), *summer 2005*

Williamson, Edward, *summer 2005*

OTHER SOURCES

Abernathy, Ralph David. *And the Walls Came Tumbling Down: An Autobiography*. New York: Harper and Row, 1989.

Adanson, Michel. *A voyage to Senegal, the isle of Goreé and the river Gambia*. London: J. Nourse, 1759. In John Pinkerton, *A General Collection of the Best and Most Interesting Voyages and Travels in all Parts of the World* . . . . London: Longman, Hurst, Ross, Orme and Brown, 1813.

[Africanus, pseudo.]. "Remarks on the Slave Trade, and the Slavery of the Negroes." In *A Series of Letters*. London: J. Phillips, 1788.

Agassiz, Louis and Elizabeth Agassiz. *A Journey in Brazil*. Boston: Ticknor and Fields, 1868. Reprint, New York: Praeger, 1969.

Allen, William and T.R.H. Thomson. *A Narrative of the Expedition to the River Niger in 1841*, 2 vols. London: Richard Bentley, 1848. Reprint, London: Cass, 1968.

Ammi, Ben. *God, the Black Man and Truth*. 2d ed. Washington, D.C.: Communicators, 1990.

Ancelet, Barry Jean, Jay D. Edwards, and Glen Pitre. *Cajun Country*. Jackson: University Press of Mississippi, 1991.

Andrade, Margarette Sheehan de. *Brazilian Cookery: Traditional and Modern*. Rio de Janeiro: A Casa Do Livro Eldorado, 1978.

Angelou, Maya. *I Know Why the Caged Bird Sings*. 1969. Reprint, New York: Bantam, 1970.

Anonymous. "Soul Food Moves Down Town." *Sepia* (Fort Worth, Texas) 18 (May 1969).

Armstrong, Louis, *Satchmo: My Life in New Orleans*. New York: Da Capo, 1986.

Atwater, Wilbur O. and Charles D. Woods. *Dietary Studies with Reference to the Food of the Negro in Alabama in 1895 and 1896*. U.S. Department of Agriculture, Office of Experiment Stations, bulletin no. 38. Washington, D.C.: U.S. Government Printing Office, 1897.

Ball, Charles. *Slavery in the United States: A Narrative of the Life and Adventures of Charles Ball, a Black Man, Who Lived Forty Years in Maryland, South Carolina and Georgia, as a Slave* . . . . Pittsburgh: J.T. Shryock, 1854.

Baraka, Amiri. [LeRoi Jones]. *Home: Social Essays*. New York: Morrow, 1966.

Barkley Brown, Elsa and Gregg D. Kimball. "Mapping the Terrain of Black Richmond." In *The New African American Urban History*, ed. Kenneth W. Goings and Raymond A. Mohl, 66-115. Thousand Oaks, Calif.: Sage, 1996.

Barlowe, Arthur. "Captain Arthur Barlowe's Narrative of the First Voyage to The Coasts of America." In *Early English and French Voyages Chiefly from Hakluyt, 1534-1608*, ed. Henry S. Burrage, vol. 3 of *Original Narratives of Early American History*, ed. J. Franklin Jameson. New York: Scribner's, 1906.

Baro, Gene. "Soul Food." *Vogue* 155 (March 1970).

Bass, A.L. Tommie. *Plain Southern Eating from the Reminiscences of A.L. Tommie Bass, Herbalist*. Ed. John K. Crellin. Durham, N.C.: Duke University Press, 1988.

Bayley, F.W. *Four Years' Residence in the West Indies*. 3d ed. London, 1833.

Bell, David and Gill Valentine. *Consuming Geographies: We Are Where We Eat*. London: Routledge, 1997.

Berger, Bennet. "Black Culture or Lower Class Culture." In *Black Experience: Soul*, ed. Lee Rainwater, 131-142. New Brunswick, N.J.: Transaction, 1973.

Berlin, Ira, Joseph P. Reidy, and Leslie S. Rowland, eds. *Freedom's Soldiers: The Black Military Experience in the Civil War*. Cambridge: Cambridge University Press, 1998.

Biondi, Martha. *To Stand and Fight: The Struggle for Civil Rights in Postwar New York City*. Cambridge: Harvard University Press, 2003.

Blassingame, John W. *The Slave Community: Plantation Life in the Antebellum South*. Rev. ed. New York: Oxford University Press, 1979.

Blauner, Robert. "Black Culture: Lower-Class Result or Ethnic Creation?" In *Black Experience: Soul*, ed. Lee Rainwater, 143-180. New Brunswick, N.J.: Transaction, 1973.

The Booker T. Washington Papers. Vol. 4, *1895-98*. Ed. Louis R. Harlan, Stuart B. Kaufman, Barbara S. Kraft, and Raymond W. Smock. Urbana: University of Illinois Press, 1975.

——. Vol. 5, *1899-1900*. Ed. Louis R. Harlan, Raymond W. Smock, and Barbara S. Kraft. Urbana: University of Illinois Press, 1976.

Bowser, Pearl and Joan Eckstein. *A Pinch of Soul in Book Form*. New York: Avon, 1969.

Boyer, Richard and Geoffrey Spurling, eds. *Colonial Lives: Documents on Latin American History, 1550-1850*. New York: Oxford University Press, 2000.

Bradley, Hugh. *Havana: Cinderella's City*. Garden City, N.Y.: Doubleday, Doran, 1941.

Braudel, Fernand. *Capitalism and Material Life, 1400-1800*. Trans. Miriam Kochan. New York: Harper and Row, 1973.

——. *Civilization and Capitalism, 15th-18th Century*, Vol. 1, *The Structures of Everyday Life: The Limits of the Possible*. Trans. Sian Reynolds. New York: Harper and Row, 1979.

Bremer, Fredrika. *America of the Fifties: Letters of Fredrika Bremer*. Ed. Adolph B. Benson. New York: American-Scandinavian Foundation, 1924.

Brock, Lisa and Digna Castañeda Fuertes, eds. *Between Race and Empire: African-Americans and Cubans Before the Cuban Revolution*. Philadelphia: Temple University Press, 1998.

Brown, James and Bruce Tucker. *James Brown: The Godfather of Soul*. 1986. Reprint, New York: Thunder's Mouth, 1997.

Brown, Scott. *Fighting for US: Maulana Karenga, the US Organization, and Black Cultural Nationalism*. New York: New York University Press, 2003.

Buisseret, David. Introduction to *Creolization in the Americas*. Ed. David Buisseret and Steven G. Reinhardt. College Station: Texas A&M Press, for the University of Texas at Arlington, 2000.

Burgess, Mary Keyes. *Soul to Soul: A Soul Food Vegetarian Cookbook*. Santa Barbara, Calif.: Woodbridge, 1976.

Byrd, William. *The London Diary, 1717-1721, and Other Writings*. Ed. Louis B. Wright and Marion Tinling. New York: Oxford University Press, 1958.

Canot, Theodore. *Captain Canot; or, Twenty Years of an African Slaver: Being an Account of His Career and Adventures on the Coast, in the Interior, on Shipboard, and in the West Indies, Written out and edited from the Captain's Journals, Memoranda and Conversations*. New York: D. Appleton, 1854.

Carmichael, Stokely and Charles V. Hamilton. *Black Power: The Politics of Liberation in America*. New York: Vintage, 1967.

Carroll, Anne Elizabeth. *Word, Image, and the New Negro: Representation and Identity in the Harlem Renaissance*. Bloomington: Indiana University Press, 2005.

Cash, Floris Barnett. *African American Women and Social Action: The Clubwomen and Volunteerism from Jim Crow to the New Deal, 1896–1936*. Westport, Conn.: Greenwood, 2001.

Chafe, William H. *Civilities and Civil Rights: Greensboro, North Carolina, and the Black Struggle for Freedom*. New York: Oxford University Press, 1981.

Chambers, Douglas Brent. "'He Gwine Sing He Country': Africans, Afro-Virginians, and the Development of Slave Culture in Virginia, 1690–1810." Ph.D. diss., University of Virginia, 1996.

Claiborne, Craig. "Cooking with Soul." *New York Times Magazine*, November 3, 1968.

Clark Hine, Darlene and Jacqueline McLeod, eds. *Crossing Boundaries: Comparative History of Black People in Diaspora*. Bloomington: Indiana University Press, 1999.

Cleaver, Eldridge. *Soul on Ice*. New York: McGraw-Hill, 1968.

Coe, Sophie D. *America's First Cuisines*. Austin: University of Texas Press, 1994.

The Complete Cook: Expertly Prescribing the Most Ready Ways, Whether Italian, Spanish, or French, for Dressing Flesh, and Fish, Ordering of Sauces, or Making of Pastry. London: Printed for Nath. Brooke, at the Angel in Cornhill, 1659.

Crosby, Alfred W., Jr. *The Columbian Exchange: Biological and Cultural Consequences of 1492*. Westport, Conn.: Greenwood, 1973.

Cussler, Margaret and Mary L. de Give. *'Twixt the Cup and the Lip: Psychological and Socio-Cultural Factors Affecting Food Habits*. Washington, D.C.: Consortium, 1952.

Dailey, Jane, Glenda Elizabeth Gilmore, and Bryant Simon, eds. *Jumpin' Jim Crow: Southern Politics from Civil War to Civil Rights*. Princeton, N.J.: Princeton University Press, 2000.

Dana, Richard Henry. *To Cuba and Back*. Ed. C. Harvey Gardiner. Carbondale: Southern Illinois University Press, 1966.

Diner, Hasia R. *Hungering for America: Italian, Irish, and Jewish Foodways in the Age of Migration*. Cambridge: Harvard University Press, 2001.

Dittmer, John. *Black Georgia in the Progressive Era, 1900–1920*. Urbana: University of Illinois Press, 1977.

Domingo, Xavier. "La Cocina Precolombiana en España." In *Conquista y Comida: Consecuencias del Encuentro De Dos Mundos*, ed. Janet Long, 17–30. Mexico City: Universidad Nacional Autónoma de México, 1996.

Donnan, Elizabeth. *Documents Illustrative of the History of the Slave Trade to America*. Vol. 4. New York: Octagon, 1969.

Drake, St. Clair and Horace R. Cayton. *Black Metropolis: A Study of Negro Life in a Northern City*. 1945. Reprint, Chicago: University of Chicago Press, 1993.

Driver, Harold E. *Indians of North America*. 2d ed. 1961. Reprint, Chicago: University of Chicago Press, 1969.

Duckett, Alfred. "How to Eat and Love." *Sepia* 22, no. 5 (May 1973).

Dunmire, William W. *Gardens of New Spain: How Mediterranean Plants and Foods Changed America*. Austin: University of Texas Press, 2004.

Edgerton, John *Southern Food: At Home, on the Road, in History*. New York: Knopf, 1987.

Ellsworth, Scott. *Death in a Promised Land: The Tulsa Race Riot of 1921*. Baton Rouge: Louisiana State University Press, 1982.

Equiano, Olaudah. "Traditional Igbo Religion and Culture" [1791]. In *Afro-American Religious History: A Documentary Witness*, ed. Milton C. Sernett, 13-18. Durham, N.C.: Duke University Press, 1985.

"Eugene 'Hot Sauce' Williams, Barbecue Operator of Cleveland, Ohio." *Ebony*, March 1950.

Evans, Sherman E. "On the Health of Black Americans." *Ebony*, March 1977.

Ferguson, Sheila. *Soul Food: Classic Cuisine from the Deep South*. New York: Grove, 1989.

Fletcher, James C. and D. P. Kidder. *Brazil and the Brazilians Portrayed in Historical and Descriptive Sketches*. Boston: Little, Brown; London: Sampson, Low, 1866.

Fowler, Damon Lee. *Classical Southern Cooking: A Celebration of the Cuisine of the Old South*. New York: Crown, 1995.

Fox-Genovese, Elizabeth. *Within the Plantation Household: Black and White Women in the Old South*. Chapel Hill: University of North Carolina Press, 1988.

Franklin, Aretha and David Ritz. *From These Roots*. New York: Villard, 1999.

Freyre, Gilberto. *The Mansions and the Shanties (Sobrados e Mucambos): The Making of Modern Brazil*. Trans. and ed. Harriet de Onís. New York: Knopf, 1963.

——. *The Masters and the Slaves (Casa-grande & senzala): A Study in the Development of Brazilian Civilization*. Trans. Samuel Putnam. New York: Knopf, 1956.

Frissel, H.D. and Isabel Bevier. *Dietary Studies of Negroes in Eastern Virginia in 1897 and 1898*. U.S. Department of Agriculture, Office of Experiment Stations, bulletin no. 71. Washington, D.C.: Government Printing Office, 1899.

Fulop, Timothy E. and Albert J. Raboteau, eds. *African-American Religion: Interpretive Essays in History and Culture*. New York: Routledge, 1997.

Fulton, Alvenia. *Radiant Health Through Nutrition*. Chicago: Life Line, 1980.

Gabaccia, Donna R. *We Are What We Eat: Food and the Making of Americans*. Cambridge: Harvard University Press, 1998.

Gaines, Fabiola Demps and Roniece Weaver. *The New Soul Food Cookbook for People with Diabetes*. 2d ed. Alexandria, Va.: American Diabetes Association, 2006.

Gates, Henry Louis, Jr., ed. *Classic Slave Narratives*. New York: Penguin, 1987.

Genovese, Eugene D. *Roll Jordan Roll: The World the Slaves Made*. 1972. Reprint, New York: Vintage, 1976.

Gillespie, Dizzy. *Dizzy: To Be or Not to Bop. The Autobiography of Dizzy Gillespie with Al Fraser*. New York: Doubleday, 1979.

Gilroy, Paul. *"There Ain't No Black in the Union Jack": The Cultural Politics of Race and Nation*. Chicago: University of Chicago Press, 1991.

——. *The Black Atlantic: Double Consciousness, and Modernity.* Cambridge: Harvard University Press, 1993.

Glaude, Eddie S., Jr., ed. *Is It Nation Time? Contemporary Essays on Black Power and Black Nationalism.* Chicago: University of Chicago Press, 2002.

Goings, Kenneth W. and Raymond A. Mohl, eds. *The New African American Urban History.* Thousand Oaks, Calif.: Sage, 1996.

Goldman, Peter. *Report from Black America.* New York: Simon and Schuster, 1969.

Gomez, Michael A. *Exchanging Our Country Marks: The Transformation of African Identity in the Colonial and Antebellum South.* Chapel Hill: University of North Carolina Press, 1998.

Gonzalez, Evelyn. *The Bronx.* New York: Columbia University Press, 2004.

"Good Health Is a Family Affair: Good Nutrition, Exercise, Sleep, Physical Examinations, Etc." [interview with Dr. Keith W. Sehnert]. *Ebony*, May 1977.

Graham, Maria. *Journal of a Voyage to Brazil, and the Residence There, During Part of the Years 1821, 1822, 1823.* London: Longman, Hurst, Rees, Orme, Brown, and Green, 1824. Reprint, New York: Praeger, 1969.

Greenberg, Cheryl Lynn. *Or Does It Explode? Black Harlem in the Great Depression.* New York: Oxford University Press, 1991.

Greene, Jack P. "Beyond Power: Paradigm Subversion and Reformulation and the Re-creation of the Early Modern Atlantic World." In *Crossing Boundaries: Comparative History of Black People in Diaspora*, ed. Darlene Clark Hine and Jacqueline McLeod. Bloomington: Indiana University Press, 1999.

Gregory, Dick. *Callus on My Soul: A Memoir by Dick Gregory.* Atlanta: Longstreet, 2000.

——. *Dick Gregory's Natural Diet for Folks Who Eat: Cookin' with Mother Nature.* Ed James R. McGraw, with Alvenia M. Fulton. 1973. Reprint, New York: Perennial-Harper, 1974.

——. *Nigger: An Autobiography.* With Robert Lipsyte. New York: Washington Square, 1964.

Grossman, James. *Land of Hope: Chicago, Black Southerners, and the Great Migration.* Chicago: University of Chicago Press, 1989.

Grosvenor, Verta Mae. *Black Atlantic Cooking.* New York: Prentice-Hall, 1990.

——. "Racism in the Kitchen." *Black World* 19 (October 1970).

Guillory, Monique and Richard C. Green, eds. *Soul: Black Power, Politics, and Pleasure.* New York: New York University Press, 1998.

Gura, Stephen A. "The Limits of Mob Law: The Elaine Race Riot of 1919." Honor thesis, Emory University, 1983.

Haley, Alex. *Roots.* Garden City, N.Y.: Doubleday, 1976.

Hall, Abraham Oakey. *The Manhattaner in New Orleans; or, Phases of "Crescent City" Life.* New York: J. S. Redfield, 1851.

Hall, David D. *Lived Religion in America: Toward a History of Practice.* Princeton, N.J.: Princeton University Press, 1997.

Hannerz, Ulf. "The Significance of Soul." In *Black Experience: Soul*, ed. Lee Rainwater, 15-30. New Brunswick, N.J., Transaction, 1973.

Harris, Jessica B. *Iron Pots and Wooden Spoons: Africa's Gifts to New World Cooking*. New York: Atheneum, 1989.

Harrison, Molly. *The Kitchen in History*. New York: Scribner's, 1972.

Harwood, Jim and Ed Callahan, *Soul Food Cook Book*. Concord, Calif.: Nitty Gritty, 1969.

Hawkins, Joseph. *A History of a Voyage to the Coast of Africa and Travels into the Interior of that Country, Containing Particular Descriptions of the Climate and Inhabitants, and Interesting Particulars Concerning the Slave Trade*. 1796. Reprint, London: Cass, 1970.

Haynes, Robert V. *A Night of Violence: The Houston Riot of 1917*. Baton Rouge: Louisiana State University Press, 1976.

Height, Dorothy I. *The Black Family Dinner Quilt Cookbook*. With the National Council of Negro Women. Memphis, Tenn.: Wimmer Companies, 1993.

Hess, Karen. *The Carolina Rice Kitchen: The African Connection*. Columbia: University of South Carolina Press, 1992.

Heywood, Linda M, ed. *Central Africans and Cultural Transformation in the American Diaspora*. New York: Cambridge University Press, 2002.

Higginbotham, Evelyn Brooks. *Righteous Discontent: The Women's Movement in the Black Baptist Church, 1880-1920*. Cambridge: Harvard University Press, 1993.

Hilliard, Sam Bowers. *Hog Meat and Hoecake: Food Supply in the Old South, 1840-1860*. Carbondale: Southern Illinois University Press, 1972.

Hodgson, Adam. *Remarks During a Journey Through North America In the Years 1819, 1820, and 1821 in a Series of Letters*. New York: Seymour, Printer, 1823. Reprint, Westport, Conn.: Negro Universities Press, 1970.

Hughes, Langston. *The Langston Hughes Reader*. New York: Braziller, 1958.

——. *Not Without Laughter*. 1969. Reprint, New York: Touchstone, 1995.

Hughes, Louis. *Thirty Years a Slave from Bondage to Freedom: The Institution of Slavery as Seen on the Plantation and in the Home of the Planter*. Milwaukee, Wisc.: South Side, 1897.

Hurt, R. Douglas, ed. *African American Life in the Rural South, 1900-1950*. Columbia: University of Missouri Press, 2003.

Iacobbo, Karen and Michael Iacobbo. *Vegetarian America: A History*. Westport, Conn.: Praeger, 2004.

Isichei, Elizabeth. *The Igbo Peoples and the Europeans: Genesis of a Relationship—to 1906*. New York: St. Martin's, 1973.

James, Winston. *Holding Aloft the Banner of Ethiopia: Caribbean Radicalism in Early Twentieth-Century America*. London: Verso, 1998.

Jeanpierre, W. A. "African Negritude—Black American Soul." *Africa Today* 14, no. 6 (December 1967).

Jeffries, Bob. *Soul Food Cook Book*. Indianapolis, N.Y.: Bobbs-Merrill, 1969.

Johnson, Clifton. *Highways and Byways of the South*. New York: Macmillan, 1904.

Johnson, James Weldon. *Along This Way: The Autobiography of James Weldon Johnson*. New York: Viking, 1933.

Johnson, Ralph and Patricia Reed. "What's Wrong with Soul Food?" *Black Collegian*, December 1980/January 1981.

Jordan, Oscar J., III, "Jimi Hendrix and Chitlin' Circuit." *P-Funk Review*, February 2004.

Jordan, Winthrop D. *White Over Black: American Attitudes Toward the Negro, 1550-1812*. Baltimore: Penguin, 1969.

July, Robert W. *Precolonial Africa: An Economic and Social History*. New York: Scribner's, 1975.

Kelley, Robin D.G. "'We Are Not What We Seem': Rethinking Black Working-Class Opposition in the Jim Crow South." In *The New African American Urban History*, ed. Kenneth W. Goings and Raymond A. Mohl, 187-239. Thousand Oaks, Calif.: Sage, 1996.

King, Lamont Dehaven. "State and Ethnicity in Precolonial Northern Nigeria." *Journal of African American Studies* 36, no. 4 (2001).

Kiple, Kenneth F. and Kriemhild Coneè Ornelas, eds. *The Cambridge World History of Food*. Vol. 1. Cambridge: Cambridge University Press, 2000.

Klinberg, Frank J. ed., *The Carolina Chronicle of Dr. Francis Le Jau, 1706-1717*. University of California Publications in History, vol. 53, ed. J.S. Galbraith, R.N. Burr, Brainerd Dyer, and J.C. King. Berkeley: University of California Press, 1956.

Knight, Gladys. *Between Each Line of Pain and Glory: My Life Story*. New York: Hyperion, 1997.

Kolapo, Femi J. "The Igbo and Their Neighbors During the Era of the Atlantic Slave Trade." *Slavery and Abolition* 25, no. 1 (April 2004).

Kornweibel, Theodore, Jr. "An Economic Profile of Black Life in the Twenties." *Journal of Black Studies* 6, no. 4 (June 1976).

Kusmer, Kenneth L. *A Ghetto Takes Shape: Black Cleveland, 1870-1930*. Urbana: University of Illinois Press, 1976.

Laó-Montes, Agustín and Arlene Dávila. eds. *Mambo Montage: The Latinization of New York*. New York: Columbia University Press, 2001.

Law, Robin and Kristin Mann. "West Africa in the Atlantic Community: The Case of the Slave Coast." *William and Mary Quarterly*, 3d ser., 56, no. 2 (April 1999).

Leavell, R. H., T.R. Snavely, T.J. Woofter, Jr., W.T.B. Williams, and Francis D. Tyson. *Negro Migration in 1916-17* Washington, D.C.: Government Printing Office, 1919.

Lee, J. Edward Lee and Ron Chepesiuk eds. *South Carolina in the Civil War: The Confederate Experience in Letters and Diaries*. Jefferson, N.C.: McFarland, 2000.

Lerner, Gerda. "Early Community Work of Black Club Women." *Journal of Negro History* 59, no. 2 (April 1974).

Levenstein, Harvey A. *Revolution at the Table: The Transformation of the American Diet*. New York: Oxford University Press, 1988.

Lewis, Matthew Gregory. *Journal of a West India Proprietor, 1815-1817*. Ed. Mona Wilson. London: George Routledge, 1929.

Ligon, Richard. *A True and Exact History of the Island of Barbadoes* (London, 1673). In *After Africa: Extracts from British Travel Accounts and Journals of the Seventeenth, Eighteenth, and Nineteenth Centuries Concerning the Slaves, Their Manners, and Customs in the British West Indies*, ed. Roger D. Abrahams and John F. Szwed, with Leslie Baker and Adrian Stackhouse. New Haven: Yale University Press, 1983.

Lincoln, C. Eric. *The Black Muslims in America*. Grand Rapids, Mich.: Eerdsmans, 1993.

Littlefield, Daniel C. *Rice and Slaves: Ethnicity and the Slave Trade in Colonial South Carolina*. Baton Rouge: Louisiana State University Press, 1981.

Litwack, Leon F. Trouble in Mind: Black Southerners in the Age of Jim Crow. New York: Knopf, 1998.

Lockett, Samuel H. Louisiana As It Is: A Geographical and Topographical Description of the State. Baton Rouge: Louisiana State University Press, 1969.

McHatton-Ripley, Eliza. *From Flag to Flag: A Woman's Adventures and Experiences in the South During the War, in Mexico, and in Cuba*. New York, D. Appleton, 1889.

McWilliams, James E. *A Revolution in Eating: How the Quest for Food Shaped America*. New York: Columbia University Press, 2005.

Madden, Richard Robert. *A Twelve Month's Residence in the West Indies, During the Transition from Slavery to Apprenticeship: With Incidental Notices of the State of Society, Prospects, and Natural Resources of Jamaica and Other Islands*. Philadelphia: Carey, Lea and Blanchard, 1835. Reprint, Westport, Conn.: Negro Universities Press, 1970.

Maggin, Donald L. *The Life and Times of John Birks Gillespie, Dizzy*. New York: Harper Entertainment, 2005.

Malcolm X. *The Autobiography of Malcolm X*. With Alex Haley. New York: Ballantine, 1964.

Marees, Pieter de. *Description and Historical Account of the Gold Kingdom of Guinea (1602)*. Trans. and ed. Albert van Dantzig and Adam Jones. New York: Oxford University Press, 1987.

Marks, Carole. Farewell—We're Good and Gone: The Great Black Migration. Bloomington: Indiana University Press, 1989.

Mawe, John. John Mawe's Journey into the Interior of Brazil. 1809. Reprinted in Colonial Travelers in Latin America, ed. Irving A. Leonard. New York: Knopf, 1972.

"Medicine Links Soul Food with High Blood Pressure." *Jet*, November 2, 1972.

Meléndez, Theresa. "Corn." In *Rooted in America: Foodlore of Popular Fruits and Vegetables*, ed. David Scofield Wilson and Angus Kress Gillespie, 40-59. Knoxville: University of Tennessee Press, 1999.

Mendes, Helen. *The African Heritage Cookbook*. New York: Macmillan, 1971.

Mennell, Stephen. *All Manners of Food: Eating and Taste in England and France from the Middle Ages to the Present*. Urbana: University of Illinois Press, 1996.

Mintz, Sidney W. *Tasting Food, Tasting Freedom: Excursions into Eating, Culture, and the Past*. Boston: Beacon, 1996.

Moreno, Jairo. "Bauzá-Gillespie-Latin/Jazz: Difference, Modernity, and the Black Caribbean." *South Atlantic Quarterly* 103, no. 1 (Winter 2004).

Muhammad, Elijah. *How to Eat to Live*. Vol. 1. Chicago: Muhammad's Temple of Islam No. 2, 1967.

Narayan, Uma. "Eating Cultures: Incorporation, Identity, and Indian Food." *Social Identities* 1, no. 1 (1995).

Nash, Jonell. *Low-Fat Soul*. New York: Ballantine, 1996.

Naison, Mark. "'It Take a Village to Raise a Child': Growing Up in the Patterson Houses in the 1950s and Early 1960s: An Interview with Victoria Archibald-Good." *Bronx County Historical Society Journal* 40, no. 1 (Spring 2003).

Neverdon-Morton, Cynthia. "Self-Help Programs as Educative Activities of Black Women in the South, 1895–1925: Focus on Four Key Areas." *Journal of Negro Education* 51, no. 3 (Summer 1982).

"New York Bans Most Trans Fats in Restaurants." *New York Times*, December 6, 2006.

Nieuhoff's Brazil (1813). In John Pinkerton, A General Collection of the Best and Most Interesting Voyages and Travels in all Parts of the World . . . , vol. 14. London: Longman, Hurst, Ross, Orme and Brown, 1813.

Norman, Barbara. *The Spanish Cook Book: Over 200 of the Best Recipes from the Kitchens of Spain*. New York: Bantam, 1966.

Northup, Solomon. *Twelve Years a Slave*. Ed. Sue Eakin and Joseph Logsdon. Baton Rouge: Louisiana State University Press, 1968.

Olmsted, Frederick Law. *The Cotton Kingdom: A Traveler's Observations on Cotton and Slavery in the American Slave States. Based Upon Three Former Volumes of Journeys and Investigations by the Same Author*. Ed. Arthur M. Schlesinger, Sr. New York: Modern Library, 1984.

——. *A Journey in the Seaboard Slave States in the Years 1853–1854*. 1856. Reprint, New York: Knickerbockers, 1904.

Ogbar, Jeffrey O.G. *Black Power: Radical Politics and African American Identity*. Baltimore: Johns Hopkins University Press, 2004.

Opie, Frederick Douglass. "Eating, Dancing, and Courting in New York: Black and Latino Relations, 1930–1970." *Journal of Social History* (Fall 2008).

Osofsky, Gilbert. *Harlem: The Making of a Ghetto. Negro New York, 1890–1930*. New York: Harper Torchbooks, 1964.

Paige, Howard. *Aspects of African-American Foodways*. Southfield, Mich.: Aspects of Publishing, 1999.

Park, Mungo. *Travels in the Interior Districts of Africa: Performed in the Years 1795, 1796, and 1797, With an Account of a Subsequent Mission to that Country in 1805*. London: William Bulmer, 1816. Reprint, London: Dent; New York: Dutton, 1960.

Peckham, Howard H., ed. *Narratives of Colonial America, 1704-1765*. Lakeside Classics Series. Chicago: Donnelley, 1971.

Peretti, Burton W. *Jazz in American Culture*. Chicago: Dee, 1997.

Perez, Louis A., Jr. *Cuba Between Reform and Revolution*. New York: Oxford University Press, 1995.

Perman, Michael. *Struggle for Mastery: Disfranchisement in the South, 1888-1908*. Chapel Hill: University of North Carolina Press, 2001.

Pilcher, Jeffrey M. *!Que Vivan los Tamales! Food and the Making of Mexican Identity*. Albuquerque: University of New Mexico Press, 1998.

Pinckney, Eliza Lucas. *The Letterbook of Eliza Lucas Pinckney, 1739-1762*. Ed. Elise Pinckney, with Marvin R. Zahniser. Intro. Walter Muir Whitehill. Chapel Hill: University of North Carolina Press, 1972.

Poe, Tracy N. "The Origins of Soul Food in Black Urban Identity: Chicago, 1915-1947." *American Studies International* 37, no. 1 (February 1999).

Powell, Adam Clayton, Jr. *Adam by Adam: The Autobiography of Adam Clayton Powell, Jr.* New York: Dial, 1971.

Proyart, Abbé. *History of Loango, Kakongo, and Other Kingdoms*. In John Pinkerton, *A General Collection of the Best and Most Interesting Voyages and Travels in all Parts of the World* . . . , vol. 16. London: Longman, Hurst, Ross, Orme and Brown, 1813.

Raboteau, Albert J. *Slave Religion: The "Invisible Institution" in the Antebellum South*. New York: Oxford University Press, 1978.

Rainwater, Lee. Introduction to *Black Experience: Soul*, ed. Lee Rainwater, 1-14. New Brunswick, N.J.: Transaction, 1973.

——, ed. *Black Experience: Soul*. New Brunswick, N.J.: Transaction, 1973.

Redkey, Edwin S., ed. *A Grand Army of Black Men: Letters from African-American Soldiers in the Union Army, 1861-1865*. Cambridge: Cambridge University Press, 1992.

Rhoden, Bill "The 10 Worst Things You Can Do to Your Health." *Ebony*, January 10, 1978.

Ross, Diana. *Secrets of a Sparrow: Memoirs*. New York: Villard, 1993.

Rouse, Jacqueline Anne. "Out of the Shadow of Tuskegee: Margaret Murray Washington, Social Activism, and Race Vindication." *Journal of Negro History* 81, no. 1/4 (Winter 1996).

Rudwick, Elliott M. *Race Riot at East St. Louis, July 2, 1917*. Carbondale: Southern Illinois University Press, 1964.

Ruiz, Teofilo F. *Spanish Society, 1400-1600*. New York: Pearson Education, 2001.

Rustin, Bayard. "Black Folks, White Folks." In *Report from Black America*. ed. Peter Goldman, 164-169. New York: Simon and Schuster, 1969.

Sampson, Emma Speed. *Miss Minerva's Cook Book: De Way to a Man's Heart*. Chicago, 1931.

Sawyer, Charles. *The Arrival of B.B. King: The Authorized Biography*. Garden City, N.Y.: Doubleday, 1980.

Schaw, Jen. *Journal of a Lady of Quality: Being the Narrative of a Journey from Scotland to the West Indies, North Carolina, and Portugal in the Years 1774 to 1776*. Ed. Evangeline Walker Andrews, with Charles McLean Andrews. New Haven: Yale University Press, 1934.

Scott, Anne Firor. "The Most Invisible of Them All: Black Women's Voluntary Associations." *Journal of Southern History* 56, 1 (February 1990).

Scott, James C. *Domination and the Arts of Resistance: The Hidden Transcripts*. New Haven, Conn.: Yale University Press, 1990.

——. *Weapons of the Weak: Everyday Forms of Peasant Resistance*. New Haven, Conn.: Yale University Press, 1985.

Sernett, Milton C., ed. *Afro-American Religious History: A Documentary Witness*. Durham, N.C.: Duke University Press, 1985.

Simone, Nina. *The Autobiography of Nina Simone: I Put A Spell On You*. With Stephen Cleary. New York: Da Capo, 1993.

Smalls, Alexander. *Grace the Table: Stories and Recipes from My Southern Revival*. With Hattie Jones. New York: HarperCollins, 1997.

Smart-Grosvenor, Verta Mae. "Soul Food." *McCall's* 97 (September 1970).

Smedes, Susan Dabney. *Memorials of a Southern Planter*. Ed. Fletcher M. Green. 1887. Reprint, New York: Knopf, 1965.

Smith, John. "Descriptions of Virginia and Proceedings of the Colonie by Captain John Smith, 1612." In *Narratives of Early Virginia 1606-1625*, ed. Lyon Gardiner Tyler. Vol. 5 of *Original Narratives of Early American History*, ed. J. Franklin Jameson. New York: Scribner's, 1907.

Smith, Mark M. *How Race Is Made: Slavery, Segregation, and the Senses*. Chapel Hill: University of North Carolina Press, 2006.

"Soul Cookery Described on TV Series." *Daily Defender* (Chicago), January 9, 1969.

"Soul Food Moves Down Town." *Sepia* (Fort Worth, Tex.) 18 (May 1969).

Spencer, Colin. *Heretic's Feast: A History of Vegetarianism*. Hanover, N.H.: University Press of New England, 1996.

Spencer, Maryellen. "Food in Seventeenth-Century Tidewater Virginia: A Method for Studying Historical Cuisines." Ph.D. diss., Virginia Polytechnic Institute and State University, 1982.

Spivey, Diane M. *Migration of African Cuisine*. Albany: State University of New York Press, 1999.

Sprott, Samuel H. *Cush: A Civil War Memoir*. Ed. Louis R. Smith, Jr., and Andrew Quist. Livingston: University of West Alabama, Livingston Press, 1999.

Srygley, Fletcher Douglas. *Seventy Years in Dixie: Recollections and Sayings of T.W. Caskey and Others*. Nashville, Tenn.: Gospel Advocate, 1893.

Steele, James W. *Cuban Sketches*. New York: Putnam's, 1881.

Stevenson, Brenda E. *Life in Black and White: Family and Community in the Slave South*. New York: Oxford University Press, 1996.

Stewart, John J. *Account of Jamaica, and Its Inhabitants: By a Gentleman, a Long Resident in the West Indies*. London: Longman, Hurst, Rees, and Orme, 1808.

——. *A View of the Past and Present State of the Island of Jamaica; with Remarks on the Moral and Physical Condition of the Slaves, and on the Abolition of Slavery in the Colonies.* 1823. Reprint, New York, Negro Universities Press, 1969.

Sundstrom, William A. "Last Hired, First Fired? Unemployment and Urban Black Workers During the Great Depression." *Journal of Economic History* 52, no. 2 (June 1992).

"Tarry Town's Cuban Flavor." *New York Times*, March 20, 1977.

Taylor, Joe Gray. *Eating, Drinking, and Visiting in the South: An Informal History.* Baton Rouge: Louisiana State University Press, 1982.

Thomas, Hugh. *The Slave Trade: The History of the Atlantic Slave Trade, 1440–1870.* New York: Simon and Schuster, 1997.

Tomson, Robert. "Voyage to the West Indies and Mexico (1555–1558)." In *Colonial Travelers in Latin America*, ed. Irving A. Leonard. New York: Knopf, 1972.

Trotter, Joe W., Jr. *Black Milwaukee: The Making of an Industrial Proletariat, 1915–45.* Urbana: University of Illinois Press, 1985.

Toussaint-Samson, Adèle. *A Parisian in Brazil: A Travel Account of a Frenchwoman in Nineteenth-Century Rio De Janeiro.* Ed. Emma Toussaint. Wilmington, Del.: Scholarly Resources, 2001.

Van Deburg, William L. *Hoodlums: Black Villains and Social Bandits in American Life.* Chicago: University of Chicago Press, 2004.

——. *New Day in Babylon: The Black Power Movement and American Culture, 1965–1975.* Chicago: University of Chicago Press, 1992.

Vaughn, Alden, ed. *America Before the Revolution, 1725–1775.* Englewood Cliffs, N.J.: Prentice-Hall, 1967.

Von Hesse-Wartegg, Ernest. *Travels on the Lower Mississippi, 1879–1880: A Memoir by Ernest Von Hesse-Wartegy.* Trans. and ed. Frederic Trautman. Columbia: University of Missouri Press, 1990.

Voyage of Don Manoel Gonzales (Late Merchant) of the City of Lisbon in Portugal, to Great Britain, about 1788. In John Pinkerton, *A General Collection of the Best and Most Interesting Voyages and Travels in all Parts of the World* . . . , vol. 2. London: Longman, Hurst, Ross, Orme and Brown, 1813.

Watkins-Owens, Irma. *Blood Relations: Caribbean Immigrants and the Harlem Community, 1900–1930.* Bloomington: Indiana University Press, 1996.

Weems, Robert E., Jr. *Desegregating the Dollar: African American Consumerism in the Twentieth Century.* New York: New York University Press, 1998.

Weisbrot, Robert. *Father Divine: The Utopian Evangelist of the Depression Era Who Became an American Legend.* Boston: Beacon, 1983.

White, Deborah Gray. *Too Heavy a Load: Black Women in Defense of Themselves, 1894–1994.* New York: Norton, 1999.

White, Joyce. *Soul Food: Recipes and Reflections from African-American Churches.* New York: HarperCollins, 1998.

The Whole Body of Cookery Dissected, Taught, and Fully Manifested, Methodically, Artificially, and According to the Best Tradition of the English, French, Italian, Dutch, etc.

or, A Sympathie of All Varieties in Natural Compounds in that Mysterie: wherein is Contained Certain Bills of Fare for the Seasons of the Year, for Feasts and Common Diets: Whereunto is Annexed a Second Part of Rare Receipts of Cookery, with Certain Useful Traditions: with a Book of Preserving, Conserving and Candying, After the Most Exquisite and Newest Manner: Delectable for Ladies and Gentlewomen. London: Printed by R.W. for Giles Calvert, at the Sign of the black Spread Eagle, at the West End of Pauls, 1661.

Wickins, Peter Lionel. *Economic History of Africa from the Earliest Times to Partition.* New York: Oxford University Press, 1981.

Wiese, Andrew. Places of Their Own: African American Suburbanization in the Twentieth Century. Chicago: University of Chicago Press, 2004.

Wiley, Bell Irvin. *The Life of Johnny Reb: The Common Soldier of the Confederacy.* Garden City, N.Y.: Doubleday, 1971.

Williams, Lee E. and Lee E. Williams II. *Anatomy of Four Race Riots: Racial Conflict in Knoxville, Elaine (Arkansas), Tulsa, and Chicago, 1919–1921.* Hattiesburg: University and College Press of Mississippi, 1972.

Williams, Cynric. *A Tour Through the Island of Jamaica* .... London, 1826. In *After Africa: Extracts from British Travel Accounts and Journals of the Seventeenth, Eighteenth, and Nineteenth Centuries Concerning the Slaves, Their Manners, and Customs in the British West Indies,* ed. Roger D. Abrahams and John F. Szwed, with Leslie Baker and Adrian Stackhouse. New Haven: Yale University Press, 1983.

Williams-Forson, Psyche A. *Building Houses Out of Chicken Legs: Black Women, Food, and Power.* Chapel Hill: University of North Carolina Press, 2006.

Wilson, David Scofield and Angus Kress Gillespie, eds. *Rooted in America: Foodlore of Popular Fruits and Vegetables.* Knoxville: University of Tennessee Press, 1999.

Witt, Doris. *Black Hunger: Food and the Politics of U.S. Identity.* New York: Oxford University Press, 1999.

Wood, Peter H. *Black Majority: Negroes in Colonial South Carolina from 1670 through the Stono Rebellion.* New York: Norton, 1974.

Woodard, Komozi. *A Nation Within a Nation: Amiri Baraka (LeRoi Jones) and Black Power Politics.* Chapel Hill: University of New Carolina Press, 1999.

Zinn, Howard. *SNCC: The New Abolitionists.* Boston: Beacon, 1965.

Index

Printed in the USA
CPSIA information can be obtained
at www.ICGtesting.com
LVHW091919041124
795688LV00034B/1029